The Crosses of Pompeii

The Crosses of Pompeii

Jesus-Devotion in a Vesuvian Town

Bruce W. Longenecker

Fortress Press
Minneapolis

THE CROSSES OF POMPEII

Jesus-Devotion in a Vesuvian Town

Copyright © 2016 Fortress Press. All rights reserved. Except for brief quotations in critical articles or reviews, no part of this book may be reproduced in any manner without prior written permission from the publisher. Visit http://www.augsburgfortress.org/copyrights/ or write to Permissions, Augsburg Fortress, Box 1209, Minneapolis, MN 55440.

Cover image: Stone T. Cross © Bruce W. Longenecker

Cover design: Laurie Ingram

Library of Congress Cataloging-in-Publication Data

Print ISBN: 978-1-4514-9012-1

eBook ISBN: 978-1-5064-1041-8

This book was produced using Pressbooks.com, and PDF rendering was done by PrinceXML.

*For Mike Parsons
and in memory of Graham Stanton*

Contents

Part I. Introduction

1. Questions and Answers — 3
2. In Advance — 19

Part II. Setting Up

3. The Starting Point — 37
4. The Debate — 49
5. The Cross in Early Christianity and Beyond — 63
6. The Perpendicular Equilateral — 79

Part III. The Primary Evidence

7. Jesus-Devotion in Relief — 101
8. Jesus-Devotion in the Insula — 117
9. Jesus-Devotion in the Letters — 145
10. Jesus-Devotion and the Inn — 153
11. Jesus-Devotion in Transactions — 167

Part IV. The Supplemental Evidence

12.	Crossing the Streets	*191*
13.	Jesus-Devotion in the Streets	*217*

Part V. And So

14.	Belief and Skepticism	*253*
15.	Here and Beyond	*261*
	Appendix: Positioning Pompeii's Street Crosses	*285*
	Credits and Abbreviations	*307*
	Bibliography	*311*
	Index of Ancient Sources	*341*
	Index of Modern Authors	*349*
	Index of Vesuvian Locations	*355*

PART I

Introduction

Pompeii displays "the uninterrupted pulse of everyday life,
the pulse of a heart already two thousand years old,
a heart whose fragile and relentless echo continues to resonate."
(Lessing and Varone, *Pompeii* [1995], 193)

"Our fascination with Pompeii . . . brings with it,
just below the surface,
an unwelcome relevance to the present."
(Franklin and Potts, foreword to *The Last Days of Pompeii* [2012], 6)

1

Questions and Answers

In many ways, their lives were not much different from ours. One of them tried to capture the essence of life in two simple Latin words written on a wall: *Amamus, invidemus,* or "We love, we envy."[1] Then one day, quite unexpectedly, many of them died. They died horribly. Some died alone. Some died huddled together. Some died clutching statues of their deities. All those who died shared in incalculable terror.

Down from the top of Mount Vesuvius came six intermittent surges of volcanic ash, flowing at tremendous speeds with scorching hot temperatures. For the inhabitants of the towns of Pompeii and Herculaneum and the surrounding regions, fearful hours of panic had given way to tragic moments of horror.

---

1. *CIL* 4.1222. Compare also *CIL* 4.3149: "All who love are at war."

Figure 1.1. An artist's depiction of the eruption of Vesuvius. Johan Christian Dahl, 1823; in the public domain.

These enclaves of the Greco-Roman population lay within the Bay of Naples in the region of Campania. That stretch of the Italian peninsula had become the playground for the Roman elite prior to the eruption of Vesuvius.[2] In December 88, less than a decade after the eruption, the Roman poet Martial described the pre-eruption Vesuvian slopes as a place beloved by the deities, a place where "the noble grape [had] loaded the dripping vats"; after the eruption, however, "all lies drowned in fire and melancholy ash" – to which Martial adds the note that "even the high gods could have wished this had not been permitted of them" (*Epigrams* 4.44).

---

2. Woolf 2012: 157 describes it as "half Las Vegas and half the Left Bank of the Seine."

Figure 1.2. Skeletal remains of victims in Herculaneum. The reproduction of images of realia from the Vesuvian towns contained in this book is prohibited by the Superintendency for Archaeological Heritage of Pompeii, Herculaneum and Stabiae.

Asking Questions

Thousands of lives were snuffed out, erased from history in the eruption of Vesuvius – an eruption traditionally dated to August 24 in the year 79 (although some data favor an autumn eruption).[3] But if they were removed from the human population, their imprint has not been removed from the record of human culture. This is because archaeological initiatives have uncovered much about the daily lives of the people of these towns. The Roman towns of Pompeii and Herculaneum, subjected to intermittent archaeological efforts since the mid-eighteenth century, now lie exposed to both the eroding forces of nature and the probes of scholars and tourists. Or as someone has well said: "History did not allow Pompeii two thousand years of

---

3. On the date of the eruption, see Joanne Berry 2007: 20; Beard 2008: 17–19; and especially Roberts 2013: 278–79. If the eruption is dated to August, then the graffito of "Apollinaris the physician of the emperor Titus" who "had a good shit" in Herculaneum (CIL 4.10619) needs to be accounted for in some way, since Titus became emperor in June 79, just two months before the eruption on the traditional dating.

cleansing by the rain and bleaching by the sun. The observer in Pompeii is not a visitor, but an intruder.... The house is not prepared, the unsightly marks have not been removed."[4]

From these "unprepared" centers of the Greco-Roman population, numerous artifacts from the first century have been discovered and studied in detail. Among their number are a few artifacts that will form the focus of this book. Those artifacts help to pose questions that occasionally surface in archaeological explorations of the Vesuvian remains: Were Christians already present in the Vesuvian towns prior to August 79? Could Jesus-devotees have been among those whose lives were destroyed in the devastating eruption? Had the Jesus-movement infiltrated the walls of Pompeii and Herculaneum? Do any artifacts suggest that a Jew crucified outside the walls of Jerusalem was an object of religious devotion in the Vesuvian towns less than fifty years after his death?

These are simple questions. Many have thought that there are simple answers to them. We will see in the course of this book, however, that the issue is far from simple, and it is far more intriguing than has been recognized thus far.

Where the Answer Lies

This book presents a fresh case for the presence of Christian devotion in the shadow of Mount Vesuvius. This position is currently a minority view, but I am not alone in holding it. Nor is it held for ideological reasons, or in complete disregard of the historical record. In fact, as I will demonstrate, this interpretation of a number of significant data avoids the mistakes of earlier interpreters, whose methodological blind spots and unfounded assumptions caused them to misinterpret the material record. Of course, my case will rightly be put to the test in the court of historical inquiry, and no doubt there will be dissent. But the consensus view itself is not free of dissent, nor am I the first historian

---

4. Paul Berry 1995: 38.

to challenge it in the twenty-first century, even if my case is the most developed.

It was never my intention to write a book on this particular subject. Initially I was little more than a casual reader of Vesuvian scholarship. Having completed a major research project on the early Jesus-movement in relation to economic structures of the Greco-Roman world, my attention began to focus specifically on life within the Vesuvian towns, as a way of further exploring more of the concrete realities of first-century life.[5] Besides the exhilaration that comes from exploring an ancient culture, my primary interest was in stimulating further research questions about the emergence of the early Jesus-movement within its first-century context. How was religious devotion configured in civic centers of the Roman world? How intertwined were political and religious spheres of life? How did differences in socioeconomic profiles affect people's perspectives on issues that most pressingly affected their lives? How might the omnipresent concern for social honor have impacted on the everyday lives of ordinary people?

As my investigations into the Vesuvian towns developed, I began to notice weaknesses in the interpretation of certain artifacts that frame the question of whether Jesus-devotion may have been present in the Vesuvian towns. The more I familiarized myself with the scholarship of the past, the more I became dissatisfied with the answers given by the majority today. Many of the arguments of the past have filtered down to the present without being properly adjudicated. Long-standing interpretations rested on illegitimate and outmoded ways of interpreting the emergence of the Jesus-movement in the Greco-Roman world. Moreover, significant evidence had been left out of the debate altogether. As a consequence, standard calculations failed to add up, and established estimates failed to be convincing. I began to see the issue in a different light, with the Vesuvian evidence stacking up in ways that challenged the consensus.

---

5. For my earlier work on Greco-Roman economic structures, poverty, and the early Jesus-movement, see Longenecker 2010.

Pamela Bradley depicts Vesuvian research as being in an exciting phase today because it is shedding some of its traditional constraints and breaking out of old habits in bold, new ways. She notes how researchers are "now challenging the [inherited] story of the sites" by "questioning widely-held concepts about Roman life," by "asking different questions about the material finds," by "shifting away from the old certainties of 'fact' and 'truth,'" and by "recognising the ways in which the views [of previous generations of scholars] were affected by the politics and ideologies [of their day]."[6]

This book shares the spirit described by Bradley. The chapters that follow in this book make an unconventional case that proves to be more historically robust than the current consensus. The case will demonstrate that first-century Jesus-devotion did, in fact, have a Vesuvian foothold in the town of Pompeii. Along the way we will find ourselves able to locate particular residences in which Jesus-followers dwelled. We will be able to identify the occupations of a few of them. And we will be able to name one of them. A few shadowy glimpses, then, enable us to peer into the life stories of a few Vesuvian residents who devoted themselves to Jesus Christ and who seem to have called themselves Christians.

Amplifying the Answer

If the claims of this book are right, the consequences are both significant and multiform. Their import can be sketched here, at the outset of this book, in order to enable readers to capture the sense of where we are going as the ensuing argument rolls along from artifact to artifact.

The material record, covered for centuries under Vesuvian ash,

---

6. Bradley 2005: 38. One of the best examples of this is the overthrowing of the view that after the earthquake of 62 or 63, the Vesuvian towns were abandoned by the elite and in a state of serious decline, being taken over by an infestation of commercial workers and artisans. This view was advocated by Amedeo Maiuri (director of Pompeii excavations from 1924-61) and, to a lesser extent, by August Mau in the late nineteenth century – both highly influential figures. Some recent scholarship has attempted to overturn this longstanding view; see esp. Wallace-Hadrill 1994: 122-29; Roberts 2013: 274-78; Ling 2009: 90-91. But Maiuri's view continues to have strong advocacy; see its influence, for instance, in Butterworth and Laurence 2005; Magagnini 2010: 12-13.

offers us valuable access into some of the earliest days of the Jesus-movement. The early years of that movement are among the most hidden of all in the history of Christianity. In the process of setting the historical record straight about Jesus-devotion in Pompeii, we will be able to fill in some of the gaps about a largely inaccessible period in the history of early Christianity.

Further, we will find ourselves not only with fresh historical data but also with a new historical laboratory in which to test hypotheses and study results. Scientists enjoy sterile labs in which to conduct experiments under highly controlled settings. By contrast, historians often have to formulate their hypotheses using "surrogate laboratories" that replicate the setting they seek to reconstruct as closely as possible. For instance, in the pursuit of long-standing questions about the rise of the early Jesus-movement, historians have carried out reconstructions imagining what it might have been like if a Jesus-group had been based in a specific context – a house from here, a shop from there, this space, that space, on and on. This allows historians to test out theories about how Jesus-followers may have conducted their corporate life with reference both to themselves and to outsiders, while accounting for the various identities of a group's hypothesized membership. If the argument of this book is correct, Pompeii can function as a fruitful laboratory for the historian of early Christianity – one in which we know a bit about who Jesus-followers were, thereby allowing us a greater amount of control over our historical reconstructions.

This introduces another feature of the findings of this book. The little that we already know about Christianity in this very early period comes almost exclusively from literary texts rather than from material evidence. Those texts were written by people with prominent voices within the early Jesus-movement – the "apostolic voice" in a sense. By contrast, however, the Vesuvian remains contain remnants of Jesus-devotion that derive from a much different provenance. What we will be seeing in the course of this book is the Jesus-devotion of everyday people who were probably not great theologians. They were probably not well versed in the intricacies of scriptural interpretation. They probably did not have an overarching program for the spread of the Jesus-movement throughout the Mediterranean basin. They probably were not taught in the schools of rhetoric, and they probably did not distinguish themselves with eloquent speech. Most likely, they were just simple people going about their daily routines – undertaking their businesses, serving in households, and just getting by.

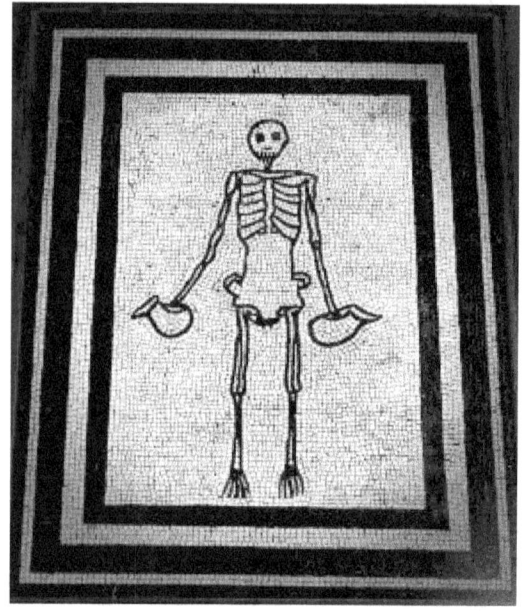

Figure 1.3. A mosaic capturing the cognizance of the ominous fate that awaits one and all (MANN 9978). The mosaic, with the skeleton holding two wine pitchers, may have been intended to endorse an Epicurean mantra: "Drink today, for tomorrow we die."

Further still, our survey has ramifications beyond early Jesus-groups themselves. When placed in their historical context, artifacts of Jesus-devotees from Pompeii reveal as much about the fragile complexities of Greco-Roman life as they do about the religious sentiments of those devotees themselves. If a few ordinary people in the vicinity of Mount

Vesuvius adopted devotion to a deity who was said to have risen from the dead, the artifacts of their devotion consistently reveal one important aspect of their lives. They were people who felt that danger was all around them, and they were anxious about what lay outside their control. In this way, they were much like many people of their day – people who lived in residences on each side of them, within their neighborhood, throughout their town, and across the whole of the Mediterranean basin. Their world was one in which suprahuman forces were alive and well, a world in which evil spells and curses coursed through the streets of their town in a highly charged competition for survival and, in a few cases, success. Death was everywhere and could not be hidden away from the view of anyone. Life was cherished, fragile, and, for many, fleeting. One person from Pompeii articulated the point in this way: "While I am alive, you, hateful death, are coming."[7]

In their world, mechanisms to ensure stability for the benefit and flourishing of all were not robust. The streets of Vesuvian towns, for instance, did not benefit from the omnipresent patrolling of police who operated according to legal stipulations determined by a democratic society.[8] Legal systems were usually skewed in favor of the elite and the successful, often at the expense of those less securely positioned and, therefore, less valued.[9] So, for instance, Pliny the Younger held the view that judges hearing legal cases should make sure that "the distinctions of rank and dignity" are maintained in their judgments, for "to level and confound [i.e., confuse] the different orders of humanity is far from producing equality among them; it is, in truth, the most unequal thing imaginable" (*Epistulae* 9.5).

---

7. *CIL* 4.5112.
8. In 6 CE, emperor Augustus created "protector groups" (*cohortes vigilum*) to patrol the city of Rome in order to crack down on burglaries within the city and to stamp out fires. This initiative was largely restricted to the city of Rome and was hardly comparable to a modern police force or fire brigade.
9. Stegemann and Stegemann capture this well when they write (1999: 64): "not only did criminal law have two tracks [one for the elite and another for the subelite], but also different standards were applied before the court. Thus the statements of high-ranking citizens were given more credence." In reality, it was not so much a "two track" system but a system in which the balance was skewed in favor of those with superior status, relatively speaking.

Figure 1.4. The precariousness of life in the balance, with Fate ready to tip toward poverty (right) or riches (left) with little more than a flutter of a butterfly's wings, and with death as the plumb line of all existence (MANN 109982).

Theirs was a world of insecurity and danger, driven by "the distinctions of rank and dignity." If ordinary people sought protection against evildoers or sought redress for wrongs committed against them, their best prospects lay not with a "jury of their peers" or with social structures derived to protect the majority of the population. Instead, their best prospects lay with suprahuman forces that populated their imaginations. These included the almost-innumerable deities of their worldview and the spirits of the departed. Some of these spirits or daimons were especially pernicious, hovering in graveyards beyond the town walls and lurking throughout the streets, being called on to demolish the prospects of love, success, and well-being for ordinary people trapped in the envious schemes of their competitors. The ancient mind-set imagined the world to be multilayered, with spiritual forces above and below the human sphere ready to impact the life of the material world in which humanity dwelled, when coaxed to do so by what amounted to little more than a human bribe. Pliny the Elder, who died in the eruption of Vesuvius, stated it this way: "There is indeed nobody who does not fear to be spell-bound [i.e., cursed] by imprecations" from others (*Natural History* 28.19). The ancients imagined that their neighbors could unleash terrible powers against them. The world beyond one's own household could be seen and experienced as menacing.

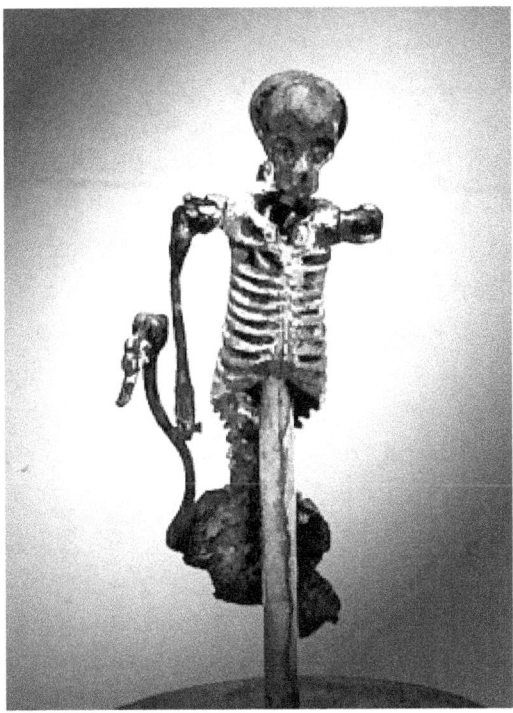

Figure 1.5. A miniature skeleton that probably adorned place settings at Pompeian meals (MANN 109688).

Protection and retribution were offshoots of a person's devotion to the deities and the successful manipulation of these suprahuman spirits. When the Christian apostle Paul recited Jewish Scripture in the mid-50s to articulate the Judeo-Christian deity's words "Vengeance is mine, I will repay" (Romans 12:19, citing Deuteronomy 32:35), he was trading in the currency that predominated in the ancient world – a world in which access to suprahuman power was much like taking out an insurance policy: the more you had, the better your chances of survival and, perhaps, success. The prospect of an almighty deity undertaking vengeance or orchestrating profitable initiatives on behalf of his devotees would have held notable attraction in the dangerous world of the first century.

It is also in this context that some of the earliest Christian preaching is best understood. Paul himself may regularly have framed his message to urbanites of the Greco-Roman world in words like these from his earliest letter: "Turn to God from idols, serve a living and true God, and wait for his Son from heaven, whom he raised from the dead – Jesus, who rescues his followers from the wrath that is coming" (1 Thessalonians 1:9–10).[10] Many who felt they had been dealt an unjust hand in life would have warmed to hear that the wrath of the Most High deity, who stood over and above all intimidating forms of suprahuman powers, was coming to rescue his devotees from injustice.[11] So Paul lauds Jesus-followers for their faithfulness and assures them that the deity whom he proclaims will show that he is "just" because he will "repay with affliction those who afflict you . . . when the Lord Jesus is revealed from heaven with his mighty angels in flaming fire, inflicting vengeance" and "the punishment of eternal destruction" (2 Thessalonians 2:4–9).[12] Whatever cautions we might want to register about these lines of thought, there is little doubt that discourse of this kind addressed anxieties that ran deeply within

---

10. Compare also Romans 1:23–25; 1 Corinthians 10:14; 2 Corinthians 6:16–18; Acts 19:26.
11. In his analysis of Paul's letter to the Romans, Oakes rightly notes (2009: 134–35) that although the oppressed of the first century would have taken significant notice of the theme of wrath and justice in that letter, many Christians in the affluent West "'airbrush' the theme of judgement out of Paul's gospel." See also 2009: 176–77.
12. Paul also had other forms of theological discourse in his rhetorical arsenal, but this is one form of discourse that he occasionally employed. See, for instance, Hays 1996: 39–41.

the Greco-Roman world. Paul captured all this in a nutshell when he wrote, "If God is for us, who can be against us?" (Romans 8:31).

Those who adopted devotion to Jesus in the Vesuvian towns were probably little different from any of their neighbors. They were people who sought protection from perceived evils all around them. They were people desperate for security. They were people who, had they ever encountered them, might have nodded in agreement at the words of Jesus' prayer, "Deliver us from evil" (Matthew 6:13) – whether that be "the evil one" per se or the fiendish spirits that, in the predominant ancient imagination, surrounded humans on every side. Similar words may have been circulating that offered comfort along different lines. The same Christian Gospel includes this promise:

> Do not worry, saying, "What will we eat?" or "What will we drink?" or "What will we wear?" . . . Indeed your heavenly Father knows that you need all these things. . . . Strive first for the kingdom of God and his righteousness, and all these things will be given to you as well. (Matthew 6:31–34)

Of course, these words derive from a Gospel whose final composition derives from a few years after the eruption of Vesuvius, but it is not unlikely that prospects of this kind were embedded within the Christian proclamation before their appearance in this particular text. In a world dominated by the powerful, for the benefit of the powerful, and often at the expense of those who were often little more than cogs in the machinery of elite power, the average person might well have had interest in the prospect of a "heavenly Father" who knew the needs of his devotees in the present and promised that justice would be carried out on their behalf in the future.

In a dangerous world such as theirs, suprahuman assistance was an essential feature of everyday life. Only the exceptional person would have failed to prick up his ears when hearing that "Death has been swallowed up in victory" (1 Corinthians 15:54). Only the exceptional person would have been uninterested in hearing about "the immeasurable greatness of his power for us" – a power that was "put to work in Christ" who was raised from the dead and a power that is now on tap for those whose deity is now "far above all rule and authority and power and dominion" (Ephesians 1:19-21). Only the exceptional person would have failed to take note of claims that that deity had already encountered the spirits of the underworld and trounced them "with authority," having "command[ed] even the unclean spirits" so that "they obey[ed] him" (Mark 1:27). Only the exceptional person would have been uninterested in a deity who, supplying "seed to the sower and bread for food," will also "supply and increase your store of seed" (2 Corinthians 9:10) – with the word "seed" representing financial resources.[13] The gospel of Christ crucified, said Paul, is not just about fine eloquent words; if that were all it was, then the cross of Christ would be "emptied of its power" (1 Corinthians 1:18). As Stephen Westerholm writes, "Jews and non-Jews alike had always been concerned to keep on good terms with the supernatural powers that influenced, or even controlled, their destinies. With such concerns, [the Christian] message found a natural resonance."[14]

The common thread uniting most of the artifacts examined in the following chapters falls along the axis of enhancing protection in a dangerous world and bolstering life prospects. Evidently, in their efforts to capture suprahuman power most effectively, some residents in a Vesuvian town imagined that devotion to Jesus would increase their prospects, in both their everyday existence and beyond it.

But I have gotten ahead of myself. The point is simply that, if my case is correct in the following chapters, we will be seeing more than neglected artifacts from the past. We will be doing more than simply shedding new light on the emergence of Christianity in the ancient world and understanding how it could have been a message that attracted the attention of Greco-Roman urbanites. In essence, we will be peering into the soul of the ancient world, a world that, more than our own, was supremely conscious of and exposed to the clutches of

---

13. It is important to note that, in the context in which this is spoken, those resources are to be used in support of others. The metaphor of "supplying seed," then, is not a "get rich quick" scheme but is more about bearing one another's burdens (as in Galatians 6:2). On this aspect of 2 Corinthians 9:10, see further Longenecker 2010: 290-91.
14. Westerholm 2013: 5 (with the word "Paul's" appearing where I have inserted "the Christian"). See also Sanders 1983: 153.

death, "the final enemy" (1 Corinthians 15:26). We will be witnessing the multilayered architecture of life in the Greco-Roman world, where fear of dangerous forces beyond one's control fostered a variety of innovative strategies for survival. For a small number of people in the proximity of Mount Vesuvius, those strategies included devotion to a deity reputedly raised to life after having died on a Roman cross.

2

In Advance

Before he could accomplish his task of tossing the Ring of Power into the heart of Mount Doom, the hobbit Frodo Baggins had to pass through great stretches of dangerous territory. Fortunately, the task before us is less lengthy than Frodo's in Tolkien's The Lord of the Rings trilogy, and it is certainly far less dangerous an undertaking. But there is some "territory" that needs to be crossed in the early stages of this adventure before we can arrive at our own mountainside destination to carry out our own tasks. While it is not ominous territory to traverse, it will offer the occasion to sharpen our interpretative tools prior to entering a world far removed from our own. We begin by noting how others have traversed this territory in the past, often with less interest in historical veracity than in defending inherited worldviews.

Pompeii: No Place for Theological Apologists

Had Jesus-followers walked on the streets preserved by the volcanic ash from Mount Vesuvius? The first person known to have asked a question of this sort was the Christian theologian Tertullian, who lived in northern Africa in the late second and early third century. In his work *To the Heathen* that dates to the year 197, Tertullian claimed that Christians could not have been resident in the Vesuvian towns (1.9.7).[1] Tertullian did not have 120-year-old census records from the towns to justify his view. His claim was simply an inference derived from theological first principles that he thought were self-evident. In the process of making a larger case that Christians are not the cause of natural disasters (the counterargument being that Christians cause the deities to be angry), Tertullian lists a series of natural disasters that cannot be interpreted as moments of divine wrath against Christians. These examples include the sinking of the lost continent of Atlantis, a disaster that happened long before Christians ever existed. For Tertullian, just as there were no Christians in Atlantis prior to its sinking, so too there had been no Christians in the Vesuvian region prior to the eruption of the local mountain.

What Tertullian offers us is a kind of historical reconstruction through deductive reasoning rooted in and predetermined by Christian apologetics – discourse intent on proving the truthfulness of Christianity. In the course of Tertullian's argument, the reputation of Christianity is defended against its detractors. Tertullian's claim about the absence of Christians from the Vesuvian region did not emerge from historical analysis. In fact, in another text Tertullian compounds his claim by stating that Christians were absent from the whole of the region of Campania (*Apology* 40.8). That claim is contradicted by Acts 28:13–14, which notes the presence of Jesus-followers (by 60 CE) in Puteoli, a coastal town in Campania not far from Herculaneum and Pompeii.[2] The questions asked in this study, then, cannot be answered for us by the apologist Tertullian, whose historical pronouncements on this matter are simply theological constructs without any historical basis.

A theologically driven estimate of a different kind is evidenced in

---

1. Last (1954: 114) disputes this common interpretation of Tertullian: "it would rather appear to me that Tertullian implies the presence of Christians at Pompeii." Others, including me, do not share Last's interpretation. See especially Hoffmann 1974.
2. Lampe (2003: 8n1) rightly observes that the presence of Jesus-followers in Puteoli is "pre-Lukan," in the sense that it "is superfluous" to Luke's interests and is thereby historically reliable.

the second or third century. Originally a Jewish text, the text of the *Sibylline Oracles* was updated by later Christians, to the extent that it is virtually impossible to disentangle the Jewish original from subsequent Christian contributions. In the fourth book of this text, we hear prophecies (after the fact) about the rise of Roman rule and the destruction of Jerusalem (4.102–29). In that context, the eruption of Mount Vesuvius is afforded a theological interpretation.[3] Pretending to prophesy about the future, *Sibylline Oracles* 4.130–36 speaks about the coming time when a "firebrand" will be severed "from a cleft in the earth in the land of Italy." At that time, "smoking ashes will fill the great sky, and showers will fall from heaven like red earth"; "it will burn many cities and destroy men" because of "the wrath of the heavenly God." This is the wrath of the Judeo-Christian deity – wrath provoked by the Roman destruction of Jerusalem in 70 and evidenced in Vesuvius's eruption in 79. The atrocities perpetrated by Rome against the Jews, "the blameless tribe of the pious," had provoked the divine retribution evident in the destruction of Pompeii and Herculaneum.[4]

For anyone who adopted this point of view, it might make better sense to imagine that followers of the Judeo-Christian deity (whether Jesus-followers or non-Christian Jews) were not already in the Vesuvian region. If Rome's atrocities against the people of the Judeo-Christian deity caused that deity to wipe out Roman towns in retaliation, it would have been a cleaner counterinsurgence if his own people were not resident in those towns. It is unfortunate for this view that there are artifacts testifying to a Jewish presence in the Vesuvian towns. So if the eruption was divine retribution in a tit-for-tat retaliation for the killing of Jews and the destruction of their Judean city, it is odd that the Judeo-Christian deity could not target his sights more precisely, reducing the incidents of "friendly fire" against his own people. Here again, theological apologetics is at the forefront, not historical reconstruction.

---

3. Another ancient theological interpretation of the event might be evident in the *Apocalypse of Adam*; see Goedicke 1968.
4. This view is also adopted by some characters in Harris's popular novel, *Pompeii* (2003).

Tertullian and the *Sibylline Oracles* are not alone in constructing apologetically driven estimates on the subject of this study. Apologetic reasoning is also offered by twenty-first-century Christian apologists seeking to influence viewers on popular media sites like YouTube. There, unsuspecting viewers can learn from amateur videos that Christianity was alive and well in the Vesuvian towns.[5] The extravagant claims of these videos are usually plagued by misinformation regarding the data and by optimism regarding the apologetic potential of the historical data. Creators of amateur videos seem to imagine that a Christian presence within the Vesuvian towns helps to prove the veracity of Christianity, on the unwarranted assumption that the quick spread of Christianity throughout the Greco-Roman world is a testimony to its truthfulness. This kind of apologetic is exactly the opposite of the view of Tertullian, who imagined that good apologetics require Christians to have been absent from the Vesuvian towns.

Use of the Vesuvian sites for the purpose of enhancing the reputation of Christianity is not merely an ancient or twenty-first-century phenomenon. It was also extremely popular in nineteenth-century novels about Pompeii. The first of these was Thomas Gray's 1830 novel *The Vestal*. Gray places Christians at the forefront of his novel, set in Pompeii in the mid-90s – a decade when, according to Gray, Christians were hunted down and slaughtered through the crazed initiatives of the emperor Domitian (emperor from 81 to 96). Despite the fact that the town of Pompeii had actually laid under Vesuvian ash for fifteen years or so when this story purportedly takes place, Gray's extreme literary license is part of his strategy to set Christians within the most dangerous of situations in order then to magnify their heroism and laud their faith.[6]

---

5. For the sake of curiosity (rather than enlightenment), consult the nine-minute YouTube video "Evidence of Christianity in First Century Pompeii" (https://www.youtube.com/watch?v=aakJEflzVdk). The middle three minutes (roughly 4 through 6) are simply riddled with errors when discussing the Vesuvian data (especially with regard to where artifacts were found and how they were positions). The surrounding six minutes contain no material of relevance to the issue.
6. The last decade of the Vesuvian towns was probably one of the most peaceful times for Jesus-followers in the pre-Constantinian period.

Early in Gray's *The Vestal*, for instance, the reader is taken to the Pompeii amphitheater, where an initial drama unfolds. After "a score of soldiers" enter the arena, it is time for the Christians to emerge. Soon they are forced either "to acknowledge or deny their Saviour." The "real Christians" do not recant of their faith in their savior, and they meet gruesome fates. The last Christian to be slaughtered is an old and venerable man who holds a "calm, fixed gaze" as a lion leaps to tear him apart, whereupon "the old man's voice was heard, as he turned upward his gaze, 'Father, into thy hands I commit my spirit.'" The moment is emotive, and the drama is high. Who could fail to be moved by the man's unwavering heroism?[7]

But we are only at page forty-four in what the novelist hopes will be a motivational page-turner. Throughout the rest of the imaginative story, the main male character, Lucius, converts to Christianity and is filled with unprecedented peace and fulfillment. The narrative weaves in and out of people's lives until the obvious conclusion – the eruption of Vesuvius. When the mountain explodes, the pagan population scurries about, clamoring for life in wild desperation. The Christians, while fearful, go to their deaths with a much different demeanor, filled with grace and virtue, transitioning to their heavenly life in the final frames of the story. For instance, one Christian by the name of Vetullius, who is presented throughout as a good and valiant man, meets his death with expected nobility, free from terror. With volcanic ash falling all around him, Vetullius "gathered his garments closely about him, and wrapped his face in his mantle. 'Lord, now lettest thou thy servant depart in peace,' he said, as he laid himself down upon the earth from which he never arose."[8] Fantastic stuff! But, of course, all of this emerges from the imagination of a nineteenth-century novelist, not from the historical artifacts of the first-century Greco-Roman towns.

Novelistic placements of Christians in Pompeii were given a significant boost in the popular imagination only four years after

---

7. The quotations in this paragraph are from Gray 1830: 37–38 and 44.
8. Gray 1830: 177.

Gray's novel, with the publication of the novel *The Last Days of Pompeii*. Written by Edward Bulwer-Lytton, this blockbuster went on to enjoy tremendous success in a variety of media. Inspiring operas, theater productions, and (much later) films, this 1834 classic depicts the Greco-Roman world as a swamp of moral decadence. Against that backdrop we read a love story in which Christian morality is a new, refreshing, and honorable insertion into a world in which corrosive immorality was the all-engulfing norm. Embedded within the story line, then, is a clear Christian apologetic, with the Judeo-Christian deity punishing the Vesuvian towns for their flagrant disregard of divine morality in a replay of the destruction of the cities of Sodom and Gomorrah in the Old Testament (Genesis 18–19).[9] This is high drama, to be sure. But placing Christians within the town of Pompeii is easily done when the genre is fiction; when the genre shifts to historical reconstruction, it is another story altogether.[10]

It is, of course, the job of the novelist to allure readers into a world of intrigue.[11] If there is intrigue in subsequent chapters of this book, it does not arise from the imaginative sensationalism of the modern novelist, nor is it the product of theological apologetics. There is some

---

9. Much the same is evident in Wordsworth three years later (1837: 2, 32–33): "I profess gratitude to God, by whose wonderful order this city was overwhelmed.... [The town's erotic inscriptions] show us with what moral depravity these graceful embellishments were allied. Therefore we neither envy them, nor are we prone to believe that man's Art or Intellect will ever reform the world. We no longer indulge in such a dream, nor question the justice of Providence which buried Pompeii in the dust."
10. When discussing this novel, St Clair and Bautz (2012: 54) note that Bulwer-Lytton's imagination was clearly unimpeded by historical realia, since "no unequivocal evidence that there were Christians in Pompeii had been found by 1834," adding "nor indeed has been found subsequently." The novel inspired a film of the same name (produced in 1933, RKO Radio Pictures), which had very little to do with the novel and took the Christian elements to the forefront. See Stähli 2012: 84.

   The moralism of Bulwer-Lytton's novel was frequently echoed by others, not least Francis and Harriet Clark (1895: 572): "[Pompeii] was overwhelmed by the wrath of God in a single night: its polluted streets and houses, which even now indicate depths of depravity that have seldom been witnessed in the history of the world, ruined and utterly destroyed as habitations for the living. Surely the moralist will be excused for drawing his lesson from the destruction of this comparatively modern Sodom and Gomorrah." On the tendency to see the Vesuvian towns as part of a decadent society against which to depict the glory of Christianity, see Seydl 2012.
11. The same is true of ancient orators, who frequently adopted sensationalistic measures when depicting historical events. We might suspect something of this order to have crept into Pliny the Younger's account of Vesuvius's eruption, for instance. There is little reason to doubt the relative accuracy of his description of the eruption, but how much are we to believe when he depicts his uncle's own heroic part in the narrative, or about his own enthusiastic interest in carrying on with his studies while his world was being torn apart around him (*Letters to Tacitus* 6.16, 20)?

scope, at times, for allowing disciplined theorizing to fill in some of the blanks in the historical database (which does not interpret itself), but there is no scope for placing the issue of our study within a theological context in which faith-based apologetics of one kind or another predetermines the terms of engagement. (As we will see, faith-based apologetics has contributed to the rise of the consensus view itself.) The apologetic thread could run and run, but in the end, it gets us nowhere, theologically or historically. The issue of whether Jesus-devotion was present in Vesuvian towns needs to be stripped of traditional apologetics and situated solely as a matter of historical inquiry. Apologists would do better traversing other terrain than this.

First-Century Jesus-followers on the Italian Peninsula

Before exploring artifacts from Pompeii for their relevance to the question of Jesus-devotion in that town, the larger context of first-century Jesus-devotion on the Italian peninsula needs to be outlined in brief, allowing our purported Pompeian Jesus-followers to slot into those larger parameters.

Italy housed many Christians in the first century. As noted above, we know that Jesus-followers were already established in Puteoli by the time Paul arrived there in 60. Puteoli, Italy's leading port city in the first half of the first century, lay just beyond a day's walk from Pompeii. According to Scottish archaeologist and New Testament scholar William Ramsay, Puteoli was one of the leading centers "from which Christianity radiated" (along with Corinth, Ephesus, Syrian Antioch, Rome, etc.).[12] If this is right, a power plant helping to generate the emergence of Christianity was just down the road from the Vesuvian towns.

Further afield, a good number of Jesus-devotees were based in the imperial city, Rome. In the year 109 or so, Tacitus described Rome as an important base for the spread of the early Jesus-movement, stating that the "most mischievous superstition" spread by Christians "broke

---

12. Ramsay 1895: 346. Puteoli remained one of Rome's main ports, even more so than Ostia, up to the time of Nero. On this, see Lampe 2003: 10.

out not only in Judea, the first source of the evil, but even in Rome" (*Annals* 15.44).

This dovetails well with what we know from other sources. The apostle Paul wrote to Jesus-followers based in Rome in 57. Organized within a variety of Jesus-groups (as Romans 16 suggests), those Jesus-followers seem to have had a presence in Rome dating back to the early years of the Jesus-movement, perhaps the early 30s.[13] Among those Jesus-groups were several people who were important within the early Jesus-movement. Andronicus and Junia, for instance, are identified by Paul as "prominent among the apostles," having been Jesus-followers before him and perhaps even having been imprisoned with him at some point.[14] So too Prisca and Aquila were highly significant mission partners of Paul, having resided with him in both Corinth (50–51) and Ephesus (53–55); by the time Paul wrote to Christians in Rome, Prisca and Aquila were living there once again (Romans 16:3–4).[15] Evidently, Jesus-groups were fairly well ensconced within Rome by the late 50s and included some prominent figures within the early days of Christian history.

In the early 60s, Paul spoke of Christians in Rome as fervent in their proclamation of the gospel, being emboldened by their association with him during his time of imprisonment in the imperial city. He writes: "Most of the brothers and sisters have become confident in the Lord [by my imprisonment] and dare all the more to proclaim the gospel without fear" (Philippians 1:14).[16] During this time, Jesus-followers inhabited Rome in fairly impressive numbers. Robert Jewett estimates that by the mid-60s, Jesus-groups "had grown to several

---

13. Acts 2:10 mentions people from Rome being present in Jerusalem to celebrate Pentecost and experiencing the moving of the Spirit on the nascent Jesus-movement. On this, see especially Richard Longenecker 2011: 69-72. And on Romans 16 being integral to the letter to Jesus-groups in Rome, see Longenecker and Still 2014: 165–66.
14. For interpretative issues that these verses pose, see Longenecker and Still 2014: 171, especially note 6.
15. Departing Rome, Prisca and Aquila relocated in Corinth (Acts 18:2) and then moved to Ephesus (1 Corinthians 16:19, written from that city), before returning to Rome, evidently after the death of Claudius in 54.
16. On Philippians having been written from Rome in the early 60s, see Longenecker and Still 2014: 197–99.

thousand adherents" (although that estimate probably requires some downward revision).[17]

Just a few years after receiving Paul's letter to them, however, these same Christians were to become the target of persecution, devised by the emperor himself. Tacitus tells us that when Nero required a scapegoat for the burning of Rome in July 64, he "fastened the guilt and inflicted the most exquisite tortures on a class hated for their abominations, called Christians by the populace" (*Annals* 15.44). In mid-60s Rome (beginning perhaps in late 64 or possibly in 65), some Christians were slaughtered; others kept their heads below the parapet (implied by 2 Timothy 4:16); still others must have fled the city, perhaps returning in the late 60s when Nero's pogrom against them tailed off.[18]

Subsequent to Nero's persecution, Jesus-groups in Rome seem to have thrived again. According to Ignatius (early second century), Christians at Rome were well known to have "taught others" in locations beyond their own city (*To the Romans* 3:1). This is illustrated well by the text of *1 Clement*. Writing from Rome in the late first century, the author of *1 Clement* instructs Christians in Corinth about situations they were facing.

Tucked within this context is a historical gem regarding the emergence of Christianity in the initial years after the Neronian period. As history attests repeatedly, persecution against a targeted group easily fosters a dialectical form of empathy for that group, especially if the persecution against them is seen to be ill-founded. According to Tacitus, this is precisely what happened in the wake of Nero's persecution against Christians, as "compassion began to arise" (*miseratio oriebatur*) toward Christians, who were seen as "being

---

17. Jewett 2007: 61–62.
18. We know that some Christians were forced to leave Rome in 49, when Claudius expelled some Jews from the city due to a disturbance regarding "Chrestos" (probably a misunderstanding of "Christos"; see Suetonius, *Claudius* 25). Some Jewish Christians were included in this expulsion from the capital city – including Prisca and Aquila (Acts 18:2), who returned to Rome sometime after Claudius's death in 54, when his edict was no longer in effect. On the situation of Roman Christians up to the late 60s, see Longenecker and Still 2014: 171–74.

eliminated not for the public utility but for the savagery of one man" (*Annals* 15.44.5).

This may explain why the two decades immediately following Nero's persecution were a notably quiet time in the register of persecution against Christians. No historical source suggests that Christians feared for their lives as a consequence of the initiatives of Vespasian, emperor from July 1, 69, to June 23, 79. Just the opposite is the case, in fact. Whereas Melito of Sardis identifies only Nero and Domitian as persecutors (Eusebius, *Ecclesiastical History* 4.26), Tertullian explicitly names Vespasian in his list of emperors who did not persecute Christians (*Apology* 5), and Eusebius claims that Vespasian did no harm to Christians during his reign (*Ecclesiastical History* 3.17).[19] The twenty-five-year period between the death of Nero and the (alleged?) persecution of Christians under Domitian in the mid-90s was not remembered as a fearful time for Christians.[20] If we take our cues from Tacitus and others, it seems that Vespasian's emperorship was a period during which early Christianity was able to spawn without much external impediment or internal anxiety overwhelming it.

As we will see, it was within this period, from the late 60s onwards, that Jesus-devotion is evident within the vibrant town of Pompeii. Nonetheless, even if Jesus-devotion had a foothold within Pompeii, it was not a prominent form of devotion there. Although Tertullian's argument about the absence of Jesus-followers in the Vesuvian towns is not historically robust, it does reveal that those towns could not have

---

19. Vespasian was frequently remembered as an emperor of moderation, in contrast to other early emperors. An example of this sentiment is given to us by Tacitus, *Histories* 4.42. There, the senator Curtius Montanus makes a speech to fellow senators during the time of Vespasian that includes these words: "Do you think that Nero was the last tyrant? The same belief was held by those who survived Tiberius and Gaius [Caligula]; yet meantime Nero arose more implacable and more cruel. We do not fear Vespasian, such are his years and his moderation."
20. In fact, if the surviving texts from that period are anything to go by (e.g., the New Testament Gospels, Acts, the deuteropauline literature, Hebrews, the Petrine texts), it was a time in which Christians were finding their voice and their feet within the empire. No wonder the Gospel of Matthew, written in the 80s, can end with words that imagine Christians taking their faith boldly to their contemporaries (Matthew 28:19–20). At around the same time, the Lukan Gospel was being composed, which Richard Hays depicts in the following fashion (1996: 134): "Luke's deep confidence in God's providence imparts to the story a positive, robust, *world-affirming* character. . . . [T]he church is not a defensive community withdrawing from an evil world; instead, it acts boldly on the stage of public affairs, commending the gospel in reasoned terms to all persons of goodwill and expecting an open-minded response."

been an important hub in the spread of the early Jesus-movement; if they had, Tertullian could not have made his theologically motivated claim about the absence of Christians in those towns. Consequently, if Jesus-followers did reside within Pompeii (with population estimates currently at about ten thousand), they must have had a relatively insignificant profile among the population.[21]

Nomenclature

Before starting down the road of this adventure into ancient artifacts, several preliminary explanations are required to help the reader get around the data with relative ease.

First, when discussing locations in Pompeii, the standard practice for listing locations will be followed. In the mid-nineteenth century, the esteemed archaeologist Giuseppe Fiorelli divided Pompeii into regions; within those regions, he assigned numbers to the street blocks; and within those street blocks he enumerated entryways into houses and businesses. That method of enumerating locations will be adopted throughout this book. So, for instance, the House of the Faun is situated in region 6 of Pompeii and in block number 12, with its main entrance being entryway number 2 within that block. In other words, the House of the Faun is located at 6.12.2 in Pompeii. A rough map of the nine designated regions of Pompeii appears below (figure 2.1). Within those regions, street blocks are called *insulae* or "islands" (the singular being *insula*, a self-contained block of houses and commercial properties surrounded by streets, giving the block a certain identity as a conglomeration of properties).

---

21. The number of inhabitants of the Vesuvian towns is difficult to determine. Previous estimates of twenty thousand Pompeii inhabitants or above (Grant 1971: 27; Brilliant 1979: 3; Etienne 1992: 75) have tended to be brought down in more recent years. See, for instance, Bradley 2005: 82.

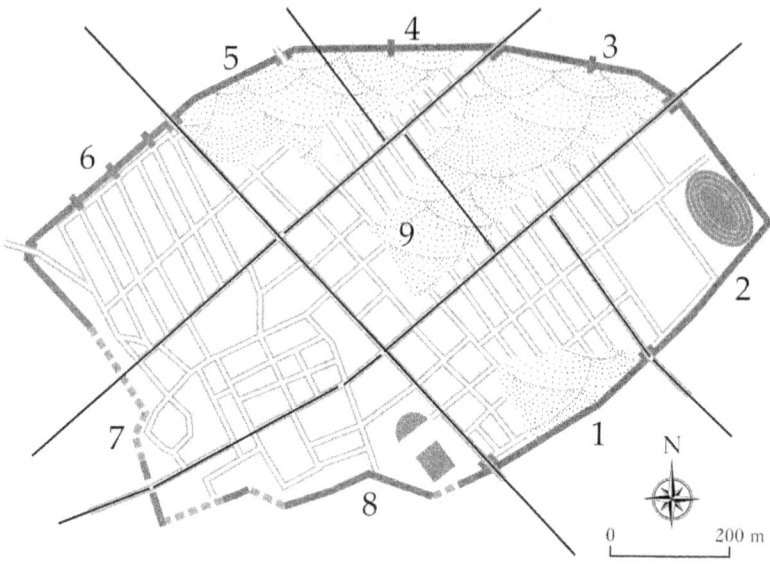

Figure 2.1. Pompeii divided into nine regions (shaded areas have not yet been excavated).

Second, inscriptions from the ancient world are sometimes referred to in the chapters that follow. These inscription have been collected in the standard reference work *Corpus Inscriptionum Latinarum,* or "the corpus of Latin inscriptions." The fourth volume of this massive project (together with the tenth volume) contains the majority of inscriptions found from Pompeii and Herculaneum, of which there are over eleven thousand. So when an inscription is mentioned and a reference appears next to it, such as "*CIL* 4.5112," the reader knows that this inscription comes from the fourth volume of *Corpus Inscriptionum Latinarum,* where it appears as inscription number 5112.

Third, the reader will soon be immersed in a world of ancient cross-shaped artifacts, and a case will be made that some of these derive from early Jesus-devotion. In this regard, it is important to note that ancient Christian crosses often differed in their appearances. There is, first, what I call "the T cross." Traditionally referred to by the Latin term *crux commissa,* the T cross has the appearance of a capital *T*, with the crossbar at the top of the vertical stave (see figure 2.2).

Figure 2.2. A Byzantine T cross.

A second formation of the Christian cross is what I call "the body cross" (for reasons that I explain elsewhere).[22] Traditionally referred to by the Latin term *crux immissa* and later known as "the Latin cross," the body cross is formed with the crossbar below the top of the stave but above the middle: † (see figure 2.3).

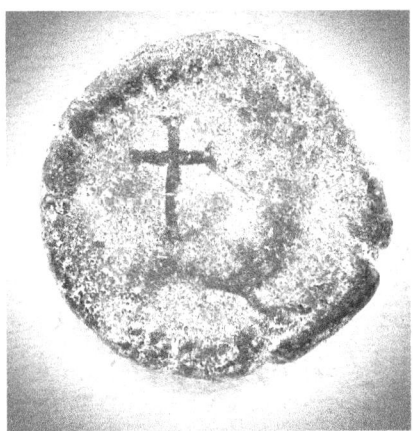

Figure 2.3. A "body cross" on an ancient coin from Israel.

---

22. See especially Longenecker 2015: 70.

What I call the equilateral cross is a third way of depicting this symbol. Traditionally referred to by the Latin term *crux quadrata*, this is a balanced cross in which all of the appendages are of roughly equal length: (see figure 2.4).

Figure 2.4. An ancient ring displaying an equilateral cross with flared ends.

A fourth formation of the cross is the handled cross or the Ankh. Traditionally referred to by the Latin term *crux ansata*, this cross is formed by combining either the T cross or the body cross with a loop attached to the top, as if the cross were being carried by a piece of rope or a handle at the top (see figure 2.5). This Egyptian symbol of life was frequently used as an amulet against evil. It had embedded itself within Egyptian religious imagery for more than a thousand years prior to the emergence of Christianity. Egyptian Pharaohs and deities are commonly seen with it in their hands or are associated with it in some way on inscriptions or coins. With the rise of devotion to the Egyptian deity Isis in the centuries just prior to the Common Era, she too is frequently depicted in association with the Ankh. This symbol will play a key role in our discussion in chapter 7 below.

Figure 2.5. A stylized Egyptian Ankh, formed by placing a circular handle above a T cross.

***

Preliminaries such as the ones dealt with in this chapter are important for setting up the task at hand, but they themselves cannot match the intrigue of studying the artifacts that lie ahead of us in subsequent chapters. But before setting out our case in relation to those artifacts (parts 3 and 4 below), we need first to determine the most feasible starting point for our trek. Sifting through the various artifacts is critical in this enterprise, in order to ensure that our starting point provides the best traction. Chapters 3 and 4 below will tease out that starting point and place it within the broader stream of academic debate. Having established our starting point and seen issues that pertain to it, we will then broaden our focus in chapters 5 and 6, entertaining further issues in order to ensure that we know what we should be expecting when setting out on our journey. These are the things of part 2, below.

PART II

Setting Up

"Because Pompeii and the surrounding areas
were buried so suddenly and completely,
much is preserved there which did not survive
from elsewhere in the Roman Empire."
(Milnor, *Graffiti and the Literary Landscape in Roman Pompeii* [2014], 5)

"The lack of Christian crosses from the first century A.D.
may be due to the vagaries of survival.
Little else has come down from this early period,
but the picture might look very different
if more towns like Pompeii and Herculaneum
had survived in toto."
(Barnard, "The 'Cross of Herculaneum' Reconsidered" [1984], 23)

3

The Starting Point

Were Jesus-followers resident in the Greco-Roman centers that were decimated by the eruption of Mount Vesuvius in 79? Historians, classicists, and archaeologists from previous generations have answered the question in different ways at different times in relation to different pieces of evidence. The pendulum has swung from one side to the other, depending on the currents of scholarship. It was sometimes fashionable among specialists to claim that Jesus-followers did, in fact, reside in the Vesuvian towns and that there is solid evidence for this view among select artifacts. But there were always detractors from this position. Some found the evidence less than compelling, thinking that the artifacts could be explained in other ways. In fact, this has been the strongest current among the opinion makers regarding this matter.

In this project, I will propose a fresh interpretation of the relevant historical data (nearly two dozen artifacts). I will suggest that, when all the data are in play and interpreted in light of the most up-to-date scholarship, the much stronger current runs contrary to the flow of the consensus. This will involve (1) reevaluating judgments already thought to be sound regarding certain artifacts, and (2) introducing new artifacts that have thus far been neglected.

In the process, it will become clear that some of the things our predecessors considered to be certainties have proved not to be certainties at all. The point has recently been made by Edinburgh classicist Alastair Small when discussing the issue in 2007:

> The evidence for Christianity in Pompeii and Herculaneum is of uneven value, and has been much debated, but when the more dubious arguments are discounted, there remains a residue of archaeological documentation which should leave no doubt that there were Christians in Pompeii before the eruption.[1]

These words indicate that the consensus of our predecessors is not wholly robust and that the same is true for its handling of the evidence. This book involves the task of "discounting the more dubious arguments" while taking on the burden of proof and demonstrating that the evidential base is, in fact, best interpreted as indicating the presence of Jesus-devotion in the shadow of Mount Vesuvius.

Starting-Point Candidates

What data present themselves in this task? The debate thus far has generally been informed by only a few artifacts that are not free from interpretative snags, regardless of which side of the debate they are used to support. The following artifacts have been placed front and center at different times in past rounds of the debate:

1. two cross-shaped artifacts mounted on walls: (a) one in a bakery in Pompeii's Insula Arriana Polliana (6.6.17/20–21), and (b) one in a small upper apartment in Herculaneum's House of the Bicentenary (5.15–16);
2. a charcoal inscription (*CIL* 4.679) in which the Latin word *Christianos* (i.e., "Christians") was etched in the so-called House of the Christian Inscription at Pompeii (7.11.11); and

---

1. Small 2007: 194.

3. a word-square inscribed into plaster (at two places in Pompeii) that features the word *rotas* (Latin for "wheels") and might contain a highly ingenious cryptic message allegedly hidden within it – that is, the phrase *Pater Noster*, or "Our Father," in the shape of a cross (the letter *N* functioning as the center point of the cross), along with two occurrences of the theological title "Alpha Omega" (*CIL* 4.8623).

Artifacts other than these are sometimes considered as well, but usually their viability is so weak as to be virtually negligible.[2]

Of course, none of these artifacts is self-interpreting. Each has been evaluated in support of quite different interpretations. But this should not be seen as an instance of rolling the dice until you get the number that you want. Some arguments are better than others, and fresh evidence will help us to weigh "which ones are which."

To demonstrate, here is an example of a bad argument – one that is especially notable since it comes from a prominent scholar of the Vesuvian towns. In his influential book from the early twentieth century (*Pompeii: Its Life and Art*), August Mau argued that the *Christianos* inscription could not have been referring to local Christians. How did he know this? He held this view simply on the basis that Tertullian had long ago stated that there were no Christians in the Vesuvian towns. Accordingly, Mau claimed that the inscription only allows "the inference that Christians were known at Pompeii, not that they lived and worshipped there. According to Tertullian (*Apology* 40) there were no Christians in Campania before 79."[3]

Mau's case was clear and simple. No doubt, it contributed significantly to bolster the consensus view, since Mau is one of the

---

2. Other artifacts deserving mention include: (1) graffiti that mention the word "faith," such as the phrase *fidelis in p (pace? perpetuum? CIL* 4.3200); (2) an amphora bearing a chi-rho symbol; and (3) a graffito simply reading "Sodom(a) Gomora" (*CIL* 4.4976). Lampe is right to list these as finds that "cannot convincingly be connected with Christianity" (2003: 8). The "Sodom(a) Gomora" graffito may have been inscribed by a Jew without any Christian commitment; the chi-rho symbol had currency as a simple abbreviation of various terms (see Finegan 1992: 353) prior to its adoption by Christians as a truncation of the name "Christos." Lampe lists other inscriptions that may have Christian relevance as follows: *CIL* 4.679; 4976; 10477; 10062; 10193; 8123; 10000; cf. 6175. There is also the occurrence of the name "Iesus" in *CIL* 4.4287.
3. Mau 1902: 18.

foremost Vesuvian scholars of the past two hundred years.[4] Nonetheless, since Tertullian's claim is historically unreliable (as we saw in chapter 2), this is quite simply a bad argument, despite being advocated by an influential Vesuvian archaeologist.[5] (And what made a bad argument worse is that Mau never discussed other evidence that had been discovered in Pompeii nearly a century before his pronouncement.)

Karl Zangemeister made precisely the same argument in 1909 in the *CIL* entry for the *Christianos* inscription.[6] In essence, the standard reference work of Pompeii inscriptions incorporates second-rate argumentation in its handling of the issue regarding the possibility of a Christian presence within the Vesuvian towns.

If Mau and Zangemeister thought Tertullian's specious comment was the starting point (and the determining factor) when considering whether Christians were in the Vesuvian towns, other starting points have sometimes been preferred. At times, the *rotas* word-square has been used as the artifact that frames the whole issue, especially when that inscription is interpreted as a cryptic proclamation of Christian faith. But since the word-square's credentials as a Christian artifact are tenuous, that artifact falls beyond the confines of this book. And since any interpretation of the *rotas* word-square is inevitably fragile, that artifact should not be given pride of place in the discussion; at best, it can only trail behind at the end. Even if it is a Christian artifact, it will not serve as a support for my case here, not least since significant advances can be made without its presence in the mix.

What then of other starting points? The *Christianos* inscription cannot serve in that role, not least because it has proved extremely

---

4. In an obituary (Bates 1909: 346), Mau was heralded as having known Pompeii "more intimately than any other man," adding "except, perhaps, Fiorelli" (the influential inspector and later director of the site of Pompeii from 1860 through 1875).
5. Lampe advocates this same bad argument (2003: 7): "Tertullian knows that no Christians lived in Pompeii in 79 C.E." Lampe is, however, critical of Tertullian's claim that no Christians lived in Campania, since Lampe recognizes that Acts 28:13–14 places Christians in Campania (Puteoli). Lampe (2003: 7n2) calls this aspect of Tertullian's case "a hasty rhetorical exaggeration." It is unfortunate that Lampe, like Mau, failed to recognize the rhetorical dimension in Tertullian's apologetic claim regarding the towns destroyed in the eruption of Vesuvius.
6. See Zangemeister's entry on the Christianos graffito (*CIL* 4.679) in Mau and Zangemeister 1909: 461.

difficult to interpret. Moreover, although it makes reference to Christians, as Mau rightly noted (before wrongly employing Tertullian to decide the matter) we can never be sure whether the Christians mentioned in that inscription were already within the Vesuvian towns – unless, that is, other data give confirmation of that fact.

Of the usual candidates, only two artifacts remain as possible contenders for framing the issue, both of them being artifacts that contained cross-shaped figures – the artifacts found in the Pompeii bakery and in Herculaneum's House of the Bicentenary. Neither of these artifacts is available to us today. The Herculaneum artifact was removed from the walls by someone in the first century, and the Pompeii artifact was removed by Mother Nature once the artifact was exposed to the elements in the early nineteenth century.

Of the two, the Herculaneum artifact has frequently taken pride of place when addressing the issue of the presence of Jesus-devotion in the Vesuvian towns. When it was first discovered in the late 1930s, archaeologists were eager to present it as a Christian cross. With that established, other artifacts coalesced around it within a web of ancient artifacts. But the pendulum was soon to swing the other direction, for reasons that will become clear in chapter 4 below. For now, it is enough to say that the Herculaneum artifact is not a viable starting point for establishing the presence of Jesus-followers in the Vesuvian towns, since it may well be an artifact of another kind altogether (although even that view is not as robust as it is sometimes thought).

Of the usual candidates, then, the best starting point for fruitful consideration of the issue is the cross-shaped artifact on the wall of the Pompeii bakery. And as we will see in later chapters, this artifact will not disappoint, since it frames the issue with considerable clarity.

The Artifact in the Pompeii Bakery

The cross-shaped artifact in a ground-level room in Pompeii's Insula Arriana Polliana (insula 6 of Pompeii's region 6; see figure 3.1) was discovered on January 28, 1813. At that time, the excavations at Pompeii were under the direction of François Mazois, a French expert in ancient architecture. Mazois reported on the cross-shaped artifact in his *Les Ruines de Pompeii*, published in 1824, two years before his death in 1826.[7]

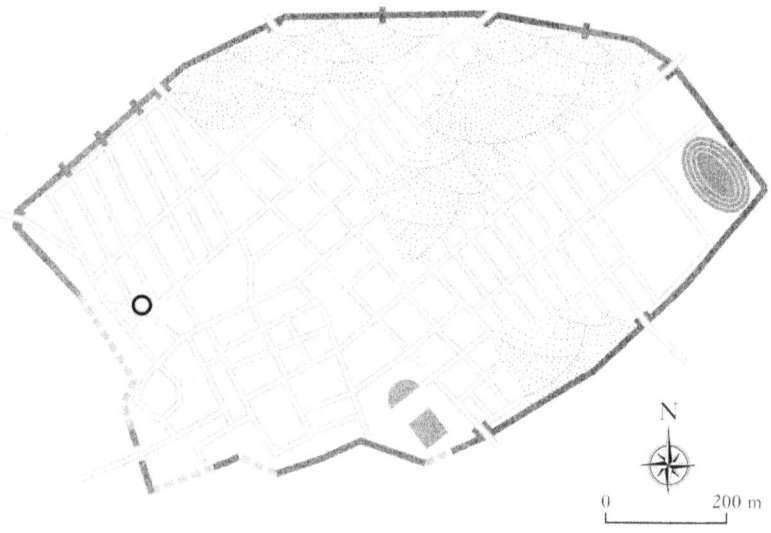

Figure 3.1. The bold circle marks the location of the bakery where the cross-shaped artifact was found.

As is true for most parts of Pompeii today, everything above ground level in this insula was lost in the ancient eruption or the modern excavations. Consequently, the cross-shaped artifact in this insula was exposed to the elements of nature and eventually destroyed by them.[8] It is uncertain when that destruction occurred, but it probably happened within the first two decades of the artifact having been uncovered.

This bakery, which had no direct access into the main house of the insula, was one of ten or so premises around the outer ribbon of the

---

7. Mazois 1824: 84–85.
8. This sort of thing happens all the time in the ruins of Pompeii and Herculaneum. William Clarke (1847: 91) makes mention of one house in Pompeii that "was formerly decorated with paintings taken from the Odyssey, and from the elegant fictions of Grecian mythology. When Mazois visited it in 1812, two paintings in the atrium were still in existence, though in a very perishable state. Shortly after he had copied them they fell, owing to the plaster detaching itself from the wall."

insula, most of which were self-contained (see figure 3.2).[9] These were (predominantly?) rental properties (as testified to by the inscription *CIL* 4.138).[10] The Insula Arriana Polliana was extensive and lavish, with a crop garden at the back that occupied a third of its space, perhaps supplying goods that could be sold in some of the properties dotted around the outer ribbon of the insula (e.g., 6.6.22).

As a corner shop with entrances to the south and west, the bakery at 6.6.17/20–21 had easy access to two streets, both of them major arteries for Pompeii's flow of traffic. (Entryways 18 and 19 facilitated stairways leading to upper residences and were not part of the bakery complex.) These streets have been given the modern names "Via del Terme" to the southern front of its shop (part of a main east-west axis in the north of the town) and "Via Consolare" to the western side of its shop (the route leading to the Herculaneum Gate in the northwest corner of the town). Since the bakery's entrances were easily accessible to passersby on these two main routes (see entryways 20 and 21 in figure 3.2 [right]), the bakery was ideally located to attract trade, probably enjoying a lively business. Another smaller bakery (probably more a pastry bakery than a bread bakery) stood at the other front corner of the insula (6.6.4–5, at the southeast of the insula) and also benefited from a double aspect onto two streets (the Via del Terme to its southern front and Vico della Fullonica to its eastern side).

The cross-shaped artifact found in this bakery was worked in bas-relief within a larger stucco panel. Placed on the wall in the corner shop that could have been entered by way of entries 20 or 21, the cross-shaped artifact faced outward toward Via Consolare (see figure 3.3).[11] We cannot date when the artifact was erected. The premises where the bakery now resides were significantly remodeled in the aftermath of the earthquake that shook the Vesuvian towns in 62 or 63, and the artifact may have been part of that remodeling, or it could have

---

9. These were entryways 2, 3, 4/5, 6/7, 9, 10/10a, 14, 15, 16, and 17/20/21; probably entryways 8, 18, and 19 led up to residential areas as well. The shop at 6.6.22 had access to the main house. The same was probably true of 6.6.13.
10. On the premises surrounding the insula's main house as rental premises, see Pirson 1997.
11. See della Corte 1965: 115.

been added after the main remodeling.[12] Either way, it is likely to be a postquake feature.

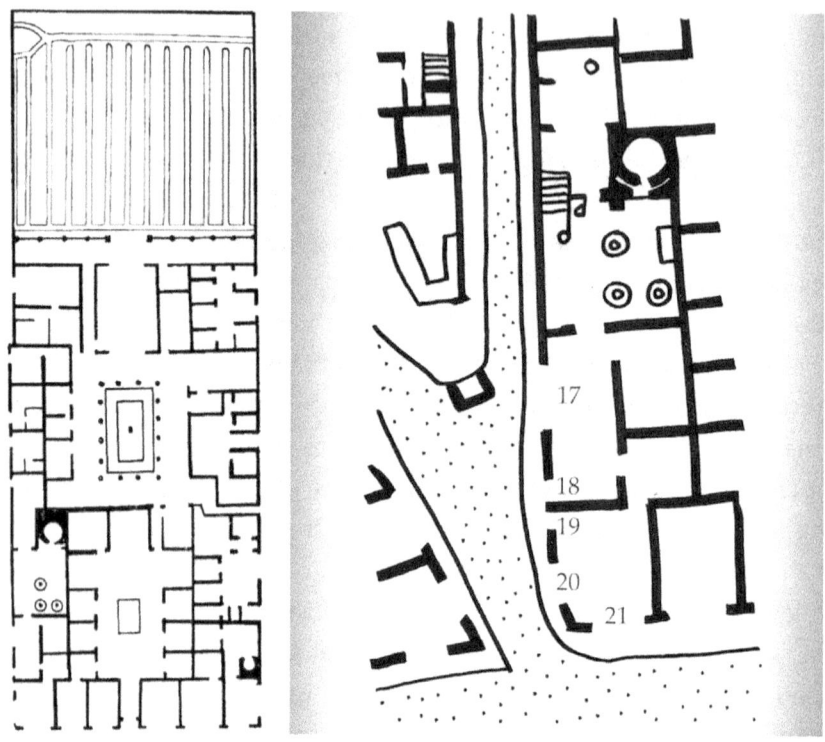

Figure 3.2. Left: the plan of the Insula Arriana Polliana, with the bakery in the southwest corner (from Jashemski 1979: 37); right: the bakery itself, with entryways listed.

We know what the cross looked like only because Mazois included an elaborate drawing of it in his report of 1824 (see figure 3.4). There is no reason to think that Mazois's illustration is deficient in its precision. His illustrations are widely lauded for their precision, with Mazois having "eschewed the creative license" of some earlier illustrators.[13] His drawings are "filled with learned commentary on Pompeian

---

12. At some point, a series of small shops along the southwestern edge of the insula was incorporated into a single bakery, with residential premises built upstairs, accessed by stairways within the oven room (for the baker and his household, presumably) and at entryways 18 and 19 (for separate households, presumably). This conversion of the premises may have happened after the earthquake.
13. Gardner Coates 2012: 100.

architecture ... and crowned by numerous plates" that are known for "the accuracy of [their] architectural renderings."[14]

Figure 3.3. Looking from Via Consolare through entryway 20 into the bakery shop and the wall where the cross-shaped artifact was found.

The insula in which the bakery stands is often referred to by way of the main house of the insula – traditionally described as the House of Pansa. This descriptor arose when a political advertisement on an exterior wall of the insula was interpreted to mean that the insula was owned by the prestigious Pansa family. But it is now recognized that the advertisement cannot carry the weight of that interpretation.[15] In fact, another inscription (*CIL* 4.138) suggests that at the time of Vesuvius's eruption, it was Gnaeus Alleius Nigidius Maius who owned the insula.[16] (Maius was an extremely wealthy resident of Pompeii and,

---

14. Brilliant 1979: 142.
15. The inscription is a political endorsement and reads: *Pansam aed[ile], Paratus rogat* (*CIL* 4.251). This inscription suggests that Paratus lived within the house, but it does not place a member of the Pansa family in that location. Pansa is simply a candidate for the position of aedile and is receiving Paratus's public support. Programmata of this kind were frequently placed on walls throughout the town.
16. The inscription read: "Insula Arriana Polliana owned by Cn. Alleius Nigidius Maius: to rent, from

especially prior to and after Nero's reign, was a prominent civic leader there.)[17] The same inscription informs us that the insula itself was known at that time as the Insula Arriana Polliana – perhaps having earlier been owned by an Arrius Pollio.[18] We cannot be sure that Maius lived in the main residence of the insula; perhaps he resided elsewhere in the town.[19]

---

1 July next, shops with their own mezzanines, respectable upstairs apartments, and a house [or houses]. A prospective tenant should apply to Pirmus, Cn. Alleius Nigidius Maius's slave."

17. Maius was one of the most prominent among civic elite at the time of the eruption. He had been adopted into the powerful Alleius family. His adoptive mother was buried in the massive and elaborate Tomb of Eumanchia, herself an extremely influential woman of the Augustan period at the beginning of the Common Era. Maius's daughter Alleia became a prominent priestess of Venus before her premature death, with her tomb then being paid for from the civic treasury (see *CIL Supp* 8.855). Maius himself had been elected to a high public office (*quinquennial duumvir*) for the year 55–56, which suggests that he had already served in roles only slightly less celebrated (*aedile* and *duumvir*) prior to that date. All three were extremely influential positions within the local government. Maius frequently sponsored lavish gladiatorial games (see *CIL* 4.7991) and was known as the "chief of games" (*CIL* 4.7990). One inscription identifies him as "leader of the colony" (*CIL* 4.1177). After the death of Nero, he became a priest of the emperor Vespasian and seems to have sponsored celebratory games in the town's impressive amphitheater on the day that a temple altar was dedicated to Vespasian and his children (*CIL* 4.1180) – perhaps the impressive altar residing at the front of the temple of Vespasian.
    Maius, then, was clearly a man of high social standing with vast economic resources. Renting out a number of accommodations and shops dotted around the southern half of his insula was merely a drop in his much larger economic bucket. At least one of those rental spaces is advertised as being suitable even for members of the equestrian order of Roman society (*CIL* 4.138). Clearly, Maius enjoyed notable streams of income and a profile of influence. On Maius, see Franklin 1997; van Buren 1947.
18. Visitors to Pompeii today will find the house bearing a double signage; the official signage lists it as Casa di Pansa, but a much larger plaque has also been erected next to it that states *Domus Cn Allei Nigidi Mai*.
19. On Maius's possible ownership of the equally impressive House of the Dioscuri (6.9.6), see Romizzi 2006a: 58–64; 2006b. Pirson (1997: 172), however, makes the case that the main house of the Insula Arriana Polliana was not a rental property. Ling (2009: 143) simply notes that Maius "may have resided in the dominant central house" of insula 6.6.
    It is possible that two occupants in the insula's main residence included men mentioned in inscriptions *CIL* 4.250 and 4.251. One inscription names Paratus (as noted in note 60 above), and the other names Olius Primus. These two men were asking others to support their favored political candidates. See della Corte 1965: 113–15. Ollius Primus had connections with the Neronian imperial household, back when that was fashionable in Pompeii (in the early to mid-60s). See Franklin 2001: 127.

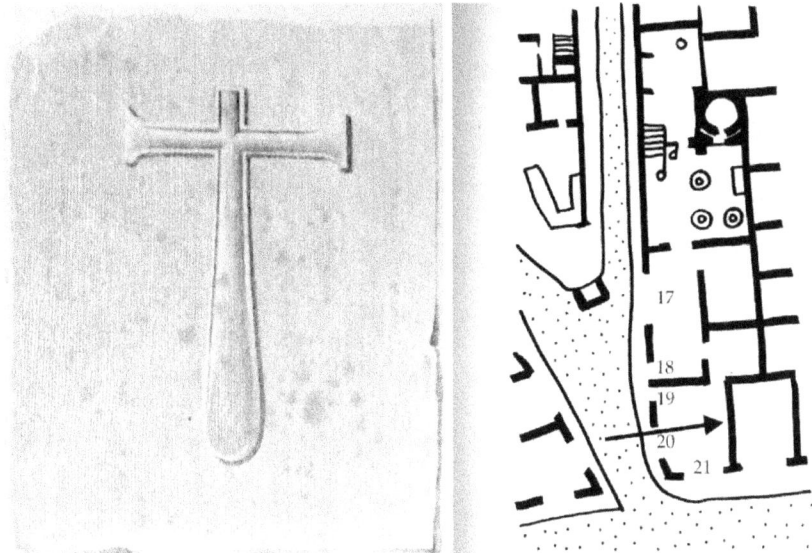

Figure 3.4. Left: Mazois's drawing of the Pompeian cross (with defacement spots from paper deterioration); right: the arrow identifies the position of the artifact in the shop of the bakery. Left photo from Mazois 1824: vol. 2, 88.

***

In this chapter, we have narrowed the starting point of our project to the cross-shaped object in the bakery of the Insula Arriana Polliana, and have reconstructed its placement within its environs. We move now to a survey of how that artifact has been interpreted in the years since its discovery.

4

The Debate

The cross is so closely associated with the religious symbolism of Christianity that to see the shape of a cross on a wall (as in the Insula Arriana Polliana) almost inevitably tilts perceptions toward the assumption that it must be articulating a form of Jesus-devotion. It was for this reason, for instance, that Matteo della Corte (the director of excavations in Pompeii in the mid-twentieth century) made this bold claim in his 1962 guidebook to Pompeii: "It has been definitely established that a nucleus of Christians was present in Pompeii before the catastrophe."[1]

Appearances can be deceiving, of course.[2] The fact that the cross has been intertwined with Jesus-devotion throughout so much of Christian history does not necessarily mean that we can import the same significance to a cross-shaped object on a wall from the second half of the first century. So, keeping to the guidebook genre, we can see that other tourists have been given a much different impression from

---

1. Della Corte 1962: 5.
2. So, for instance, the appearances of other Pompeian artifacts frequently led della Corte to claim Christian influence in ways deriving more from wishful thinking than from compelling argumentation.

those who purchased della Corte's guidebook. In a 1985 guidebook to Herculaneum, for instance, Alphonso de Franciscis noted that a cross-shaped object originally hung from a wall of the House of the Bicentenary, but he left his readers with the clear impression that the artifact has nothing to do with Christianity: "In one of the rooms . . . can be seen a cross-shaped impression in the white plaster, a discovery which at the time created a sensation, being widely interpreted as evidence for the spread of Christianity to Herculaneum before A.D. 79."[3] Discussion of the cross-shaped artifact simply ends at that point, the implication being that this sensational interpretation is no longer valid. A 2011 guidebook makes that point explicitly:

> A very interesting discovery was made on the upper floor: for decades, it was considered the most important find at the home – a cross-shaped emblem on a wall inside a stucco panel. Many archaeologists . . . thought it had religious significance as the oldest known reference to the cross before 79 AD. Recent theories suggest that the wall marking might have been left by the imprint of a bracket that once hung on the wall.[4]

Clearly these artifacts have been subject to different conclusions over the years. In order to clarify the issues at stake, we will undertake here a short history of interpretation, laying out the reasoning behind different conclusions, highlighting how opinions have changed, and noting why the current consensus sees no basis for thinking that we have artifacts of Jesus-devotion within the Vesuvian remains.

Although an interpretation of the cross-shaped artifact from Herculaneum is not featured in this book, discussion about that artifact is so intertwined with discourse about the cross-shaped artifact in the bakery of the Insula Arriana Polliana that we will occasionally benefit by including debate about the Herculaneum object in order to help frame the contours of scholarly debate about the bakery artifact.

---

3. De Franciscis 1985: 75.
4. Bonaventura 2011: 40. Understandably, the artifact is not even raised to the visiting public's attention. For instance, visitors to the Herculaneum House of the Bicentenary (at least in 2013, when I visited the site on three occasions throughout the year) are greeted with a sign saying that the house is closed for repairs. The notice advertises the house as the location where a beautiful painting was found, with the painting shown on the notice. No mention is made of the cross-shaped impression that once "was considered the most important find at the home" and caused such a stir when it was first discovered, on the basis that it might be a cross of Jesus-devotion.

First Reactions

When the cross-shaped object in the bakery of the Insula Arriana Polliana was discovered in 1813, François Mazois showed his carefully drawn picture of the artifact to others who did not have access to the site, asking for their view of the artifact's function and purpose. Here is a short extract of his reflections on the matter: "I cannot bring myself to see some unknown instrument in it, as claimed by a few people to whom I have shown this drawing of it. In truth, it is difficult not to recognize in it the Latin cross" (called here a "body cross").[5] While Mazois found it hard to regard this artifact as anything other than a relic of Jesus-devotion, some of his contemporaries preferred to see it as an "instrument" of some kind, but evidently they could not provide an explanation as to its precise function. For Mazois, it was most likely a symbol of Christianity, although a symbol that would have had meaning only to insiders to the Jesus-group that met in the bakery. So he wrote:

> Perhaps at this time the cross was still a mysterious hieroglyphic whose meaning was unknown to the common people, except to those who had embraced the Christian faith, which, placed here among the symbols of paganism as if in testimony of gratitude, informed the faithful that the truth had here found an asylum with a poor man, under the safeguard of all the popular superstitions.[6]

Mazois imagined that the cross may have been an enigmatic symbol that circulated stealthily among Jesus-followers, the only ones to know of its true religious significance. In this way, although the cross was in a "clearly visible" position and was "placed in a manner to be seen by all who passed by, as if someone had wanted to make a sign," nonetheless the symbol did not draw negative attention to the Christians in the

---

5. Mazois 1824: vol. 2, 84: "je ne peux me résoudre à y voir un instrument inconnu, comme le prétendent quelques personnes auxquelles j'ai communiqué ce dessin. Il est véritablement difficile de ne pas y reconnaitre une croix latine."
6. Mazois 1824, vol. 2, 84: "Peut-etre la croix était-elle encore à cette époque un hiéroglyphe mystique inconnu au vulgaire, dont les initiés au christianisme connaissaient seuls la signification, et qui, placé là, comme un signe de reconnaissance au milieu des simu lacres du paganisme, avertissait les fidèles que la vérité naissante s'était cachée dans l'asile d'un pauvre homme, sous la sauve-garde de toutes les superstitions populaires."

bakery because none of their contemporaries understood what it signified.⁷

Nonetheless, Mazois also seemed somewhat uncomfortable with his view that the cross-shaped artifact in the bakery was a relic of Jesus-devotion. There were no other signs of Jesus-devotion in the insula. Instead, pagan devotion typical of the Greco-Roman world was everywhere, in the form of devotion to particular deities who performed certain functions to enhance the household. Mazois made the point this way: "But if it be a [Christian] cross, how can we explain the juxtaposition – the mixture of this symbol of a new and pure religion with the images and practices of one of the most absurd superstitions of antiquity?"⁸ Here we see something of Mazois's nervousness about identifying the artifact as Christian in character. A symbol of this "new and pure religion" seemed to him to be completely out of place in the Insula Arriana Polliana, where the "absurd superstitions of antiquity" (i.e., pagan worship practices) were rampant. We will examine the reliability of this assumption in chapter 8 below. For now, it is enough to note both (1) Mazois's affirmation that the cross-shaped object was probably a Christian relic, and (2) his hesitation with this view, owing to his estimate that Christianity was a "new and pure religion."

If Mazois maintained that the cross-shaped artifact in the Insula Arriana Polliana was a cross symbolizing devotion to Jesus, so too did the supervisor of the archaeological excavations at Herculaneum when the impression of a cross-shaped object was discovered in the House of Bicentenary in 1938 (see figure 4.1). Professor Amedeo Maiuri (Director of Excavations from 1924–61) reported the discovery to the Pontifical Academy of Archaeology in 1939. In his essay on the artifact, Maiuri suggested that a Christian interpretation of the artifact was the only viable one. What had been uncovered, he believed, was a place of

---

7. Mazois 1824, vol. 2, 84: "bien en évidence . . . placée de manière à etre vue de tous les passants, comme si l'on eût voulu en faire une enseigne."
8. Mazois, 1824, vol. 2, 84: "Mais si c'est une croix, comment expliquer le rapprochement, le mélange de ce symbole d'une religion nouvelle et pure, avec les images et les pratiques d'une des superstitions les plus ridicules de l'antiquité?"

Jesus-worship. A wooden cabinet discovered within the upper room had probably served as an altar below the cross, and the nails on the wall (evident from the existence of various nail holes) had probably supported an elaborate shrine that enhanced the cross in the middle – with the shrine having been removed from the wall at some point (see figures 4.2[9] and 4.3[10]).

Figure 4.1. The House of the Bicentenary (the residence with the elongated entryway in the middle of the photo) on Herculaneum's Decumanus Maximus.

Maiuri was no doubt familiar with the criticism leveled against the view that the cross-shaped artifact in the Pompeian bakery was a symbol of Jesus-devotion in that town, but this did not deter him from seeing in the Herculaneum artifact what Mazois had seen in the Pompeii artifact more than a century earlier. Accordingly, nearly two decades after the discovery of the artifact, Mazois wrote the following

---

9. This photo was originally circulated by M. C. Ceruti in May 2006 and can be viewed here: www.micro-solus.com/abbe-carmignac/bulletins/n30.pdf.
10. Sukenik 1947: plate 88.

in his 1956 guidebook to the little room where this artifact was found: "[T]he interpretation given at the moment of the discovery that it would be a private Christian oratory is at present strengthened by the most widespread and authoritative assents, notwithstanding lively polemics and discussions."[11]

Both Mazois and Maiuri considered these cross-shaped artifacts hanging on Vesuvian walls to defy the odds by being, in fact, relics of first-century Jesus-devotion. At the same time, both recognized that their views were subject to "lively polemic and discussions." It is to those discussions that we now turn.

Figure 4.2. A cross-shaped artifact in a small upper room in the House of the Bicentenary (with the cabinet moved directly under the artifact by archaeologists).

---

11. Maiuri 1956: 46.

Figure 4.3. The artifact soon after it was discovered.

Lively Discussions

If the cross-shaped artifact from the Pompeii bakery did little to raise the prospect of a Christian presence in the Vesuvian towns in the early nineteenth century, it was the cross-shaped artifact from Herculaneum that raised the prospect to real heights – as testified to by Maiuri's confidence that it had "the most widespread and authoritative assents" in 1956. This was echoed, as we have seen, in della Corte's confident 1962 declaration that the presence of Jesus-followers in Pompeii "has been definitely established" – a claim he reasserted in 1965, where he noted that scholars were almost all agreed on this point.[12] In 1960,

---

12. Della Corte 1965: 116. There he notes that the question as to the presence of Christians in Pompeii is now being "answered in the affirmative" ("per la soluzione positiva") by the majority of scholars. See also Maiuri's popular guide to the town of Herculaneum, which was still being published after his death; it notes that the wall-cross in the House of the Bicentenary gave the room "the character of a primitive Christian oratory" (1973: 23). For early critiques of Maiuri's

Jack Lindsay translated this view into narrative form by imaginatively postulating a situation in which a Greco-Roman tour guide leads newcomers through Pompeii in the year 79. That ancient tour guide says the following to those accompanying him: "I heard recently of a slave in Herculaneum who was found worshipping a cross which he'd hidden behind a piece of furniture – it was inset in the wall. The cross was removed as a dangerous magical object and the slave was whipped."[13] In 1983 Raymond Brown, the renowned scholar of early Christianity, held the view that "there were Christians at Pompeii and Herculaneum."[14] The same claim was made by Leslie Barnard in 1984 and was expressed again in relation to Pompeii by Alastair Small in 2007, as noted in chapter 3 above.[15]

But the tide had turned long before that, and counterclaims had already been firmly established. In 1959, for instance, Duncan Fishwick had declared that interpreting Vesuvian cross-shaped artifacts as relics of Jesus-devotion was "tenuous in the extreme," adding that "the cross at Pompeii [= the bakery cross] has never been accepted as genuine" in its association with Jesus-devotion – a claim only slightly overstated.[16] With regard to the cross-shaped artifact in Herculaneum, Fishwick argued that it could not have been a product of Jesus-devotion because "the character of the find spot at Herculaneum, with its wooden dice box and loose die," precludes such an interpretation.[17] In his estimation, such everyday objects used for gaming would not be

case, see de Jerphanion 1941; de Bruyne 1945. Their points are casually batted away in Catalano 2002: 183.
13. Lindsay 1960: 251.
14. Brown 1983b: 147.
15. Barnard 1984; Small 2007.
16. Fishwick 1959: 37. Even after Mazois declared the bakery artifact to be a Christian cross, very little was done with that view in the generations that followed. Fiorelli does not even mention the bakery artifact in his 1877 guide to Pompeii, despite giving two pages to the Insula Arriana Polliana (1877: 25–26). The same is true for the 1898 version, updated by Antonio Sogliano (1898: 22)..Della Corte, however, declared the artifact in the bakery of the Insula Arriana Polliana to be a Christian artifact in 1936: 16.
17. In view of the multifunctional purposes of ancient space, Fishwick's claim carries little weight. And to claim that the presence of a die in the room rules out a devotional ethos within the room overlooks the role that dice played in determining the will of the divine (so Cicero, *De Divinatione* 1.13; 2.21, 59). On these two scores, Fishwick's conceptualization is distinctly anachronistic and misinformed. That is not to say that the artifact was a product of Jesus-devotion, but the suppositions supporting Fishwick's conclusions are extremely weak.

present in a room marked out by Jesus-devotion (echoing the claim that Jesus-devotion was out of place in the pagan context of the Insula Arriana Polliana).

In 1970, Olivieri Farioli adopted a more nuanced view of the matter. On the one hand, he intimated that Maiuri's elaborate reconstruction of a Christian chapel (complete with the cross in a wall-shrine and a kneeling stool) was motivated by his own "personal conviction" (i.e., his religious commitments).[18] In this, Farioli is expressing one of the concerns that rightly supports the consensus view: archaeology should be free from the illegitimate burden of propping up Christian apologetics. On the other hand, Farioli maintained that no interpretation of the Herculaneum wall-cross has ever been free of problems. According to him, the Herculaneum wall-cross is likely to remain simply an "unexplained" artifact.[19]

Such cautious nuances were soon to disappear, however, and confident claims were soon the staple of the consensus diet. In 1987, for instance, Everett Ferguson noted how the Herculaneum cross had initially been thought of as evidence of early Christianity within that town, but added that "[f]urther consideration . . . has given a more utilitarian purpose: the imprint in the plaster was left by wooden brackets for a wall cabinet or perhaps a shelf or mantel with a supporting upright piece."[20] That same year Peter Lampe made the same point. According to him, the Herculaneum artifact was simply the support "for a wall cabinet or perhaps a shelf or mantel," the "simplest interpretation" being that "a secular console hung here on the wall, which was secured in the plaster by a cruciform holder."[21] A decade later, Carolyn Osiek and David Balch concurred, stating in 1997

---

18. For instance, the stool was not found directly under the cross-shaped artifact on the wall but, instead, was a bit to the right side of it, perhaps having little direct connection with the cross-shaped artifact (see figure 4.3). Placing the two in direct relationship was Maiuri's initiative (as illustrated in figure 4.2). This would not have been the first time that Maiuri assisted in the interpretation of artifacts by reconstructing rooms according to his own interpretation (compare his reconstruction of the "room of the weaving girl"). As Beard whimsically notes (2008: 22), "in the modern imagination, an awful lot of Pompeians have ended up in the wrong place."
19. Farioli 1970: 70 and 71.
20. Ferguson 1987 (rev. 2003): 590.
21. Lampe 2003 (original 1987): 9.

that "the cross as a visual symbol is otherwise wholly unattested for the first several Christian centuries, and is unlikely to be a Christian symbol here."[22] In 2005 Alex Butterworth and Ray Laurence maintained the same view, claiming that the artifact had not been a Christian cross, which would be "iconographically anachronistic"; instead, it was simply "a shelf unit that had become detached from the wall."[23] In 2007, Joanne Berry identified the Herculaneum artifact as "a cupboard support," while in 2011 Andrew Wallace-Hadrill summarized the consensus view as maintaining that the artifact encompasses "the support brackets for a cupboard."[24] This view is asserted by those in charge of the sites today. In a letter written to me in April 2013, Teresa Elena Cinquantaquattro (the current Superintendent of Archaeology for the Vesuvian towns) and Greta Stefani (the current Director of the site of Pompeii) informed me that "the cross [on the Herculaneum wall] was not actually a cross but the mark left by a shelf."[25]

The same interpretation has consistently been applied to the cross-shaped artifact discovered in the Pompeian bakery. In 1992, Robert Etienne made the point simply: "In the 70s of the first century, the new Christian religion had yet to reach the people of Pompeii" – the simple inference being that the bakery cross could not be a Christian artifact.[26] In 2003, Graydon Snyder argued that Christian crosses could not have appeared in Pompeii or Herculaneum since the cross was not a Christian symbol at this period; they would be out of their natural historical sequence by three hundred years.[27] In 2005, Stefani could simply note that the cross in the Pompeian bakery had been "erroneously interpreted as a cross" – a claim made without defense, demonstrating the extent to which a scholarly consensus had already been established.[28] And in 2014 Peter Keegan reiterated the consensus

---

22. Osiek and Balch 1997: 86. Both scholars have recently related to me that they are dissatisfied with their previous formulation of this issue.
23. Butterworth and Laurence 2005: 383n22.
24. Joanne Berry 2007: 201; Wallace-Hadrill 2011: 313.
25. My translation of the phrase "la croce non è tale, ma il segno di una mensola," included an email sent to me from Cinquantaquattro, signed by Stefani, and sent on April 14, 2013.
26. Etienne 1992: 124.
27. Or as he says, they would have come "300 years too soon" (Snyder 2003: 61).
28. Stefani 2005: 139 ("erroneamente interpretato come una croce").

with the confident claim that "Christians did not employ publicly any form of the cross prior to Constantine" – which removes the artifact displayed to the public in the Pompeii bakery from consideration.[29]

But old habits die hard, and every now and then the old view enjoys a temporary revival (even beyond spurious YouTube videos, as mentioned in chapter 2). In 2012, a television series entitled "The Dark Ages" was produced by the British Broadcasting Corporation (in this case, BBC4). In the third minute of the first episode of that series, the presenter takes the viewers to Pompeii and, before the fourth minute of the series is under way, tells them boldly that archaeologists have discovered "proof that there were Christians here by 79 AD." The proof shown to viewers is not the cross-shaped artifacts nor even the *Christianos* inscription but, instead, the tenuous *rotas* word-square. He goes on to articulate the case for seeing this word-square as an artifact of Christian devotion (although he fails to mention that the consensus of scholarly opinion runs contrary to that view, and several details were incorrectly presented).

In the aftermath of the program, a few blogs in Britain were alight with discussions about whether Jesus-followers had in fact been present in Pompeii. The popular Cambridge classicist Mary Beard dedicated one blog posting to setting the record straight, having been inundated with people asking her about the matter after the program was aired. While most of her blog comments pertained to the *rotas* word-square, she expanded her reply to include the cross-shaped artifacts as well. According to her, "the most famous sign of the cross appears to have been the traces left by a set of shelves" (a reference to the wall-cross in Herculaneum's House of the Bicentenary). Moreover, she stated that the symbol of the cross "does not appear (so far as we know) to have been a distinctively Christian symbol until much later than 79." With these arguments in play, she concludes as follows: "I'm afraid that ideas of Christians at Pompeii are a bit of a fantasy. Sorry."[30]

---

29. Keegan 2014: 108.
30. Mary Beard, "Were There Christians at Pompeii? The Word-Square Evidence," *A Don's Life* (blog), The Times Literary Supplement, November 30, 2012, http://timesonline.typepad.com/dons_life/2012/11/were-there-christians-at-pompeii-the-word-square-evidence.html.

The single word of that apology articulates the current consensus in a nutshell.

Historical Plausibility

What we have seen in the foregoing paragraphs is a conversation that runs almost like this:

Voice 1: "It sure looks like a Christian cross, and try as I might, I can't imagine it being anything else."

Voice 2: "Yes, but the cross didn't come into use as a Christian symbol until much later, and these cross-shaped artifacts were found in contexts that rule out Christian devotion. They must have been shelf holders instead. Look at all the nail holes on the wall in the House of the Bicentenary, for instance."

In the last fifty years or so, the second voice has characterized the articulations of all but a few of the participants in the conversation. It comprises, then, a consensus view. Consensus views are often firmly based on reliable evidence and sound critical thinking. But every now and then a consensus emerges that is less than sound in its evidential base. Is this one of those instances?

It is my view that errors have been made on both sides of this debate during the past two centuries. As archaeologist Paul Bahn has rightly said, "true scientists constantly question and return to their earlier conclusions, to check them again."[31] As I will demonstrate in subsequent chapters of this book, there is need to reassess the situation with regard to the material evidence from Pompeii (leaving to one side the consensus on the cross-shaped artifact of Herculaneum's House of the Bicentenary). This reassessment will involve testing the foundations of the consensus, introducing neglected evidence into the discussion, and recalibrating the agenda of the debate.

What will readers find as they engage these arguments? They will not find historical certainties or historically assured results. The following chapters comprise what I take to be the most historically

---

31. Bahn 2012: 79.

probable scenarios – or, at times, the least implausible scenarios. I will simply use the tools of the historical trade to interpret a selection of artifacts, applying not only reasoned deduction but also sometimes disciplined inference. This is simply required by the subject matter itself and is an essential part of any historical reconstruction, with the gaps and silences that inevitably plague the material record.[32] In fact, the consensus view is based on these same procedures and is characterized by the same instability that inevitably comes into play when interpreting ancient artifacts. No matter which side of the argument one adopts, there is an interpretative dimension that overlays the "brute evidence." The task is to determine which interpretative overlay does the most justice to the material record.

The historian deals with various possibilities and seeks to find which of them rises to the top as the most likely candidate among a group of contenders. When we get to the main argumentation in later parts of this book, we will explore interpretative possibilities and assess which of them is the best contender for the title "most probable," or, at times, "least implausible." In the process, readers will discover that it is an exciting time to ask the question, Were Jesus-followers resident in the Vesuvian towns?

Before addressing that question specifically, we need to give consideration to a few issues concerning the cross in Christianity and beyond – issues addressed in chapters 5 and 6 below.

---

32. Brown (1983a: ix): Historians "must and do operate on the basis of reconstructions that fill in gaps left by evidence."

5

The Cross in Early Christianity and Beyond

As we saw in chapter 4 above, one of the perennial objections to the prospect of finding a Christian cross in Pompeii is the claim that the cross was not a symbol within Christianity until the fourth century and beyond. In 1951, erudite historian and archaeologist of early Christianity Erich Dinkler regarded it as "absolute dogma" that "the symbol of the cross makes its first appearance in the age of Constantine."[1] This dogma holds fast today, as recently as Peter Keegan's bold declaration of 2014 (noted in chapter 4) that "Christians did not employ publicly any form of the cross prior to Constantine."[2] If correct, a "dogma" of this scope and magnitude would be the scholarly equivalent to the blast of a nuclear bomb. It would decimate the whole of the pre-Constantinian period with regard to crosses of Jesus-devotion and would render that temporal terrain radioactive to all who might sift through its rubble and foolishly imagine that they have stumbled on a Christian symbol of the cross.

In this chapter, we will explore this objection and, in turn, some

---

1. Dinkler 1965: 132, the article first having been published in German in 1951, the quotation here being from 1951: 157.
2. Keegan 2014: 108.

others that arise from it. First, however, it will be instructive to consider how "the Constantinian objection" has been handled by scholars of the mid-twentieth century who argued that Christian crosses are found within the Vesuvian remains. Since the debate was provoked by the cross-shaped impression within Herculaneum's House of the Bicentenary, we will feature that discussion here, even though our attention will be on artifacts from Pompeii. Listening in on a debate of the past will help inform us in the present as to routes that might best be taken or avoided.

Previous Attempts to Dismantle the Nuke

If some twentieth-century scholars argued that the cross in the House of the Bicentenary was a Christian artifact, they were also cognizant of the need to articulate their argument in relation to the "absolute dogma" regarding the absence of Christian crosses in the pre-Constantinian record. Three of their positions on this matter are instructive, assisting us in viewing the contours of the discursive terrain.

In 1947, Eleazar Sukenik accepted the view that the cross was not a symbol of Christian devotion until the fourth century. Thinking it "unwise to insist that the cross had already become a venerated symbol of Christianity" by 79, Sukenik nonetheless held that the cross in the House of the Bicentenary was, in fact, an artifact of Jesus-devotion. He ironed out the apparent discrepancy by avoiding the claim that the cross-shaped impression was a symbol. For him, that Herculaneum artifact was simply "a pictorial expression of the event, tantamount to exclaiming, 'He was crucified'"; it amounted to little more than "a lamentation for the crucifixion of Jesus by some of His disciples" in Herculaneum.[3] Sukenik, then, invoked a distinction between a "pictorial expression" and a "symbol" in his proposed solution to "the Constantinian objection."

In 1956, Amedeo Maiuri tackled the issue in a different fashion.

---

3. Sukenik 1947: 365.

Accepting that the Herculaneum wall-cross was a symbol of Jesus-devotion, Maiuri imagined that it was simply one of various exceptions to the pre-Constantinian "dogma," an exception that challenges that rule. So he wrote:

> Thanks to this discovery, the Christian cult of the Cross, officially established after Constantin's [sic] edict and till now documented by few monuments as belonging to the II and III century, would date back to the time anterior to the 79 A.D., i.e. to the earliest time of Apostolic Preaching. The introduction of this cult to Herculaneum would be attributed to St. Paul's preaching. This humble room of the House of the Bicentenario preserves, therefore, one of the most precious testimonies of the oldest history of the Church.[4]

Maiuri did not allow the identity of the wall-cross to be predetermined by a view of the absence of the Christian cross throughout the whole of the Mediterranean world prior to Constantine. Instead, referring to Christian crosses in the second and third century, Maiuri added the Herculaneum wall-cross as one of the few data that challenge "the Constantinian objection."

In 1984, Leslie W. Barnard adopted a different view. Like Sukenik, Barnard accepted that the cross functioned as a symbol "only from the time of Constantine," but he argued that there was one simple exception to this periodization of things. According to Barnard, "[t]he circumstances of Christians in the first century differed markedly from those which obtained in the second and third centuries."[5] So he concluded his study in this fashion:

> [I]t is no longer possible to hold the dogma that the symbol of the Christian cross first appeared in the time of Constantine. Our contention is that it was used by humble Christians before the year A.D. 79, but that its use was dropped when Christians came into wider contact with the pagan world and had to face pagan attacks and slanders.[6]

Although the cross-shaped impression in Herculaneum's House of the Bicentenary played a key role in Barnard's case, he also

---

4. Maiuri 1956: 46.
5. Barnard 1984: 20.
6. Barnard 1984: 26.

incorporated another piece of evidence in support of this conclusion – an artifact that was discovered only in the mid-1950s, and one from Pompeii that we will give consideration to in chapter 9 below. For now, it is enough to recognize how Barnard challenged the consensus view by postulating a period in history in which Christians could have included the cross as a symbol of their devotion. Regarding Christians during the time that the Vesuvian towns were still thriving, Barnard claimed the following: "Christians kept to themselves and met in small groups. There were, as yet, no Christian monuments or buildings per se. In such a milieu as this, tolerated as they appear to have been by their pagan neighbors, they were perhaps not afraid to confess their faith by the use of a simple cross."[7]

As we can see, these three scholars (Sukenik, Maiuri, and Barnard) have proposed different routes in relation to "the Constantinian objection." Sukenik skirted around the controversial word "symbol." Maiuri traced a thin line from third- and second-century artifacts back to the first-century House of the Bicentenary in order to establish that the cross has a traceable lineage as a pre-Constantinian Christian symbol. Barnard was not cognizant of second- and third-century cross artifacts but imagined that the first century was different from the second and third centuries, with first-century Christians being able to devise visible expressions of faith in ways that later Christians could not.

Of course, these scholars were discussing the cross-shaped artifact in the House of the Bicentenary – an artifact that we will not be assessing in this project. Our focus instead is on cross-shaped artifacts within Pompeii. In relation to those artifacts, three things can be said about the way forward in relation to "the Constantinian objection."

1. Sukenik, with his distinction between "pictorial expression" and "symbol," does not offer a viable route.
2. Maiuri is right in recognizing the relevance of second- and third-

---

7. Barnard 1984: 27.

century Christian symbols of the cross but needs to be further supplemented with a small dose of Barnard.
3. Barnard is wrong in his contention that Christian crosses are absent from the material remains of the second and third century (needing a dose of Maiuri on this) but is on the right lines regarding the possibilities for the articulation of Christian faith in the period that concerns us.

These claims now require substantiation.

Is the "Dogma" Robust?

Despite the claims of Dinkler and others, the Constantinian objection is not the "bomb" that it is sometimes made out to be. There are several reasons for this. Although I have already dealt with them substantially in my book *The Cross before Constantine: The Early Life of a Christian Symbol*, the main points need to be outlined briefly here.

Since the time of Dinkler, scholarship has increasingly recognized that pre-Constantinian Christianity was anything but uniform. There may have been overarching trajectories within which certain forms of Christianity flowed, but those trajectories and the forms within them were marked by diversity.[8] It is now commonplace for scholars to speak of a variety of "Christianities" within the pre-Constantinian period.[9] That fact alone makes it difficult to advocate any "dogma" that runs across the board for each and every indigenous form of Christian devotion. Even if it were the case that the cross is absent from a good number of pre-Constantinian Christianities, the historian must still allow for the occurrence of a distinctive development within an indigenous context. Even if there might be little foothold for the Christian cross in the pre-Constantinian era, that fact alone should not be allowed to foreclose the matter of the identity of Vesuvian wall-crosses altogether. At the very least, if we could ascertain that the Vesuvian remains testify to the symbol of the cross as an artifact

---

8. See, for instance, Dunn 1990; Hurtado 2013. For an early statement of this, see Bauer 1934.
9. See, for instance, Ehrman 2003.

of first-century Jesus-devotion, this might simply be a feature of a localized Christianity, perhaps distinct and distinguished from other forms of Jesus-devotion. No scenario should be squelched from the outset. History shuns "absolute dogma" on almost any matter. Historians should shun absolute dogmatism.

But is the dogma itself robust? Did Christians shun the cross before Constantine christened it a symbol of the Christian empire? As I have shown in *The Cross before Constantine*, at times the cross was fashioned as an artistic and symbolic expression of Christian devotion even within the pre-Constantinian period. It is certainly true that the cross was not the primary symbol that unified disperse Christianities prior to Constantine. Nonetheless, it is also true that the cross as an expression of Christian devotion is found in an impressive variety of contexts within the pre-Constantinian record, requiring us (in the words of William Tabbernee) to "revis[e] our traditional view of the time when crosses first came to be used."[10]

If only one example were allowed to make the point, it would have to be the interesting collection of inscriptions featured in figure 5.1[11] (not least for their relevance to the artifact discussed in chapter 11 below). These symbols were incised into one area of flooring in Room 6 of Ostia's Baths of Neptune (region 2, insula 4). In his definitive study of Ostia Antica, Giovanni Becatti claims that these inscriptions are Christian symbols (an interpretation shared more recently by Ostian scholar Jan Theo Bakker).[12] Whether or not that is true for all the inscriptional marks on this floor, it is nonetheless notable that a number of these figures incorporate the symbol of the cross (as I have demonstrated elsewhere). For our purposes, the most interesting of these will be examined here.

---

10. Tabbernee 1997: 158.
11. From Becatti 1961: figure 17. The symbols are not as they were found but have been extracted from their positions and grouped together in this figure. I have rotated the top right inscription ninety degrees counterclockwise, since I take it to include a staurogram – something that was not clear from Becatti's orientation of the symbol. I have done the same to the square inscription, to give the inscription symmetry between its left and right halves. (The circle in the middle of the square may be an attempt to replicate the defense against the evil eye.) Moreover, Becatti includes further symbols in his figure (to the right), which I have not replicated here.
12. See Bakker's website at www.ostia-antica.org/regio2/4/4-2.htm.

Figure 5.1. Symbols incised in the Baths of Neptune from Ostia Antica.

Although the inscription at the bottom left of figure 5.1 looks like a series of artistic scribbles, it unpacks to spell out the Latin word *Iesus* or "Jesus" twice (or at least twice) – with the clever styler of this fascinating construction having laid the letters along the two axes of an equilateral cross.[13] It is constructed in the following fashion, from left to right (compare also figure 5.2):

1. *I* (a single stroke)
2. *E* (two vertical strokes, connected to the *I* by a horizontal line above the three vertical strokes)
3. *S* (in the middle)
4. *U* (beneath the middle *S*)
5. *S* (below the middle *S* and the *U*)

The pattern then repeats from other side with inverse procedures (so that the second *U* appears upside-down), with the center *S* doing double duty.

---

13. It is possible that there are two further formations of the name *Iesus* within this inscription; see Longenecker 2015: 79–80.

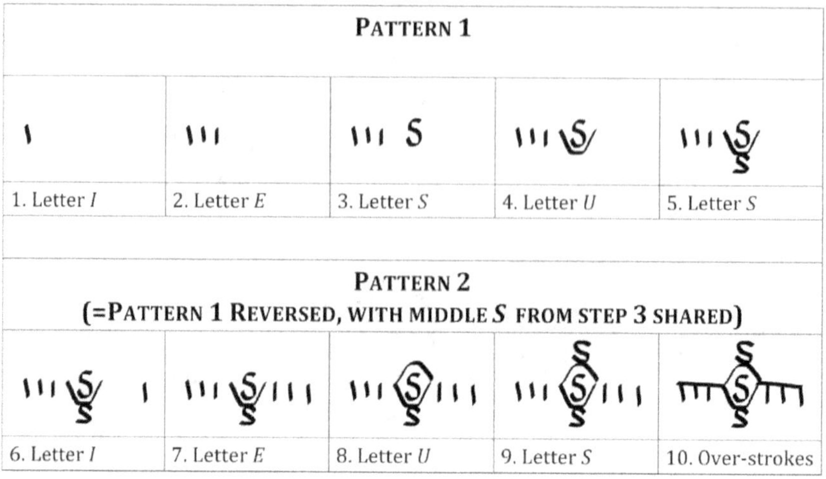

PATTERN 1				
❙	❙❙❙	❙❙❙ S	❙❙❙ ⓢ⁄	❙❙❙ ⓢ⁄ₛ
1. Letter *I*	2. Letter *E*	3. Letter *S*	4. Letter *U*	5. Letter *S*

PATTERN 2 (=PATTERN 1 REVERSED, WITH MIDDLE *S* FROM STEP 3 SHARED)				
❙❙❙ ⓢ⁄ₛ	❙❙❙ ⓢ⁄ₛ ❙❙❙	❙❙❙ ⓢ⁄ₛ ❙❙❙	❙❙❙ ⓢ⁄ₛ ❙❙❙	▱ ⓢ⁄ₛ ▱
6. Letter *I*	7. Letter *E*	8. Letter *U*	9. Letter *S*	10. Over-strokes

Figure 5.2. The Ostian "Iesus" inscription, built up stage by stage.

Notably, then, the pre-Constantinian Christian who devised this clever inscription was interested in using the shape of the equilateral cross as the backbone for his theological artistry. In fact, of the various symbols assembled in this part of the floor in Room 6 of Ostia's Baths of Neptune, the cross is the predominant shape. Moreover, these crosses are embedded in quite different structures in each of its five instances. Evidently the cross was the primary shape that undergirded the theological imagination of the Christians who crafted these symbols and who looked for artistic ways of depicting it. Their attachment to and interest in the symbol of the cross appears in the incisions they left behind.

Note also that these crosses were inscribed prior to Constantine. Becatti dates them to "the period in which there had not yet been a full official recognition of the new religion but Christianity had already deeply penetrated Roman society."[14] That would put the date of these symbols in the second half of the third century or, perhaps, the very early fourth century. If Christians could be constructing the cross as

---

14. Becatti 1961: 58–59, my translation ("in un periodo in cui ancora non v'era stato un pieno riconoscimento ufficiale della nuova religione, ma il cristianesimo era gia profondamente infiltrato nella societa romana").

a symbol in the years prior to Constantine, might they have been doing similar things in generations before that? The material record demonstrates that they were.

The third century finds Christians occasionally engraving crosses on rings, alongside other affirmations of their faith (for example, the name "Jesus," the title "Savior," or the term *ichthus*). This seems to have been a development from practices seen in the late second century and throughout the third century, in which Christians were occasionally embedding or painting crosses on their tombstones. A few of these have been found in the Roman catacombs, but more often they were erected in public places as well, occasionally with the additional notice that the tombstones had been set up by "Christians for Christians."

Around the turn from the second to the third century, several manuscripts were written that incorporated a staurogram in places where the text refers to Jesus' cross or crucifixion (P46, P66, and P75). The staurogram was a ligature combining two Greek letters – a rho (P) superimposed onto a tau (T). When the stems of the two letters share the same space and the loop of the rho peeks out above the cross-bar of the tau, a miniature picture of a crucified person emerges. Scholars of textual traditions have noted that there is no reason to imagine that these manuscripts from around 200 CE were the first to have incorporated the staurogram; it may have been a Christian scribal practice that preceded that time by a decade to two.

At about the same time, someone crafted a beautiful protective amulet that depicts Jesus on a cross as its focal point.[15] The amulet contains a number of other features too, but Jesus on his cross carries the most import in this device, whose owner imagined it to have protective powers in deflecting evil. Again, the late second or early third century is the best time frame for this artifact. And again, scholars have noted that there is little reason to imagine that this artifact was the first of its kind.

---

15. This apotropaic gemstone is held by the British Museum (artifact inv. MME 1986.05-01.1). For further discussion, see Longenecker 2015: 100–105.

A full survey of these artifacts would testify that the cross appears in a variety of streams of pre-Constantinian Christianity/Christianities. Some arose within proto-orthodox Christianity; some within Manichaean Christianity; some are unidentifiable beyond deriving from a basic Christian allegiance. There is even evidence suggesting that the cross was adopted as a symbol in some "gnostic" forms of Christianity in the second half of the second century and beyond. This makes the most sense if gnostic use of the cross was derived from proto-orthodox Christian practice rather than being the originating point for proto-orthodox usage.

That proto-orthodox Christianities were the originating point for employing the cross as a symbol gains support from a neglected text originating from about the year 140 CE – the Latin text of 5 Ezra.[16] Readers of 5 Ezra are instructed that, when they come across a dead body (surely a not-uncommon experience in the Greco-Roman world), they should bury it in a grave "and mark it" (2:23). The Christian audience of 5 Ezra was expected to understand what was meant by "mark it." The data discussed in chapter 6 below helps to explain why this was the case. For now, it is enough to note that the most obvious candidate for the shape of the mark is the cross. As Jacob Myers suggests, the mark is "a cross sign placed on grave [sic] as a sign of victory."[17] Of course, within the text itself there is no description of

---

16. On the date of 5 Ezra as quite soon after the Bar Kochba revolt of 132–135 CE, see Stanton 1993: 260–72; Longenecker 1995: 114–20; Elgvin 2007: 300–301; Dunn 2015: 230. Bergren (2013: 467, 472–73) dates it to the second half of the second century or third century, but Stanton's case for dating it to "the middle of the second century, perhaps shortly after the Bar Kokhba rebellion" (1993: 260) is stronger; Elgvin rightly calls Stanton's case "persuasive" (2007: 301).
17. Myers 1974: 151. Bergren (2013: 480) interprets the verse in different terms: "When I [= God] find your dead, I will raise them; I will watch for signs, and will give your dead the place of honor in my resurrection." This interpretation derives from Bergren's preference for the Spanish recension of the Latin text over the traditionally preferred French recension (see also Bergren 1990). But even if the Spanish recension is deemed original in this instance, the French recension must nonetheless be recognized as testifying to an ancient sentiment that is articulated here. The only issue to resolve is how far back in time the sentiment can be dated. In fact, however, in this instance it is the French recension that benefits from being the *lectio difficilior* (the more difficult reading) and therefore more likely to embody the original text. Problematically, the French recension mentions nothing about the dead who benefit from the cross mark having been Christians in life; the religious commitments adopted in life by the deceased person whose grave is marked by a cross is an irrelevancy in the French recension. This is a very "undeveloped" theology. Moreover, it is not wholly obvious why the one who does the marking of a grave should be awarded with the splendid reward promised to him/her in the French recension

the shape to be used and no explanation as to what that shape accomplishes. But that itself is significant. If the author assumed that eschatological protection comes to the person who is marked by the cross of Jesus, this seems not to be a theological innovation or idiosyncratic novelty of the author; what he instructs was expected to be readily sensible to his Christian audience – and all this within the second quarter of the second century. This neglected text itself opens a significant window onto Christian conviction in the first half of the second century. If some Christians were marking the graves of the deceased that they happened to come upon, they must certainly have been marking their own graves as well, using a cross formation to ensure eschatological protection.

This text, then, testifies to the fact that the cross was being put to use in ways that went beyond abstract conceptualization and mental visualization even prior to the middle of the second century CE. For some followers of Jesus, the cross was not simply an abstract symbol in the realm of theological mind mapping. It also served a role within the concrete realm of physical representation during the imperial reign of either Hadrian or Antonius Pius – distant predecessors of Constantine. Even before that time, Christians were posturing themselves in the shape of cross to replicate the "sign" of their lord. Sometime prior to 120, the author of the Christian text *The Odes of Solomon* spoke of holding out one's arms in praise of Jesus Christ, since "the expansion of my hands is his sign," noting that "my extension is the upright cross" (*Ode* 27).

It was not the case, of course, that Christians regularly embedded

---

– that is, having a prime position in the eschatological procession (French recension, 2:23). These theological oddities are ironed out in the Spanish recension, which improves the verse by clarifying that the beneficiaries of the resurrection are "your dead" (not just any dead) and by dropping the curious notion that one who marks the graves of the deceased will be given priority in the resurrection procession. In the process of making these improvements, the Spanish recension awkwardly introduces its own theological curiosity; in an effort to preserve the original notion of the mark or sign, it ends up depicting God as a watcher of signs – a theological oddity that testifies to an editor's attempt to conserve the original while also improving the deficiencies of the original text. For these reasons, even if Bergren is right in preferring the Spanish recension in general, in this instance the French recension is far more likely to retain the sense of the original text (dating from around 140) – a sense that has been lost in the theologically motivated adjustments evidenced in the Spanish recension.

crosses into all sort of different materials. Nor was the cross primary within pre-Constantinian Christian symbolism. But it makes an appearance within the material remains of pre-Constantinian Christianity nonetheless, and across considerable distances within the Mediterranean basin – often at key geographical growth points in pre-Constantian Christianity. And, as noted above, the cross was being used as a symbol of Christian devotion across any number of forms of Christianity – or "Christianities." And more often than not, the pre-Constantinian data suggest that the cross was seen as a symbol of protection again the forces of evil that, in the ancient mind, were ever-present and ever-threatening.[18]

This collection of data (amplified in much more detail elsewhere) puts us well within striking distance of any crosses that might crop up from within the late first century. While any artifacts of that nature would need to be historically assessed in order to determine whether they are, in fact, expressions of Jesus-devotion, there is some scope to reopen the debate regarding the presence of Jesus-devotion in the Vesuvian towns in relation to cross-shaped artifacts that have been found there. Although we cannot simply assume from pre-Constantinian data that Vesuvian cross-shaped artifacts *are* expressions of early Jesus-devotion, we would be foolish to assume a priori that they could not be. No longer can we simply say, as Graydon Snyder does, that cross-shaped artifacts in the Vesuvian towns cannot be Christian crosses since they would have appeared "300 years too soon" within the material record.[19] The cross seems to have served as a theological symbol for some Christians as far back as two centuries prior to Constantine – well within the temporal striking distance of the pre-eruption Vesuvian towns.

Further

With these historical data in view, three adjacent issues need also

---

18. See, for instance, Tabbernee (1997: 159): "The major issue to be settled is what such an early cross would have symbolized. Perhaps it was merely seen as a symbol of protection rather than as a kerygmatic cross, the latter probably being post-Constantinian."
19. Snyder 2003: 61.

to be adjudicated. First, when using the cross as a symbol of their devotion, pre-Constantinian Jesus-devotees formed it in one of three ways. Many preferred an equilateral cross, while others incorporated a body cross or a T cross. As data from the Johannine Apocalypse (Revelation) and the *Epistle of Barnabas* demonstrate, all three shapes were being envisioned by Christians before the first quarter of the second century. In fact, the *Epistle of Barnabas* presents the cross in two different formations within the span of four chapters, with the author's discourse relying on a T cross in chapter 9 and a body cross in chapter 12.[20] At times, the shape of the cross that a Christian employed depended on the theological context in which that cross was to function. Perhaps at other times there was little in it. But there seems to have been no standard form of the cross. Instead, different formations emerged, sometimes in relation to a particular function.

Second, it seems not to have been the case that Christians prior to Constantine were inevitably hiding behind locked doors in fear of persecution, being loath to devise public proclamations of their faith. Of course, that may have been true for many of them, especially in times of persecution.[21] But those times had peaks and troughs in the pre-Constantinian period and were not sustained throughout the whole of that period, nor in each and every place throughout the Mediterranean basin. I have made the point elsewhere in relation to the literary and material records of the pre-Constantinian period, but it is enough to allow the point to be made here by Felicity Harley-McGowan. In her 2011 study, she sought "to raise awareness of the evidence" of the "existence of Crucifixion iconography" in the pre-Constantinian record and to point to "manifestations of that existence in art used in magical and Christian contexts" prior to the fourth century; on the basis of that data, Harley-McGowan notes that her work "directly challeng[es] that persistent belief that persecuted Christians were too scared or too ashamed to name and depict the subject [of their faith] explicitly."[22]

---

20. For further demonstration of these points, see Longenecker 2015: 61–72.
21. On *6 Ezra* (or *2 Esdras* 15–16) as a Christian text written during a time of persecution, see Longenecker 1995: 112–14.

Third, and following on from the second, it needs to be noted that the Vesuvian towns, captured in the eruption of 79, are temporally located within a period whose character is notably different from most others in the pre-Constantinian period. If we have to reckon with the possibility of persecution against Christians at various points within the first three centuries of the Common Era, the material remains from the Vesuvian towns derive from an exceptional time within that time frame.

This is the impression given by a variety of ancient sources that testify to the point, as we noted in chapter 2 above. Even "soft persecution" (that is, social pressure and discrimination) may have been quite minimal during the late 60s and 70s, at least if Tacitus is right in saying that Nero's persecution of Christians in mid-60s Rome caused compassion for Christians to flare up in its wake (as noted in chapter 2; see Tacitus, *Annals* 15.44.5). This does not mean that all was smooth sailing for Jesus-followers during this period, of course. For instance, someone in Pompeii may have directed a jocular insult at them in the *Christianos* inscription (residence 7.11.11/14), depicting them as "cruel" in some fashion (*CIL* 4.679; see chapter 10 below). But jocular insults are not necessarily the stuff of "hard persecution" (that is, martyrdom).

It is precisely for this reason, for instance, that Thomas Gray had to move the drama of his 1830 Pompeii novel *The Vestal* from the time of Vespasian in the late 70s to the time of Domitian in the mid-90s (as noted in chapter 2 above). This is a rather odd thing to do from a historical point of view, but it was required by the contours of the story he wanted to construct, in which Christians were being persecuted regularly by their pagan contemporaries. Quite simply, if Gray had placed his storyline in the 70s, he could not have manufactured a story in which Jesus-followers were in fear of their lives. If Tacitus was

---

22. Harley-McGowan 2011: 220. Compare Butterworth and Laurence (2005: 334) on the implications of Acts 28:13–14 (Paul's arrival in Puteoli in 60): "That the centurion guarding him had allowed the accused a week's grace to stay with Christians in the port city suggests that he was persuaded by the prospect of comfortable accommodation during their sojourn: clearly the sect was not, then, an underground movement."

right, the last decade in the life of the Vesuvian towns was a period in which Jesus-followers enjoyed a noticeable dose of goodwill from some (although clearly not all) of their contemporaries. While some Christians might have drawn the ire of Pompeian neighbors, others might have been met with a neighborly shrug of the shoulders.

In one important regard, then, the Greco-Roman town of Pompeii offers us a historical context that most resembles the Constantinian world – a pseudo-Constantinian island in the pre-Constantinian stream. The last days of Pompeii coincided with the time when Christians were seeking to demonstrate that "virtue shines brightest in misfortune," with the misfortunate death of Jesus being interpreted in relation to certain virtues and advantages for his followers – as demonstrated in the texts of the New Testament from the second half of the first century. If the cross was propelled as the preeminent symbol of Christianity in the wake of Constantine's initiatives, the world of Pompeii may offer us a precursor to the Constantinian period, with conditions being as optimal as possible for the emergence of the cross as a symbol of Christian devotion.

6

The Perpendicular Equilateral

Even if the cross was a symbol among Christians at a much earlier date than the consensus has previously recognized, we need to ask whether the cross was the exclusive possession of some early Christianities. Might it also have been a general symbol of the ancient world, or a symbol of a pre-Christian religion?[1] If so, a cross in the Vesuvian record would not, in and of itself, be evidence of Jesus-devotion per se – at least, not without corroborating evidence to demonstrate its Christian credentials. If, for instance, we should find a cross that cannot be explained as a structural feature (i.e., a wall-bracket) but seems to have

---

1. Tertullian's comments about the cross in *Apology* 16.6–8 are sometimes used to suggest that the cross was a numinous symbol in non-Christian Greco-Roman religion. But this is a misuse of Tertullian's point, since Tertullian does not refer to the use of the cross in pagan worship in that context. His point is simply that the cross is a ubiquitous symbol, if only pagans had eyes to see. He gives ordinary examples of the ubiquitous cross, such as: (1) wood is placed in the shape of a cross as a brace to hold clay when fashioning a god; (2) trophies are sometimes molded in the shape of a cross; (3) processional standards placed next to gods are sometimes in the shape of the cross. He then offers another example, one in which images placed on standards in the shape of a cross are then worshiped, but his point is not that the cross is a symbol of devotion in pagan worship. He is using irony to imply that even pagans *unwittingly* offer worship in relation to the cross, not that they *intentionally* do so. His reference to the deities Pallas and Ceres in the same context seems to refer to their position with arms reaching out (to hold a spear or a scepter, for instance) and has nothing to do with worship directed to a cross. The same images are invoked by Minucius Felix (*Octavius* 29.8), with the addition of the shape of a ship's mast. These are not instances showing that the practice of venerating the shape of a cross was alive and well in pagan worship.

served a symbolic purpose, might its symbolism point just as easily to religious devotion of a kind other than Christian?

This chapter deals with matters in and around this issue. Artifacts from the Vesuvian towns provide us with a variety of cruciform-shaped objects. Although the starting point for our discussion (that is, the bakery cross) is not an equilateral cross, our discussion will broaden out to include perpendicular equilaterals in a good number of instances, so it is important to consider that shape in relation to issues relevant to our interests. Surveying these matters provides the final opportunity to focus our interpretative lenses before finally digging into the Vesuvian material record in the chapters that follow.

Equilateral Crosses as Functional and Ornamental

Some cross-shaped artifacts in the Vesuvian remains clearly served functional purposes. Two bathing pools in Herculaneum were constructed in a cross-shaped outline: a large pool in the Palaestra (which served the general public) and a much smaller pool in the House of Galba (which served the purposes of the household and its private functions; see figure 6.1). These pools were not constructed in this shape for a symbolic reason. Quite simply, this pattern permitted the pool to be filled with a minimal amount of water without reducing the amount of space accessing the water (with pool users sitting at the poolside and dropping their feet in the water). The shape of these Herculaneum pools ensured maximal efficiency in their water usage. Rather than tapping into some numinous symbol, these pools were simply designed to allow water resources to be prudently used.

Figure 6.1. The pool in the House of Galba at Herculaneum (7.1–2).

Functionality, together with aesthetic appeal, led to the formation of another kind of perpendicular equilateral within the Vesuvian record – that is, the combination of two Latin letters, a *T* and an *I*. Inscribers or artisans occasionally placed these two letters together so that the *I* sat directly above the stave of the *T* – thereby forming a +. These ligatures can be found in Pompeii on stamp rings (or *signacula*), for instance.[2] The ring of Aulus Vettius Restitutus is a case in point (*A. Vetti Restituti*),[3] where the *TI* ligature appears twice in the second line of letters (see figure 6.2).[4] (Notice also two other ligatures in this ring: the *VE* combination toward the right of the top line, and the *TU*

---

2. Stamp rings embedded their owner's name in a bronze panel fixed to the ring, allowing the ring's owner to impress his name onto materials in order identify himself on transactional documents and other materials.
3. When used, this stamp ring left a mark meaning "of Aulus Vettius Restitutus." An amphora was engraved on the back bezel of the ring. On Restitutus as one of the two owners of the House of the Vettii, see esp. Severy-Hoven 2013: 25.
4. Figure 6.2 is my transcription of Restitutus's stamp ring. For a photo of the original, consult the following website: www.pompeiiinpictures.com/pompeiiinpictures/r6/6 15 01 entrance p4.htm. This ligature formation within stamp rings was not simply a Pompeian phenomenon. It occurs in stamps far beyond Pompeii. See examples from late first-century and second-century Jerusalem in Cotton et al. 2012: 61 (figure 757) and 66 (figure 763). Of course, it was not inevitable that the letters T and I were formed as a ligature in stamp rings. See, for instance, the stamp ring of Titiniae Saturnus found in 6.15.5, at this website: www.pompeiiinpictures.com/pompeiiinpictures/R6/6 15 05.htm.

combination toward the left of the bottom line, between the two *TI* combinations.) The same *TI* combination in the shape of an equilateral cross can be found on the stamp ring of Lucius Brittius Eros from Pompeii.[5] Ligatures of this kind were used in later Christian symbolism to signify the cross, but they cannot be taken as evidence of Jesus-devotion in first-century artifacts, unless there are other reasons for doing so.

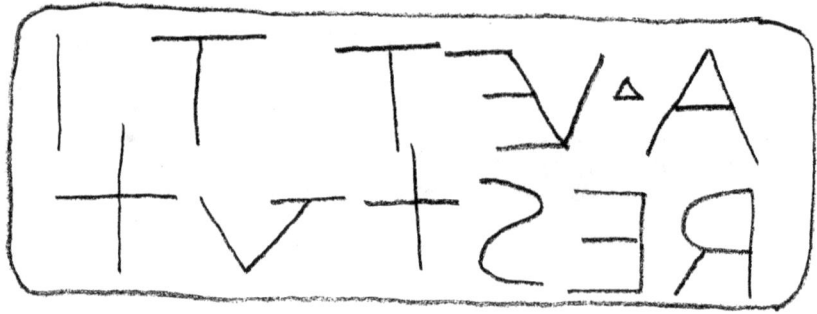

Figure 6.2. The stamp ring of Restitutus (in negative aspect), with two cross-shaped ligatures.

Further along the spectrum of aesthetic appeals, equilateral crosses occasionally appear in floor mosaics. At times, they repeat in patterns that seem to enhance a simple, often elegant, decor. This can be seen, for instance, in the mosaic flooring in Herculaneum's House of the Beautiful Courtyard (see figure 6.3) or in the large exedra of Herculaneum's House of the Inn (3.1–2/18–19). In these instances, the mosaic patterning solely features the equilateral cross.

---

5. See Stefani 2010: 107.

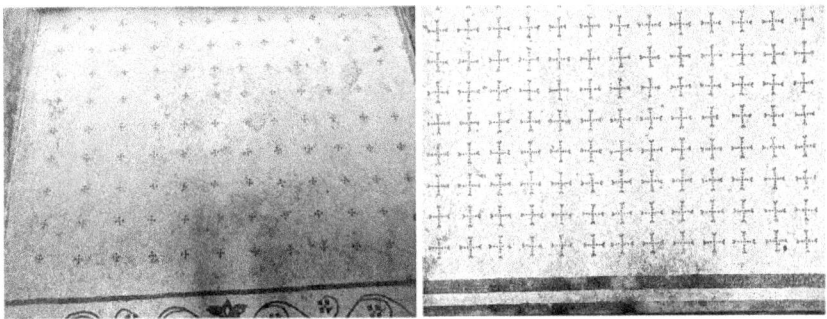

Figure 6.3. Equilateral crosses embedded within two floor mosaics in Herculaneum's House of the Beautiful Courtyard (5.8).

At other times, an equilateral cross can be found in partnership with other patterns in Vesuvian floor mosaics. This happens, for instance, in the simple flooring in Herculaneum's Samnite House, where the equilateral cross is partnered with the *gamma* cross in mosaic flooring. In a floor mosaic within the tablinum of Pompeii's House of the Gilded Cupids (6.16.7), a stylized equilateral cross appears together with cubes, circles, and other shapes (see figure 6.4). Since floor mosaics were frequently used as vehicles for exploring the intriguing interplay of various shapes and patterns, it is not surprising that shapes corresponding with the central symbol of post-Constantinian Christianity are found within the numerous Vesuvian floor mosaics. But to argue that the cross shape served a symbolic function within floor mosaics would require us also to argue that the same was true for a variety of other patterns as well, such as cubes, triangles, rosettes, flowers, circles, and a host of other patterns that crop up in Vesuvian floor mosaics. It is not evident that equilateral crosses were anything more than ornamental features in some floor mosaic designs from the Vesuvian towns.

Figure 6.4: An equilateral cross (bottom right quadrant) in a floor mosaic from the House of the Gilded Cupids.

This point is supported by the relative absence of cross patterning within Vesuvian religious paraphernalia. Although an equilateral cross appears within the ornamentation surrounding the lararium in Herculaneum's House of the Skeleton (see figure 6.5), this must be one of the few instances where this sort of design appears on a religious artifact from the Vesuvian towns. The perpendicular equilateral seems not to have been a standard feature in Vesuvian lararia, nor does its appearance in this shrine function beyond the merely decorative.

Signed, Sealed, Delivered

The Vesuvian towns provide little evidence for thinking that the residents of Pompeii would have recognized perpendicular equilaterals as some kind of symbol with unspecified but numinous meaning. Nonetheless, Jewish Scripture and tradition might provide a context for interpreting perpendicular equilaterals.

Figure 6.5. The lararium with cross-shape ornamentation (left) and close-up (right).

Jewish ossuaries (i.e., bone boxes) in Jerusalem occasionally bear the mark of a perpendicular equilateral. Attempts to interpret these marks as identifying the deceased as a follower of Jesus have been unsuccessful. Some of these burial artifacts are dated to the years between 100 BCE to about 70 CE or so – the earliest of them predating Jesus of Nazareth by a century.[6] But if they are not Christian marks, what are they?

Several ossuaries are deserving of special attention (see figures 6.6 through 6.9). They have simple cross marks, whether in erect (+) or reclining (x) position, incised or drawn in the middle of a panel or under the name of the person whose bones were inside; another has a cross etched deeply onto each of its four sides.[7] What might these curious marks have signified?

---

6. See Chapman 2008: 178–82.
7. See Finegan 1992: 358, 360, 366 (further Sukenik 1947: plate 81), 371. These appear in Longenecker 2015: 49–60.

THE CROSSES OF POMPEII

Figure 6.6. A transcription of an inscription with the name "Yehudah" written above an equilateral cross. From Finegan 1992: 360.

Figure 6.7. A deeply inscribed reclining equilateral cross (highlighted by a circle, added to the photo) under the popular female name "Shalamsion" on a Jewish ossuary near Jerusalem. From Finegan 1992: 371.

THE PERPENDICULAR EQUILATERAL

Figure 6.8. The Nicanor Ossuary with a reclining equilateral cross centrally located on the side of the ossuary. From Finegan 1992: 358.

Figure 6.9. An equilateral cross centrally located on one side of a Jewish ossuary, with a similar cross appearing on each of the other three sides. From Finegan 1992: 366; see further Sukenik 1947: plate 81.

87

They are unlikely to have been mason's marks for orienting the inscriptions, as is sometimes proposed.[8] Not all of the ossuaries on which they appear have inscriptions and, moreover, usually the inscriptions have little bearing in relation to the marks. They are also unlikely to have been "merely crude decorations, in the absence of the more expensive incised ornamentation characteristic of ossuaries."[9]

As Erich Dinkler has shown, the most compelling explanation of prominently displayed ossuary crosses is that they are symbols rooted in an interpretation of Ezekiel 9:4–6. In that passage, Israel's deity declares the following to his angelic servants:

> Go through the city, through Jerusalem, and put a mark on the foreheads of those who sigh and groan over all the abominations that are committed in it.... Pass through the city after him, and kill; your eye shall not spare, and you shall show no pity. Cut down old men, young men and young women, little children and women, but touch no one who has the mark. And begin at my sanctuary.

For our purposes, the key word here is "mark" – the Hebrew word tav. Since tav is also the name of the final character in the Hebrew and Aramaic alphabet, the word "mark" was at times written simply as a symbol instead of being spelled out, that symbol being the final letter in the Hebrew alphabet. In the ancient Hebrew script, that letter could be represented by one of two formations: either the standing cross (+) or the reclining cross, in which the standing cross is rolled onto its side (x).[10] In this way, an equilateral cross mark would serve as the sign of

---

8. This view is articulated by Meyers and Chancey (2012: 186): these markings are "mason's marks meant to indicate how to align the lid or where to place a decoration or inscription."
9. This interpretation is suggested by Jonathan Price 2012: 502. Price shows no awareness of the possibility that these marks derive from Ezekiel 9:4–6. As a consequence, he restricts the interpretative options to three: they were either (1) mason's marks, (2) crude decorations, or (3) marks of Christianity. The third option is ruled out on the basis that the cross "came into use long after these ossuaries were deposited in the cave" (2012b: 502). Price is right that they are not Christian marks, but his lack of cognizance of the possibility that Ezekiel 9 provides the theological background for these marks is a surprising weakness in his engagement with these artifacts. The same deficiency is evident in Price and Cotton (2012: 274), who identify the mark on the Yehuda ossuary as "clearly a directional mason's mark," which looks more like a case of special pleading than reliable argumentation.
10. On the cross as a character in Semitic alphabets, see esp. Finegan 1992: 339–42; Gesenius 1910: pull-out table.

protection to be placed on the foreheads of those preserved from the wrath of Israel's deity.

Although this mark was presented in Ezekiel as being worn on foreheads, it later morphed to become a transferable mark of protection. According to Dinkler, the cross mark encapsulated "a total context of faith . . . in one sign" – a claim that today might be articulated in terms of an overarching narrative of salvation that is packaged up within the single symbol.[11] For this reason, the cross mark made its way onto the side of ossuaries of those who died in faithfulness to their covenant deity. As Dinkler noted, the mark on these Jerusalem ossuaries are best seen as "the *protective sign* for salvation at the coming day of judgment," indicating that "the person marked with the sign of Yahweh is Yahweh's property and therefore stands under his protection."[12]

Jewish texts from the first and second century BCE confirm that Ezekiel 9 fostered an interest in eschatological protective marks among some Jewish constituencies. So the *Psalms of Solomon* (from the first century BCE) speaks of the sign or mark of God being "upon the righteous that they may be saved" (15:6). Similarly, in the *Damascus Document* from the Qumran community near the Dead Sea (middle of the second century BCE) we read the following in 19:9–13:

But those who give heed to God are "the poor of the flock" [Zechariah 11:7]: they will escape in the time of punishment, but all the rest will be handed over to the sword when the Messiah of Aaron and of Israel comes, just as it happened during the time of the first punishment, as Ezekiel said, "Make a mark on the foreheads of those who moan and lament" [Ezekiel 9:4], but the rest were given to the sword that makes retaliation for covenant violations.

The *Psalms of Solomon* breathe the air of mainstream Judaism (probably Pharisaic Judaism), and the *Damascus Document* serves as a defining document for the sectarian Judaism of the Dead Sea community. It is notable, therefore, that this interest in protective

---
11. Dinkler 1965: 145.
12. Dinkler 1965: 138.

signs, indebted to an interpretation of Ezekiel 9:4–6, flowed within at least two streams of Second Temple Judaism. Of course, neither of these pre-Christian Jewish texts reveals how the "mark" was to be formed. But since the word "mark" (tav) could be written as an equilateral cross, that shape is the most obvious candidate. And since neither text reveals to its readers what the shape of the "mark" actually was (even though the mark was crucial in serving as a form of eschatological protection), it must have been assumed that readers of these documents, whether they were in mainstream or sectarian sectors of Judaism, knew the shape of the mark. The *Psalms of Solomon* and the *Damascus Document* indicate that a symbol of eschatological protection had already been circulating in pre-Christian forms of Judaism, and that mark was most likely an equilateral cross.

This is probably why the Greek Septuagint refers to this "mark" in an articular construction in both Ezekiel 9:4 and 9:6 (LXX: *to sēmeion*), whereas four other occurrences of the word in Ezekiel have no article preceding them – both before Ezekiel's ninth chapter (4:3) and after it (20:12, 20; 39:15). And precisely the same distinction is maintained within the later Latin Vulgate, which generally employs the word *signum* (Ezekiel 4:3; 20:12, 20) except in 9:4 and 9:6, where it uses the word *thau*. This testifies to the existence of a long-standing tradition in which the "mark" of Ezekiel 9 was known as a "monadic" mark that was "familiar to readers" in identifying a "one-of-a-kind noun" – a mark par excellence that was "in a class by itself."[13]

In light of this convergence of evidence from both the material and the literary records, Dinkler's interpretation of particular Jewish ossuaries from first-century Jerusalem has strong explanatory force. The "mark" of two intersecting lines at right angles to each other, which figures prominently on several Jerusalem ossuaries, had already been incorporated within Jewish symbolism prior to the early Jesus movement. Rooted in the imagery of Ezekiel 9, that mark was bestowed

---

13. Here I borrow the terms Wallace uses to define the "monadic," "well-known," and *"par excellence"* articular infinitives (1996: 732).

with eschatological import as a sign of identification and a means of protection.[14]

We would be remiss, then, if we failed to ask whether this background might have fostered interest in the same symbol within earliest Christianity, not least since the Jesus-movement emerged from the cradle of Judaism, from which it drew many of its primary theological resources.[15] In fact, as I have demonstrated elsewhere, Ezekiel 9:4-6 proved to be of interest to Christian theologians throughout the first three centuries of the Common Era, where the "mark" of Ezekiel 9 was interpreted as the cross of Jesus. This was true of the author of 5 *Ezra* in the second century (see below), of Tertullian in the early third century (see *Adversus Marcionem* 3.22), and of Cyprian in the middle of the third century (see *Testimonies* 2.21-22). It was arguably also the case for the author of the Johannine Apocalypse at the end of the first century (see below) and for the third-century author of the *Testament of Solomon*.[16]

For now, it is enough to hear the interpretation of Ezekiel 9 in the time of one other Christian theologian. The mid-third-century writer Origen recounts an occasion in which he asked Jews what teachings they had passed on regarding the significance of the Hebrew letter tav (the question itself being indicative of Origen's interest in the theological interpretation of the shape of the cross). Of the three answers he received, the third came from a Christian Jew ("one of those who believe in Christ") who said "the form of the *tav* in old [Hebrew] script resembles the cross (*tou staurou*), and it predicts the mark which is to be placed on the foreheads of the Christians" (*Selecta in Ezehielem*

---

14. For this reason, McCane's claim that "no sources from the early Roman period associate the ossuary with belief in the resurrection" (2003: 43) seems to miss the mark. I see no reason to dispute his case that the ossuaries testify to a form of Hellenistic individualization within Judean Judaism (2004: 46–47), but this is not in conflict with the eschatological "mark" of Ezekiel 9 that appears on several of the Jerusalem ossuaries.
15. I remain dubious, however, about the marks found in the margins of some scrolls from the Qumran community, such as the Isaiah scroll. The claim that these are highlighters to mark passages about the messiah (see Finegan 1992: 346–48) is unconvincing, for a number of reasons. Note, for instance, that similar marks are found in non-Jewish texts as well, with the chi (Χ) probably signaling passages that the reader found to be most "useful" (*chrēstos*, which of course begins with a chi); see especially Johnson 2009.
16. For demonstration of these claims in relation to Tertullian, Cyprian, and the *Testament of Solomon*, see Longenecker 2015: 60 (*Testament of Solomon*), 151 (Cyprian), and 154 (Tertullian).

9).¹⁷ This passage testifies to the continuing knowledge, as late as the middle of the third century, that the mark of Ezekiel 9 could be formed by the intersection of two lines – a cross, taken to be a prophetic "prediction" of what was to come.¹⁸

Of course, in its non-Christian Jewish context, this symbol of eschatological protection had nothing to do with crucifixion, and certainly not the crucifixion of the Messiah. It was only when the Christian imagination began to explore scriptural precedents that it found a ready-made symbol and took that symbol to another stage in its theological development – specifically, as representing the cross of Christ, as exemplified in the quotation from Origen. In this way, the Ezekiel passage was available for acquisition and open to further theological development by the Christian imagination.

The earliest sign of this is evident in Revelation 7:2–3. The text reads as follows:

> I saw another angel ascending from the rising of the sun, having the seal of the living God, and he called with a loud voice to the four angels who had been given power to damage earth and sea, saying, "Do not damage the earth or the sea or the trees, until we have marked the servants of our God with a seal on their foreheads."

Of note here is the mention of "the seal" or signet ring (*sphragida*) "of the living God," which is used by an angel to place marks of protection on the foreheads of Jesus-followers who are thereby protected from the impending cosmic disaster. The same is referred to later in the apocalyptic narrative, as disasters come upon "only those people who do not have the seal of God [*tēn sphragida tou theou*] on their foreheads" (9:4) – in contrast to the mark of the beast that is said to be emblazoned on the foreheads of others (13:16–17; 14:9–11; 16:2; 19:20; 20:4).

Various Jewish texts depict the deity of Israel having a seal, either as a way of protecting his people and his creation or as a means of

---

17. *Patrologia Graeca* 13:800–801. Notice that the formation of the cross in this third-century text is imagined as equilateral or x, instead of conceptualizing it as a T cross, as Tertullian did in *Adversus Marcionem* 3.22.
18. Beale (1999: 410): Ezekiel 9 "facilitated a Jewish-Christian identification of the *taw* sign (or x) with the cross."

controlling malevolent forces (Job 9:7; Sirach 17:22; *Testament of Moses* 12:9; *Apocalypse of Moses* 42:1; *Prayer of Manasseh* 3). Some magical papyri display interest in this divine seal or signet ring, calling on "the powerful name and seal of the great deity" (*PGM* 7.583; cf. *PGM* 1.306; 3.226) and identifying that "great deity" who has a seal by means of names applicable to the deity of Israel (*PGM* 3.266-67; 4.1485-86, 1534-35, 1561, 1621, 2315, 2326, 3053; 7.220, 311, 595-96).[19] Clearly, the ancient imagination was enamored by the notion that an almighty deity had a protective signet ring that was used to bestow a powerful mark of protection on his people.

Ideally, an ancient signet ring displayed on its bezel either something of keen interest to its owner or the name or the identity of the owner in some fashion. So the ancient imagination would inevitably be acutely interested in what was engraved on the signet ring of the almighty deity.

If we are disappointed by the fact that the text of Revelation does not articulate what the bezel of the divine signet ring displayed, the informed ancient imagination might not have been so disappointed. When Revelation mentions "the signet ring of the living God" that marks out "the servants of our God with a seal on their foreheads" (7:2-3) and protects them from tumultuous dangers (9:4), it is building on the imagery of Ezekiel 9:4-6. This is not controversial, being commonly accepted by scholars.[20] As we have already seen, however, the material and literary records testify to the fact that Ezekiel's "mark" of protection placed on the forehead was known to be the intersection of two lines, as in the equilateral or *x* that represented the tav of the ancient Hebrew script. This notion tracks all the way from pre-Christian Jewish texts and artifacts through to several Christian texts of the second and third centuries. Right in the middle of that trajectory of tradition falls the Johannine Apocalypse. When we read,

---

19. See especially Aune 1998: 453 and the evidence he cites on 453-54, including various Jewish texts and artifacts that pertain to the seal or signet ring of Israel's deity (along with the Christian text *Testament of Solomon*, 1:6-7; 10:6; 15:7).
20. So, for instance, Bauckham 1993: 217: "The echo [within 7:2-3 and 9:4] of Ezekiel 9:4-6 . . . is clear." See also Beale 1999: 409-10; Boring 1989: 128; Yarbro Collins 1983: 52.

then, about a "signet ring of the living God" that places a seal on the foreheads of his people, and when we recognize that the imagery draws directly on that of Ezekiel 9:4-6, we must suppose that an audience having a resourceful or informed mind in its midst could have come to the view that the mark placed on the foreheads of the people of "the living God" was the mark of the cross.[21]

According to Greg Beale, the mark of the divine Lord and the mark of the beast may "connote that the followers of Christ and the beast both are stamped with the image (i.e., character) of their respective leaders."[22] In this frame of reference, the signet ring of the sovereign Lord displays his character in relation to the cross. But there is more to this than the display of divine character. The mark also plays out in relation to the divine "name" that is said to be placed on the foreheads of God's people (14:1 and 22:4).[23] Are both a mark and the divine name written on their foreheads? Apocalyptic imagery in general allows for images to be piled on top of each other, but in this case we are probably to imagine that one and the same thing is being imaged. As some have postulated, the "mark" of Ezekiel 9 was understood in Jewish circles "as representing the divine name."[24] This would make perfect sense in relation to the images in Revelation (7:2-3; 9:4; 14:1; 22:4) and in relation to the Jerusalem ossuaries considered above. The cross mark that those ossuaries exhibit may have been regarded as the representation of the name of the deity to whom the deceased owed allegiance. Understood as a mark of possession and belonging, it was a graphic way of symbolizing that the contents of the ossuary belonged to Israel's covenant deity. "Property of Israel's God," might be one way of translating the mark's significance. Since the ossuaries had the name of Israel's deity on them, no other power could tamper with them.[25]

---

21. Compare Krodel (1989: 183): the identification mark of the signet ring would have been understood to be "in the form of a cross or an X [the first letter of the name of Christ]"; so too Mounce 1977: 157.
22. Beale, 1999: 716.
23. Beyond Revelation, see 2 Timothy 2:19, where God's seal contains passages from Scripture, including one that references "the name of the Lord."
24. Beale 1999: 410. So also Sweet (1979: 148): "Ezekiel's mark (*tau*, the last letter of the Hebrew alphabet—written in the old script or x) was currently taken by Jews as the Divine Name."
25. This gives meaning to what the risen Lord says to the church at Philadelphia in Revelation 3:12:

Everett Ferguson brings all this together in his interpretation of the mark left by the divine signet ring of Revelation 7:2–3: "Some tracing (perhaps with oil) of a mark representing the divine name (Ezekiel 9:4, probably the Hebrew letter *tav*) on the forehead . . . marked that person as belonging to the Lord."[26] The Johannine seer probably assumed that his readers would recognize the point behind Revelation 7:2–3, either already being cognizant of the symbolic interpretation of Ezekiel 9:4–6 or soon to be introduced to it through Christian pedagogy. Evidently, then, the interpretation of Ezekiel 9 that was displayed on Jerusalem ossuaries and took on new meaning in Christian texts of the second and third century was already in the toolbox of Christian instruction in the late first century, from which audiences of the Johannine Apocalypse could draw interpretative resources.[27]

Here we can recall Richard Bauckham's view of the requirements for reading the Johannine Apocalypse. Bauckham demonstrates time and again that the text of Revelation is packed full of subtle, unarticulated intricacies that require the audience to operate as textual detectives if those intricacies are to be fully appreciated – detectives both of the apocalyptic text itself and its scriptural precursors. According to Bauckham, "Revelation was evidently designed to convey its message to some significant degree on first hearing (cf. 1:3), but also progressively to yield fuller meaning to closer acquaintance and assiduous study."[28] Even if some audiences happened to be unaware of the theological significance of Ezekiel 9:4–6, the author may well have imagined that the "fuller meaning" of the "signet ring of God" might

---

"I will write on him the name of my God . . . and my own new name." If the "mark" of Ezekiel 9, represented by the Paleo-Hebrew tav, was thought to represent the name of Israel's deity, it is easy to see how the same mark could be "co-opted" by the resurrected Jesus as his "new name" – a case of one symbol serving to combine traditional and novel meanings simultaneously.

26. Ferguson 2009: 196.
27. The cross would also take on new meaning in some Mithraic artistry, under the influence of Christianity within a syncretistic context. On Mithraic symbolism, see part 3 of Cumont 1896.
28. Bauckham 1993: 1. Bauckham goes on to note (1993: 33) that this level of textual artistry "would not have been easy to achieve. It is further evidence of the meticulous composition of the book. . . . We could say that [the author] buried in the literary composition of his work theological significance which few readers have subsequently unearthed, though it may well be that, among his first readers, at least his fellow-prophets would know better than later readers what to look for."

(eventually) become apparent to them in the course of an ongoing pedagogy within Christian communities.

One Christian author from before the mid-second century seems to have interpreted Revelation 7:2-3 in precisely this way, having recognized the "fuller meaning" waiting to be recognized within the text. This is the author of *5 Ezra*, whom we have already met in chapter 5 above. Speaking of the glory that awaits Christians, the author exhorts his audience to "Rise and stand, and see at the feast of the Lord the number of those who have been sealed" (2:38). As Michael Knibb has noted, "there appears to be a link with Rev. 7:2-8 [as well as] Rev. 9:4 [and] Ezek. 9:4-6," with two passages from *5 Ezra* (2:23, 38) interpreting "the sign" and "seal" as "the sign of the cross" (with the cross probably being understood as an equilateral cross, through the influence of Ezekiel 9).[29] For this author, those who sit at the Lord's table, both in the eschaton and (no doubt) in the present, are those who have been sealed or marked with the sign of the cross, whether that be on their foreheads in life or in their graves at death.

We have seen, then, that the equilateral cross was an important theological symbol for the author of Revelation by the late first century, through a christological reading of Ezekiel 9:4-6. (This gives us three different formations of the Christian cross by the early second century, with the equilateral cross of Revelation 7:2-3, the T cross of *Epistle of Barnabas* 9, and the body cross of *Epistle of Barnabas* 12.) Moreover, around the year 140, the author of *5 Ezra* illustrates the influence of Revelation, not only in his advocacy of the cross as a theological symbol of Christian identity but in expecting that that symbol should be marked visibly upon physical realia as a sign of protection ("mark it"). These important and neglected data are within the temporal neighborhood of the Vesuvian towns. Accordingly, if crosses in the Vesuvian material record cannot convincingly be explained in any other way, perhaps it is worth considering whether those artifacts were expressions of first-century Jesus-devotion.

---

29. Knibb 1979: 97 and 95 respectively. See also Myers 1974: 152, who postulates the same textual linkages. That the author of *5 Ezra* knows the text of Revelation is bolstered by the near certain allusion to Revelation 7:9–17 in *5 Ezra* 2:42; see Bergren 2013: 472, 481.

What If?

What if, against the odds, we find that the Vesuvian remains offer the first material evidence of Jesus-devotion from the ancient world? This prospect should not itself be historically suspicious. The Vesuvian material record offers firsts in other areas. For instance, the correlation between the seven primary heavenly bodies (the sun, the moon, and five planets) and the seven days of the week first finds its material testimony in the Vesuvian record. Alastair Small explains the situation in this way: "Each [of the seven main celestial bodies] was identified with a particular god, and gradually (during the first three centuries AD) the idea took hold that each planetary deity presided in turn over human destiny."[30] As a result of this conviction, a seven-day week associated with the primary heavenly bodies began to take root in the first three centuries. And in fact, the earliest evidence for this was uncovered within the Vesuvian remains.[31]

If we find firsts of this kind among the Vesuvian archaeological record, we should not preclude the possibility that that same record includes other firsts as well – perhaps even a cross of Jesus-devotion. This would move the earliest extant symbolic cross of Jesus-devotion into the last quarter of the first century, perhaps even slightly earlier.

To that end, the voices of Carolyn Osiek and David Balch need to be heard. In their book *Families in the New Testament World* of 1997, Osiek and Balch adopt the consensus view regarding the cross imprint in Herculaneum's House of the Bicentenary and subscribe to the view that there is no evidence for the cross being a visual symbol at such an early date. Nonetheless, they also display some uncertainty at the prospect that Christians went without visual symbols for the first few centuries of the Common Era. Noting that religious symbols were ubiquitous in the ancient world, they ask:

---

30. Small 2007: 197.
31. As Small notes (2007: 197), a graffito "on the wall of a triclinium in the small house at V.4.b in Pompeii [=*CIL* 4.6779] gave the names of the planetary deities in the order in which we know them in the calendar, beginning with Saturn, and a painting in the Fourth Style discovered at Pompeii somewhere in Ins. Occ. VI . . . shows the busts of Saturn, Sol, Luna, Mars, Mercury, Jupiter and Venus." See further Keegan 2014: 106–7.

Did Christians simply live in the midst of it all, despising the whole practice as idolatry? Or did they gradually begin to adapt their own forms of domestic piety, long before we have any evidence of it, using either symbols or images of religious figures in worship? No distinctive Christian art has been identified before the end of the second century. Could Christian families have held out for over a century in the Roman world without creating their own images of faith? That is an intriguing question that can become nothing more unless and until further evidence is discovered.[32]

As the reader of this book already knows, it is my view that "further evidence" is, in fact, available within the Vesuvian material remains. The next part of this book (part 3) examines the relevant artifacts that comprise the primary data set in the case for Jesus-devotion in Pompeii, while part 4 pushes beyond that to the supplemental data set that supports the primary evidence. Those data sets illustrate that Jesus-devotion had a solid foothold within Pompeii.

---

32. Osiek and Balch 1997: 86–87.

PART III

The Primary Evidence

"How earnestly the citizens of Pompeii invested in
the power of the gods – how truly they believed
that the fabric of their own reality was interwoven
with the threads of destiny or divine caprice – it is impossible
to know. But the pervasive presence in Pompeii of shrines
at which to honor or placate deities, or to ask for intercession,
suggests that the gods informed every aspect of
the existence of its inhabitants."
(Butterworth and Laurence, *Pompeii* [2005], 20)

Because you have made the Lord your refuge,
the Most High your dwelling-place,
no evil shall befall you,
no scourge come near your tent.
For he will command his angels concerning you
to guard you in all your ways.
Psalm 91:9-11[1]

---

1. This psalm from the Hebrew Bible was popularly regarded by Jews and Christians as an amuletic psalm. See Spier 2014: 47-49. That the same psalm could be interpreted christologically only added to the psalm's apotropaic attraction. For an early christological interpretation of this psalm, see Longenecker 2012: 84-111, 120-23.

7

Jesus-Devotion in Relief

Enough has been done to set the context of the debate. It is time now to mount a constructive case – the task of the five chapters that comprise part 3 of this book, followed by the two chapters in part 4. The five chapters of part 3 present the primary evidence – the evidence that the constructive case rests on most firmly. The two chapters of part 4 present the supplemental evidence – evidence that, while supporting the primary evidence, can also be detached from it, since the supplemental evidence might be deemed slightly less robust than the primary evidence. But whether the evidence of part 3 is deemed to stand alone or in association with the evidence of part 4, what follows is a multifaceted case demonstrating the existence of Jesus-devotion within Pompeii.

"To piece together a picture of antiquity," writes Andrew Wallace-Hadrill, "is to work with a giant jigsaw puzzle in which many or most of the pieces are missing, and those that survive can only too easily be confused for something else."[1] What we will see in these chapters is a combination of artifacts, a few of which have been confused for

---

1. Wallace-Hadrill 2011: 125.

something else and several of which have been missing from the puzzle altogether.

At the forefront of our case is none of the usual contenders that often lead the way in the debate. That is, the case does not lead with the *rotas* word-square, the Herculaneum cross-shaped artifact, or the inscription that makes mention of "Christians" (although that important inscription will be discussed in chapter 10 below). The place to start, instead, is the one artifact that is often hidden from the limelight of scholarly discourse. That artifact, as we have seen, once hung in stucco on the wall of the bakery in the Insula Arriana Polliana.

Structure or Symbol?

When articulating the consensus view, scholars sometimes foreground the Herculaneum artifact initially, claiming that it must be a wall-bracket of some kind; they then make a passing gesture to the Pompeian artifact, claiming that it too must have had the same function. By following this procedure, they give the appearance of working by way of historical analogy – if something is true for artifact 1, it must also be true for artifact 2 on the basis that the two are comparable phenomena.

This is how the argument plays out, for instance, in the work of Peter Lampe. Arguing that the artifact in Herculaneum's House of the Bicentenary is merely "a secular console," Lampe goes on to note the following: "The anchoring for a similar wall rack was found in a boutique in the Pansa House of Pompeii" (that is, in the Insula Arriana Polliana).[2] Figure 7.1[3] places the two artifacts side by side.

---

2. Lampe 2003: 9. Much the same argument is followed by Adams 2013: 109 together with 138.
3. Right image is from Mau 1824: vol. 2, 88.

Figure 7.1. The artifact from Herculaneum's House of the Bicentenary (left) alongside the artifact from the bakery in Pompeii's Insula Arriana Polliana.

But a moment's reflection on the matter suggests that something is wrong with this argument. Despite Lampe's claim, the two artifacts are not at all "similar" in terms of their construction, only in their basic shape. In fact, they are completely different in their construction. One (the Herculaneum artifact) was a hard object nailed onto the wall within a plaster panel; the other (the Pompeii artifact) was fashioned out of raised plaster within a self-contained bas-relief cradle. Devising a theory about their alleged shared function requires an explanation that does justice to the structural features of both artifacts. Procedurally, it is not acceptable simply to state that the Herculaneum artifact was a wall-bracket and then to claim that a similar wall-bracket was found in a Pompeii bakery; the hard work is in devising a satisfactory explanation as to how two artifacts can share a single function as wall-brackets when they have almost nothing in common structurally.

Most notably, it requires a real stretch of the imagination to believe that the artifact in the Pompeian bakery could have served as an anchor for any kind of console. When coming to grips with the construction material and the artistic design of the Pompeian artifact, it is quite natural to think, as Mazois did upon its discovery, that there's no way the artifact could be anything other than a symbol of some kind. Stucco plaster is not a material of choice for fixing anything to a wall; the plaster would simply have fragmented under the weight of the alleged console. When stucco is raised and formed (as in the case of the bakery artifact), it is for artistic effect alone, not for structural strength.[4] To speak of "stucco bas-relief" and of a "wall-bracket" in the same phrase is virtually a non sequitur, unless the two are conjoined by means of negation.

That the use of stucco would have been an ill-conceived form of wall-bracket technology is accentuated further when one considers the artistic nature of the bakery artifact itself.

1. It artistically flares out at the lower portion of the vertical stave before rounding off at the bottom;
2. the horizontal transverse gently grows in width before quickly expanding toward its two endpoints; and
3. except for the tips of the horizontal transverse, a delicate beveling adds an exquisite outline to the whole of the artifact.

Are we really to think that these three stylistic features are not artistic touches but serve merely to help hold up a wall cabinet?[5]

In truth, the artifact in the Insula Arriana Polliana is anything but an "anchor" to hold the weight of a console attached to the wall. If we are to avoid seeing it as having served a symbolic function, an argument will need to be made to explain the intricacies of its artistic design in some other way that describes how those artistic intricacies and its relatively delicate structure could enhance its proposed function as a wall-bracket. At present, however, no argument of this kind has yet been made. What is surprising is that the wall-bracket interpretation has managed to survive so well and so predominantly when simple matters of this kind have never been considered. Or put differently,

---

4. For examples of stucco reliefs, see www.ostia-antica.org/vmuseum/decor_4.htm.
5. Part of the problem in the history of debate about whether Jesus-followers were present in the Vesuvian towns is the fact that the bakery artifact is rarely depicted in scholarly literature. On several occasions, I have shown Mazois's drawing to archaeologists and classical historians, none of whom had ever seen it before. On these occasions, it is not unusual for the proverbial mouth to drop and for words to be uttered like, "That is not a shelf-holder. I don't know what it is, but it is not a shelf-holder."

perhaps the wall-bracket interpretation has survived so well only because simple matters of this kind have never been considered.

Evidently, then, the best-case scenario for the consensus view is that one of these two wall artifacts supported a console (the Herculaneum artifact) while another served a much more "artistic" or symbolic function.

What Kind of Symbolism?

The artifact in the bakery of the Insula Arriana Polliana served a symbolic function of some kind. Moreover, having been placed prominently in the front shop of the bakery, it was evidently meant for display, being viewable by both those in the shop and those passing in the street.

What kind of symbolism was contained within the stucco? Several possibilities can be excluded. Since the cross-shaped artifact was not equilateral, it is unlikely to have been a Jewish cross that ultimately derives from Ezekiel 9:4-6. For the same reason, it is unlikely to have served a simple ornamental role without further significance; when lines were placed to overlap at ninety degrees to each other for ornamental purposes, they were balanced (equilateral) in their formation and, moreover, were usually placed within grouped patterns.

Similarly, despite the claim of one scholar, this artifact is unlikely to represent a double-headed axe – an object that has left little trace in the material record as a stand-alone ornamental artifact.[6] The axe head should be far more impressive in its girth (they were generally depicted as being much broader than the vertical handle) and should be rounded at the blade (see figure 7.2). If the Pompeii artifact were intended to represent a double-headed axe, the craftsman has created such a paltry, laughable representation that he will have lost any chance at future commissions from prospective customers.

---

6. Baldi (1964: 40) held the view that the vertical stave must be an axe handle ("manubrio di un'ascia"), although he deemed the axe imagery to be a covert way in which a Christian hid his allegiance to this cryptic symbol of Christian faith ("simboli criptocristiani"). Again, Christians are seen as hiding their faith in fear of their contemporaries.

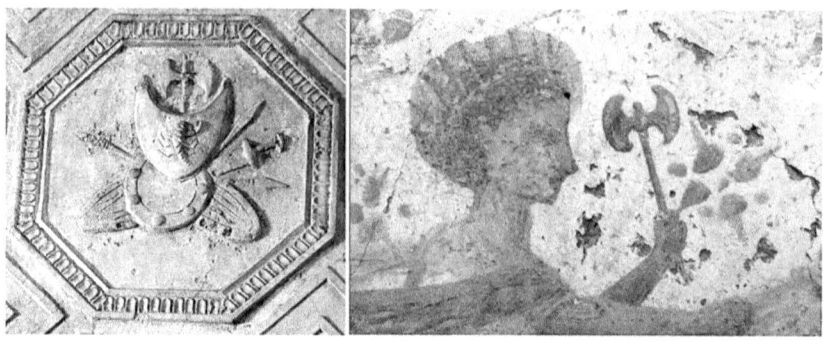

Figure 7.2. Left: A double-headed axe at the top of a stucco ceiling ornament in Pompeii's Stabian Baths; right: a double-headed axe held by Helios in a Pompeii fresco (MANN 8836).

Neither does the Pompeii artifact conform to the Egyptian Ankh, since it does not include the telltale circular aperture (i.e., a handle) at the top of the stave, nor is there space for one to have fitted there in an aesthetically acceptable fashion.

At this point, then, we find ourselves running out of options for interpreting the artifact. The symbol does not seem to conform to any pattern from the pre-Christian Greco-Roman world. The only candidate left to us, or the least improbable possibility, is that what we have on the bakery wall is a stylized cross of Jesus-devotion. With its crossbeam just below the top of the vertical stave, this cross conforms to the formation of the body cross envisaged in chapter 9 of the *Epistle of Barnabas* (as noted in chapter 5 above).

With that said, however, it is also important to recognize that the cross of Jesus-devotion that once resided on this bakery's wall shows the influence of the Egyptian Ankh (except for the absence of the Ankh's top loop). Artistic depictions of the Ankh from the ancient world generally fall into one of two categories: simple and stylistic depictions. In simple depictions, the appendages of the Ankh appear as unadorned extensions (see, for instance, the Ankh on amulet 665 in figure 7.6 below). In stylistic depictions, however, the Ankh's appendages appear more ornately, with the three straight appendages of the Ankh increasing in dimension as they get farther away from the midpoint; for the two horizontal appendages, this involved flaring at the ends. Figure 7.3 captures an example of the stylistic Ankh common to the Greco-Roman world, even though this particular depiction of it comes from a period long before the first century, thereby demonstrating the antiquity of this well-known formation (see also figures 7.4, 7.5, and 7.7 below).

Figure 7.3. Left: an Egyptian painting from the twelfth century BCE depicting two stylized Ankhs; right: a close-up of the center Ankh (MANN 976).

These characteristics of the stylistic Ankh are significant for interpreting the cross of Jesus-devotion in the Pompeii bakery (and in fact, for many crosses in centuries beyond the Constantinian era).[7] Noticing the overlap in structural composition between the stylized Ankh and the cross from the Insula Arriana Polliana, we can see that both are characterized by the same two phenomena in the three straight appendages that they share: (1) flared edges at the ends of the horizontal arms, and (2) a progressive expansion in the lower stave. Even the short stave extending above the transept arms is at home with many depictions of the Ankh.

This convergence of structural shaping is unlikely to be coincidental. Instead, the formation of the stylized Ankh seems to have influenced the presentation of the bakery cross – for reasons that will become

---

7. Catalano (2002: 185) characterizes the artifact as "un pannello a stucco con croce ansata a rilievo." Catalano would have been better to differentiate between the Ankh-like features of the artifact and the artifact itself, which cannot be an Ankh, since there is no room for the required handle and no indication that a handle was ever attached to the panel in some fashion.

clear in due course. What was once on the wall of the Pompeii bakery, then, was not simply a cross of Jesus-devotion but a cross crafted to reference the stylized Egyptian Ankh – the important symbol of life in the widespread cult of Isis. As a cross of Jesus-devotion, the bakery cross places Jesus-devotion in direct relationship with worship of Isis. The worship of Jesus, in whom the power of death was defeated, is artistically portrayed in the bakery cross in a way that inevitably alludes (in one fashion or another) to the worship of Isis. The Egyptian deity Isis was thought to have defeated death by resurrecting her husband Osiris; consequently, she was deemed to have the power to give to her devotees both enhanced life in the present and resurrected life after death.[8] In this way, Isis-devotion "answered to a spiritual need" among many Greco-Roman urbanites, offering "eschatological solutions" of a "genuine . . . religious practice."[9] In the bakery, that solution to a spiritual need has mutated in reference to a different deity whose devotees have similar prospects awaiting them.[10]

If this is a notable feature, it is not wholly surprising. As even a cursory study would illustrate, it was common for Christian artistry to be adaptive of elements from beyond its generative borders (or what we might conceive as its generative boarders).[11] The structural commonalities between the Christian cross and the Ankh are frequently depicted in religious craft-pieces subsequent to the first century, from which we can see how artistic eyes exploited the similarities between these two crosses.[12] Note, for instance, the Christian relief from Coptic Egypt in which the Ankh is flanked by two simpler crosses (figure 7.4[13]). Here, the stave of the Ankh extends a short way above the transept arms, just as in the bakery's wall-

---

8. On the Isis cult, see Bremmer 2014: 110–25, although the cult's presence in the Vesuvian towns goes unmentioned. That gap is largely filled by Brent 2007.
9. The quotations are from Feder 1978: 128 and Stefani 2010: 64, 65.
10. Butterworth and Laurence (2005: 61) note several correspondences between the Isis and Christ cults: "With the emphasis on individual responsibility that was encapsulated in its program of initiation, purgation and redemption, the Isis religion foreshadowed the other Eastern cults that would gain popular followings in the centuries to come, most familiar that of Jesus."
11. See, for instance, van den Hoek and Herrmann 2013. Cramer 1955, despite its date, is still useful.
12. See, for instance, Finegan 1992: 382–89.
13. British Museum EA 1998 [reg. 1925,1109.3]; photo © Trustees of the British Museum, used with permission.

cross; if the circular appendage of this Ankh were removed, it would be a later sibling to the cross in the Insula Arriana Polliana. The two simpler crosses in that same relief are identical to the center Ankh in their construction, with the obvious exception of the lack of a circular appendage at the top and, consequently, their taller staves above the transept arm. Three of the four appendages converge in these two cross formations. The craftsman of this artifact has linked disparate forms of religious devotion together in a fashion that keeps their differences within the context of their similarities.

Figure 7.4. A limestone relief from Coptic Egypt (perhaps fourth century), with an Ankh flanked by two simpler crosses.

Much the same is evident in the work of the fifth-century amulet maker in Syria-Palestine who crafted the two nearly identical amulets displayed in figure 7.5.[14] Depicting a giant Jesus surrounded by his twelve disciples, these amulets also display a cross shaped to imitate the Ankh (in their upper right-hand sectors); and in each case, the three appendages show flaring and/or expansion at their ends.

Figure 7.5. Two Christian amulets with a cross imitating an Egyptian Ankh.

Figure 7.6 depicts two other fifth-century amulets from the same region, with the Ankh prominently displayed on one side. These amulets are Christian. For instance, the darker amulet on the left (both sides being depicted) is inscribed with the words "One God in heaven," and on the amulet's opposite side the scene is of Genesis 22, where Abraham "sacrifices" his son Isaac – a story understood by many Christians to be a christological allegory. The amulet on the right (one side being depicted) has the inscription "One God" together with the first three letters of the name "Jesus."[15]

---

14. See also Spier 2007: nos. 636 and 637.
15. See also Spier 2007: nos. 664 (left) and 665 (right).

JESUS-DEVOTION IN RELIEF

Figure 7.6. Two fifth-century Christian amulets with the cross styled as an Ankh.

Figure 7.7. The cross and other Christian symbols embedded within the handles of Ankh imagery.

Similarly, on a cloth probably used to adorn a Christian place of worship (from perhaps the fourth or fifth century), various Christian symbols including two crosses and a chi-rho monogram appear woven

111

repeatedly into the handles of Ankhs[16] (see figure 7.7). Almost half a dozen of these fragile fabric artifacts are contained within the material record of post-Constantinian Christianity.[17]

The point of these examples, for our purposes at least, is simple. Conjoining the characteristics of the Ankh and the Christian symbol of the cross has a significant trajectory in Christian artistry of later centuries. In fact, this conjoining of characteristics may first be evidenced in the work of the artisan who styled a cross of Jesus-devotion in a Pompeii bakery prior to the eruption of Vesuvius.

This itself should not be surprising. The Vesuvian cities show a marked enthusiasm for all things Egyptian. According to Erich Lessing and Antonio Varone, "[t]he taste for Egyptian culture, an inexhaustible model for interior decoration, had become more than just a fashion, but a veritable craze."[18] But this was not simply a matter of interior design. It extended to a fascination with the Egyptian cult of Isis. It is hard to gauge at what point Isis-devotion became fashionable in Pompeii, but it was certainly in vogue at the time of the eruption in 79. It has been argued that the Isis cult had become "modish under Vespasian" in the final decade of Pompeii's life.[19] Portraits, statues, and shrines of this important female deity have been found in a number of Pompeian homes, some of those artifacts having been placed prominently within the house – including houses of wealthy residents, such as Julia Felix (2.4.3) and the owner of the House of the Gilded Cupids (6.16.7/38; see figure 7.8). Isis-followers seem even to have had a sense of corporate identity in Pompeii, at least if two graffiti are anything to go by, in which "all the worshipers of Isis" or simply "the worshipers of Isis" call on their fellow residents to vote for particular politicians (*CIL* 4.787; 4.1011) – also demonstrating the extent to which Isis-devotion had infiltrated the political and cultural arena of

---

16. London, Victoria & Albert Museum: Inv. No. 258 – 1890; © Victoria & Albert Museum; used by permission.
17. See Pillinger 2014. For other examples beyond cloth, see http://commons.wikimedia.org/wiki/File:RPM_Ägypten_282.jpg#mediaviewer/File:RPM_Ägypten_282.jpg and www.britishmuseum.org/research/collection_online/collection_object_details.aspx?objectId=124226&partId=1&searchText=1898,0315.94&page=1.
18. Lessing and Varone 1995: 125.
19. Small 2007: 187. See also Liebeschuetz 1996: 180–82.

Pompeii.[20] Isis-devotion was not simply a modish fashion; to imagine it as such would be to underestimate its cultural importance within Pompeii. According to Robert Etienne, the Isis cult had become "the city's semi-official religion."[21]

Figure 7.8. Left: foregrounded in a double fresco from the House of the Gilded Cupids are Isis and Osiris; right: a sistrum for Isis-worship from the same shrine fresco.

Nowhere is this more evident than in the case of Numerius Popidius Celsinus. After the earthquake that violently shook Pompeii and Herculaneum in 62 or 63 (foreshadowing the later eruption of Vesuvius), a massive influx of funding was needed to rebuild the edifices that had been heavily damaged within the town's central forum and beyond.[22] While some funding probably came from the town treasury and from imperial coffers in Rome, much of the rebuilding project was funded by the town's elite – or in at least one instance, by a wealthy Pompeian "wanna-be." To make a long story short, in an arrangement with civic officials, a man named Numerius Popidius Ampliatus agreed to pay for the reconstruction of the temple of Isis in return for an opportunity to promote his family status (in particular, his six-year-old son Celsinus, commemorated in *CIL* 10.846; see figure

---

20. On this, see especially Keegan 2014: 104.
21. Etienne 1992: 118.
22. Ancient sources differ as to the year of this disaster, meaning that it is uncertain whether the earthquake hit the town in 62 or 63.

7.9).²³ While many worthwhile financial initiatives could have been devised between Ampliatus and the civic officials, the restoration of the temple of Isis ranked high on the list of their civic priorities (a list that, in view of the eruption of Vesuvius less than two decades away, was in effect to be their "bucket list"). This is all the more significant in light of the fact that most of the temples to the traditional deities (i.e., the Capitoline Triad, Apollo, and Venus) were still not restored by 79 – sixteen or seventeen years after the earthquake. The restoration and enlargement of the temple of Isis would not have been carried out so quickly if the cult of the Egyptian deity was not of pressing interest among the residents of Pompeii (see figure 7.10).²⁴

Figure 7.9. The inscription above the entryway into the temple of Isis honoring Celsinus, reconstructed from thirty-seven fragments of the original stone.

Against this backdrop of civic fascination with the Isis cult (or "Egyptomania," as it has been called), the Ankh-like styling of the cross of Jesus-devotion in the Pompeii bakery makes good sense.²⁵ What once resided on the wall of the bakery was a Christian cross, but one styled to reference the Egyptian Ankh of the popular Isis cult. The Ankh was the symbol of life, and the Isis cult held out the promise of enhanced life in the present and regenerated life after death. In

---

23. What Milnor says about public benefactor inscriptions in general is obviously true in this instance (2014: 51): "[the inscription] would not only promote the reputation of the [funder] in the present day, but also support that of future generations of the same family, due to the notional permanence of the building and the inscription upon it." It is possible that Ampliatus's son Celsinus was not killed in the eruption of 79 but lived his later days in Spain, where a tomb was erected in his honor. See Butterworth and Laurence 2005: 364.
24. Butterworth and Laurence (2005: 304) date the opening of the restored temple of Isis to the year 69.
25. On "Egyptomania in Campania," see Bragantini 2012.

a similar fashion, the bakery symbol referenced life through a deity whose resurrection gave to his devotees both empowerment in the present and the overcoming of death.

Figure 7.10. The reconstructed temple of Isis in Pompeii.

More needs to be said about the bakery cross, especially its religious function within its architectural context – an issue dealt with in the following chapter.

8

Jesus-Devotion in the Insula

At least three problems have frequently been thought to plague a "Christian" interpretation of the bakery artifact (and we will see a fourth in the course of this chapter). First, the cross is commonly thought to have had currency as a Christian symbol only after Constantine. Second, Christians are commonly thought to have lived in fear because their pagan peers were vigilantly on the lookout for them, seeking to kill them off as social miscreants. Both of these assumptions have been confidently asserted over the years but prove themselves to be easily surmountable, as noted in chapter 5 above (drawn from my argument in *The Cross before Constantine*).

The third purported problem comes in the charge that Jesus-devotion would be a strange thing to find in the pagan settings where this cross was located; the polytheistic context of the bakery rules out any attempt to see the bakery artifact as a cross of Jesus-devotion. Since this has proved to be one of the main arguments in support of the consensus view on this artifact, it needs to be given full consideration – a task to which this chapter is dedicated.

The "Pagan" Context of the Artifact

As noted in chapter 4 above, François Mazois found it difficult to reconcile both (1) his conviction that the wall-cross in the Pompeii bakery really was a relic of Jesus-devotion and (2) his observations regarding the religious environment surrounding that wall-cross. Traditional forms of Greco-Roman polytheism were alive and well in the Insula Arriana Polliana, especially in the religious symbolism of the main residence that dominated that insula. Is a rental property within this polytheistic insula really a place where we would expect to find Jesus-devotion?

This puzzle has been highly influential in scholarly discourse about the artifact in the Insula Arriana Polliana. Although Mazois did not allow his hesitation about the pagan environment of the insula to overturn his conviction that the stucco cross was an artifact of Christian devotion, the environment surrounding that cross did give him pause for thought. Other scholars, however, have entertained a much higher level of skepticism. In 1870, for instance, Marc Monnier claimed that the "thoroughly Pagan" (sic) ornamentation of the Insula Arriana Polliana would be "singularly irreconcilable" with the discovery of "Christian symbol" in the same insula – that symbol purportedly being "a Latin cross in relief, very sharply marked upon a wall."[1] A little over a hundred years later, Antonio Varone held much the same view, thinking it impossible that Christian piety could be sharing the walls of such a pagan household.[2]

Of course, we might want to question the way that these scholars have framed the matter. It has often been assumed that the character of religious devotion in the bakery would have been in accord with the devotion on display within the primary residence of the insula. For instance, in Mazois's reconstruction of the situation, the baker is thought to "bow before the cross of Christ" within his bakery and yet also "pay homage to [the deities] Janus, Ferculus, Limentinus, Cardia,

---

1. Monnier 1870: 147.
2. Varone 1979: 31–34.

the deities of the thresholds and the hinges of doors" within the insula's main residence.³ This scenario seems to assume that the baker was a slave within the household of the main residence, being required to worship the deities of the householder in the insula's main residence. That scenario is not the only live option, nor is it the most likely – at least if the bakery was rented to (or owned by?) someone outside the household of the main residence. Even if the bakery was not a rental property (or a separately owned unit) but was an outpost of the household in the main residence, would worship of the householder's deities in household gatherings preclude Jesus-devotion within the bakery? Would the householder or his manager have sought control of all expressions of religious devotion in every unit dotted around the insula? We will see reasons for doubting these kinds of assumptions (both in this chapter and in chapter 15 below).

It is true, nonetheless, that there is a notable correlation between the religious artifacts in the main residence and those embedded within the insula's bakery. This only makes the point more pressing: What would a cross of Jesus-devotion be doing in a heavily polytheistic context? The answer to this emerges as we take account of the function of the religious artifacts in both the insula's main residence and the bakery at 6.6.17/20–21.

The "Pagan" Artifacts within the Bakery

Beyond the stucco cross in the baker's shop, four other forms of religious devotion adorned the bakery. Each illustrates that standard forms of ancient religious practices and devotion had once resided within that premises. Three of those artifacts hover near the bakery oven, and one of them resided in the front shop.

A fresco of a snake was found on the interior wall of the shop. The snake was commonly depicted in Greco-Roman wall paintings (see figure 8.1[4] for an example). In Vesuvian residences, paintings of snakes

---

3. Mazois 1824: vol. 2, 84.
4. From Cooke 1827: vol. 1, 70; see also Mazois 1824: vol. 1, 33. The fresco was accidentally destroyed in 1813 (the same year that the bakery cross was discovered) when carts removing rubble from the site collided with it.

(or *agathodaemoni*, "good spirits") depicted either the *genius loci* (the benign spirit of the place or household) or the *genius* of the householder.⁵ In Greco-Roman traditions untouched by Judeo-Christian traditions (in which the snake carried negative connotations), the snake was a symbol of protection, being an artistic representation of the superhuman forces that benevolently oversaw the premises. Located on the wall of the baker's shop between entryway 19 (itself a stairway leading to upstairs apartments) and entryway 20 (see figure 8.2), the snake painting was virtually opposite the wall-cross (a point to which we will return in due course).⁶

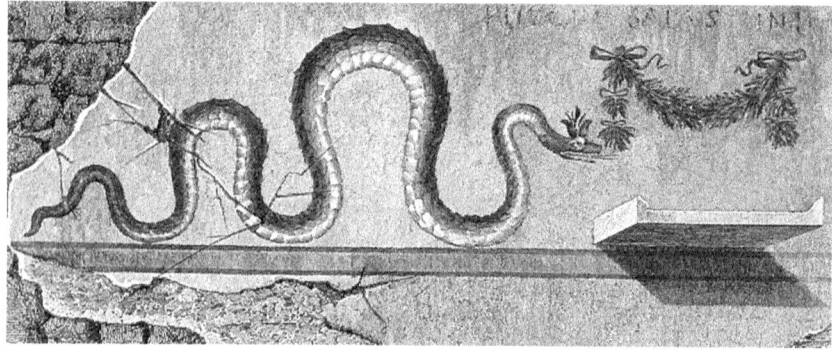

Figure 8.1. A snake moves to devour the sacrifices that would have been offered to it on the slab protruding from the wall (located in the Street of Tombs just beyond the Pompeii's Herculaneum Gate, and devised to protect against evil spirits in the tomb area).

Three further features of the bakery served religious functions, all of them concentrated in the oven room where the baked goods were produced. A small niche can be found on the left wall on entering the room (see figures 8.3 and 8.4).⁷ This concave indentation indicates that a small shrine once resided at this position (approximately sixty-one

---

5. There is uncertainty about the precise referent of the snake, which is found throughout the Vesuvian towns. See Orr 1978: 1575. Even Virgil is uncertain about its precise referent, noting that it is either the *genius* of the place or the attendant spirit of the householder (*Aeneid* 5.90–96). Evidence from the Vesuvian towns suggests that it was used for both purposes.
6. On the snake and cross-shaped artifact being opposite to each other on the west and east walls of 6.6.20/21, see della Corte 1965: 115; Stefani 2005: 139.
7. I am not aware of this small shrine having been noted in previous scholarship on this site.

centimeters [two feet] wide, forty-six centimeters [eighteen inches] in height, and twenty centimeters [eight inches] deep). Some plaster that still remains within the indentation is indicative of a small plaster platform at the bottom of the indentation. This was probably a surface upon which miniatures of household deities could be placed.[8] This household shrine may have served a double function of giving protection to the room itself and to the apartments one floor above ground level, since the niche is not far from the base of a stairway that led to the baker's residences (no longer extant).[9] The placement of shrines near stairways is evidenced elsewhere within the archaeological record of Pompeii.[10]

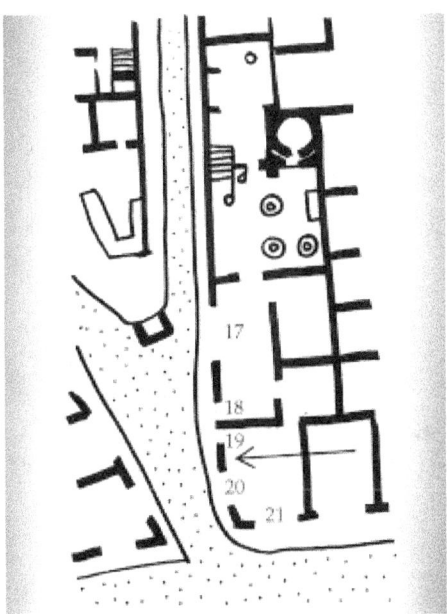

Figure 8.2. The arrow points to the find-spot of the snake fresco in the front shop of the bakery.

---

8. This location would be ideal for housing (among other deities) the *penates*, who protected storerooms and pantries especially. (Their role, however, was increasingly becoming indistinguishable from that of the *lares*, except that the *lares* were associated with the location whereas the *penates* would move with the household whenever its location changed. On this, see especially Muscettola 2013: 106.)
9. The stairs are recorded in Cooke 1827 vol. 2: plate 1.
10. For Pompeii residences with small shrines at stairways, see: 1.11.14; 5.1.20; 6.7.17; 6.15.10; and 7.3.13. See also Herculaneum 4.15.

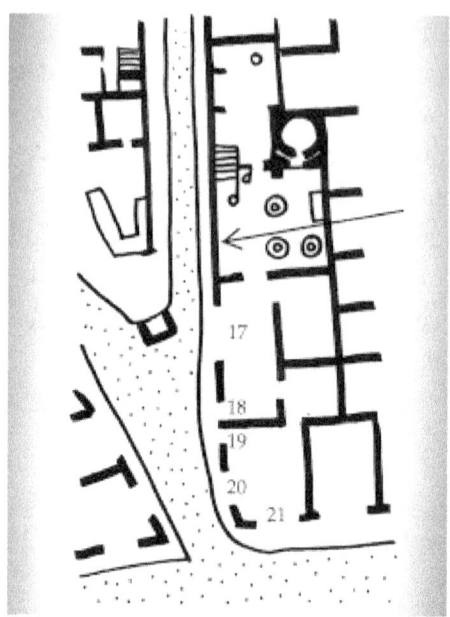

Figure 8.3. The location of a small shrine within the oven room of the bakery.

Figure 8.4. The niche for a small shrine in the bakery, highlighted by the addition of a circle.

Within the same room were found two other pieces of religious artistry (see figure 8.5 for their locations). One was removed by the forces of nature (or art hunters) not long after the bakery was excavated, while the other is enjoyed by the thousands of tourists who visit the National Archaeological Museum of Naples each year. The first, another picture of a serpent, resided next to the bakery's oven, just above a ledge on which resources needed for baking would have been kept. The second is a bas-relief of a phallus, inscribed with the words *hic habitat felicitas*, or "Here lives good fortune" (*CIL* 4.1454; see figure 8.6). Figure 8.7 replicates these two artifacts by means of digital reproduction.[11]

All four of these religious artifacts in the bakery testify to a standard form of Greco-Roman religious belief and practice. In order to put these artifacts into proper perspective, we need to recognize their importance in terms of ancient attitudes toward protection and safety.

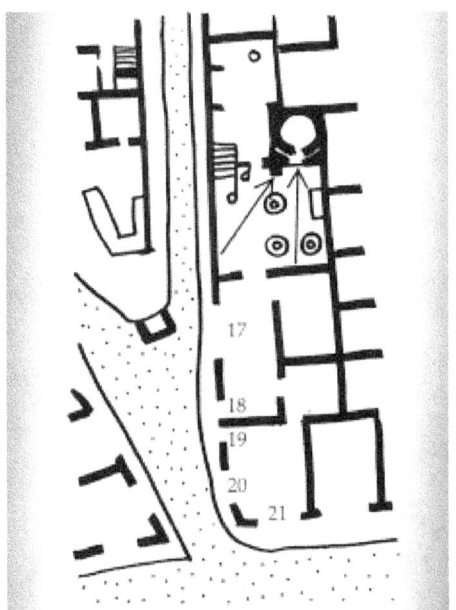

Figure 8.5. The arrows point to the placement of two further adornments in the oven room.

---

11. The photo montage in figure 8.7 replicates plate 38 from Gell and Gandy 1852.

Figure 8.6. The symbol of hopeful optimism and protection above the bakery's oven.

Figure 8.7. A reconstruction of the baker's oven with serpent and phallic symbol added to their original positions.

The Bakery, Protection, and the Deities

In the Greco-Roman world, entryways were commonly considered to be what anthropologists call "liminal spaces" – that is, corridors from one sphere of influence to another. Residential and commercial entryways were places compounded by vulnerability to evil forces that sought to gain access – whether evil spirits, evil people, or both. Ray Laurence makes the point this way: "The doorway was the entrance into the house not only for people, but also for curses and diseases."[12] Accordingly, certain architectural features and artistic representations commonly appear at precisely those points in order to increase household security. Or as Jack Lindsay makes the point, since "good and bad things enter or exit there," an entryway benefitted from "a controlling or purifying influence" – a sentiment to which the Vesuvian towns testify repeatedly.[13]

Protection from the evil was enhanced by the power of the household deities and ancestral spirits of the household.[14] Sometimes their assistance was conjured by means of inscriptions placed somewhere within the residence. In the third century, for instance, Diogenes Laertius recounts how a recently married man inscribed within his house this protective inscription about his favored deity: "The son of Zeus, victorious Heracles, lives here; let no evil enter in" (*Diogenes Laertius* 6.50). Much the same appears in a residential inscription to the same deity within Pompeii: "Hercules Callinicus, take up your dwelling here; may you live and flourish; take away all evil."[15] Images of patron deities or protective spirits could function just as well as inscriptions to deities. Such images were placed on the front of houses or in the passageway leading from the front entryway (the *fauces* or *vestibulum*) into the atrium.

---

12. Laurence 1994: 88. See also John Clarke 2007: 63–64, where he notes that "[s]uch liminal areas were highly charged and dangerous."
13. Lindsay 1960: 189. This concern to protect entryways long predates the Greco-Roman world. For Babylonian precedents, for instance, see Tuschling 2007: 16. See also Wood 2008: 141–55.
14. See for instance Barton 1995: 168–72. In a chapter entitled "Apotropaic Laughter," John Clarke (2007) shows that humor itself was recognized to serve an apotropaic function in liminal spaces.
15. The inscription is cited by Lindsay 1960: 137, who frustratingly chose not to cite inscriptional references within his work.

It is along these same lines that Pompeian residences sometimes have mosaics depicting dogs at the entryway of houses (see figure 8.8). The primary function of these canine mosaics is not to alert would-be thieves that there is a watchdog in the house that looks roughly like the one in the mosaic.[16] Instead, the mosaic claims the "canine spirit" as the watcher against evil that might otherwise enter into the house. These canine mosaics serve as an apotropaic security system against an incursion of evil. The loyal and protective canine spirit is expected to ward off evil, protecting those affiliated with the household.[17]

Figure 8.8. Dog mosaics at Pompeian entryways.

This interpretation of the canine mosaics at residential entryways is confirmed by the fact that a wild boar can also be found at the same internal location within another Pompeii residence (7.2.26; see figure 8.9). Clearly the householder who commissioned this entryway mosaic was not suggesting that a dangerous wild boar roamed through the house on protective duty – a boar that looked something like the one depicted in the mosaic.[18] The point, instead, is that this house is

16. This is not an uncommon assessment of the purpose of these canine mosaics. So Feder (1978: 30): "It was a fairly common custom to advertise the presence of a dog by depicting it in mosaic or in a wall painting at or near the threshold."
17. This is probably true even of the "sleeping dog" in the entryway of the house of Lucius Caecilius Jucundus (5.1.26). Even the contemporary expression "let sleeping dogs lie" testifies to this the sense that sleeping dogs, when wakened by the mischievous, are themselves to be feared.
18. Similarly, compare the mosaic of a phallus at the entryway of the third-century Ostian house of Jupiter Fulminator (Ostia 4.4.3). This mosaic served only to tap into the protective power of the phallus; it did not depict a particular phallus within the residence.

protected by the spirit of the wild boar – an intimidating prospect for any peddlers of ill fortune, whether they be human or suprahuman.[19]

Figure 8.9. A wild boar mosaic in a residential entryway.

The phallus was afforded the same apotropaic function at entryways of residences and at street intersections. In the male-oriented Greco-Roman world, the "ubiquitous Roman phallus" (described by Mary Beard as "exuberant") functioned primarily as a symbol of good fortune.[20] It ultimately tapped into "the divine protection of Fascinus" – the spirit of the phallus that served as the "guardian" for everyone from the least to the greatest (Pliny, *Natural History* 28.7.39). In short, it promoted well-being by keeping evil "at arm's length," ensuring that an area was afforded maximal protection.

---

19. The same probably applies to the mosaic of a wounded bear in the entryway of the House of the Bear (7.2.45). A bear is foreboding enough, but a wounded bear is a doubly fearful prospect. The salutation adjoining the wounded bear ("HAVE," or "welcome") does not distract from the clear warning in the wounded bear motif. Together, the entryway mosaic welcomes those who are friends of the household, while adding an ominous note of protection for the benefit of any who might take liberties with the hospitality of the household.
20. Beard 2012: 61, 68.

A shop in Herculaneum (4.17), for instance, had a shrine above its countertop in which Priapus was painted in a pose accentuating his magnificent penis. Maiuri refers to this as "a ritual apotropaic gesture."[21] But it was at entryways that the phallus is especially evident in the material record. It appeared in bold relief above residential entryways (see figure 8.10), and on the many *tintinnabulae* of phallic bells that frequently hung at entrances to shops and houses (see figure 8.11).[22] It famously adorned the entryway of the House of the Vettii (6.15.1), which exhibited a large painting of Priapus, a fertility deity and a protector of produce, with a perversely enlarged phallus that balances against a money bag in a weight-scale (see figure 8.12). This painting served as "a talisman against the evil eye, protecting the riches of the house" at a place where all visitors entered the residence.[23]

Moreover, phalluses were frequently placed at crossroads (see figure 8.13). One neighborhood shrine in Pompeii featured the phallus with wings centered in the shrine, with three further phalluses accenting the point (see figure 8.14[24]). Phalluses embedded at strategic points in houses and neighborhoods are so numerous that it would be impossible to replicate them all here without jeopardizing a PG-13 rating.

Because entryways were access points through which malevolent spirits might try to gain entry by stealth, they required forces of benevolence and protection to be on guard. This helps explain the function of the artifacts from the bakery cited above. Popular expectations deemed the baker's shop, like all of its Pompeian neighbors, to be vulnerable to the covert invasion of evil spirits. And beyond the spirit world, the bakery would be at risk from more ordinary and everyday abuses, such as the sticky hands of thieves. Little wonder, then, that notable initiatives had been taken to protect the bakery from malicious exploitation.

---

21. Maiuri 1958: 437.
22. Beard (2008: 228) offers an example.
23. Small 2007: 191. See also John Clarke 2007: 186. For further apotropaic devices in this house, see Butterworth and Laurence 2005: 268.
24. For an excavation photo of this artifact in pristine condition, see John Clarke 2007: 72.

Figure 8.10. Phalluses at entrance 6.14.28 (left), 7.1.36 (middle), and between entrances 9.1.13 and 9.1.14 (right).

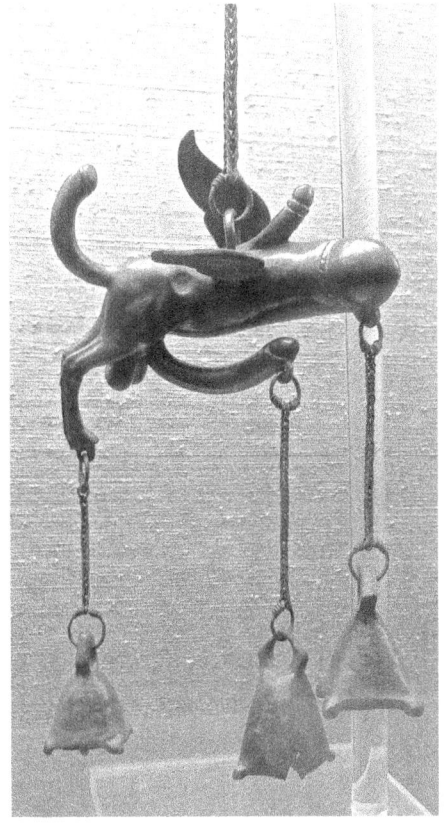

Figure 8.11. Phallic wind chimes from Pompeii (MANN 27844).

THE CROSSES OF POMPEII

Figure 8.12. The apotropaic painting in the entryway vestibule of the House of the Vettii.

Figure 8.13. Phallic symbol at neighborhood intersections in Pompeii.

Figure 8.14. Phallic shrine on the north side of Via dell'Abbondanza, with three phallic adornments helping to frame a central phallus.

An inventory of the baker's security system shows the bakery to have been under heavy guard. Moving progressively from the front street to the back of the bakery reinforces the point at each stage. The front shop contained the snake fresco. This painting benefited from a small stucco ledge protruding from the painting's base, allowing incense to be placed there. In this way, the benevolent spirit of the place or of the householder would have been kept content, enhancing the apotropaic defenses against fearful forces of evil.

The bakery's oven room was itself a miniature version of Fort Knox, containing a phallic symbol, a snake painting, and a shrine to the household deities. On entering the room, one would first encounter a small shrine on the left wall that honored benevolent deities and spirits.[25] Beyond that, the snake painted to the immediate left of the oven was also ideally located for protective purposes, with regard to both the oven room and the two back service rooms that probably functioned as a storage and preparation room for the baked produce. Near the snake painting resided a phallic symbol above the oven. Like the snake painting, this symbol also served an apotropaic function, ensuring that evil was kept far away so that good fortune could thrive within the bakery and its oven.[26]

These four artifacts noted in the bakery, then, were part of the bakery's architecture of spiritual warfare, offering protection at points that were vulnerable to invading evil. They heightened the "spiritual security" of the premises. On display within the bakery were not simply pictures of snakes, statues of deities, and a phallic symbol; instead, at a deeper level, on display was the ancient fear of evil.

Protection in the Insula's Main Residence

There is a notable convergence between the "spirituality" on display in the insula's bakery and in the insula's main residence. The deities of choice within the main residence had the reputation for offering protection against malevolent spiritual forces that threatened to invade at the weak points of liminality. As noted by Mazois, the deities that were honored in the insula's main residence included:

---

25. On the presence of deities in relation to their representation in idols and other artifacts, see Erwin 2013; Fredriksen 2002. See also Wallace-Hadrill's understanding of a collection of deities found alongside other valuables within a cabinet in the House of Wattlework (3.13–15) in Herculaneum (2011: 265): "The household gods were good at keeping their eye on valued objects." This estimate assumes a concentration of the presence of deities in the location where they were represented. This seems also to be the assumption behind Paul's comments in 1 Corinthians 10:14–22. See also Milnor's discussion of paintings of Bacchus and Primus in a garden landscape of 1.11.10 (the gardens of the Caupona of Euxinus at 1.11.11; Milnor 2014: 88–95).
26. Placed over the bakery's oven, this phallus entertains a playful double entendre. Just as the penis rises to serve its sexual function, so too the dough in the heated oven rises to serve its function. A phallus was also found above the oven in the bakery of the House of the Chaste Lovers.

1. Janus, a deity who had (at least) two faces (one looking forward and one looking backward) and who, thereby, was deemed perfectly suited for the protection of entryways;
2. Ferculus, a household deity;
3. Limentinus, the deity thought to protect the entryway leading into residences; and
4. Cardia, a deity charged with keeping the human body healthy against invading ill health.

The concern to enlist deities of household protection is not at all surprising in the insula's main residence, with its grand front entryway and its vast expanse. To counter the fears of malignant spiritual forces, the deities Janus and Limentinus were honored within the house in the hope that they would serve as divine sentries at the front and back entryways – the back entryway (6.6.12) opening into the extensive gardens at the rear of the insula (where produce was grown perhaps for consumption within the household as well as for commercial sale).[27] Meanwhile the household deity Ferculus kept vigilant watch over the well-being of things, while the deity Cardia was courted to promote the physical health of all within the house.

We witness, then, a similarity in the architectural imaginations that designed the religious adornments in the main residence and in the bakery attached to it (with Mazois simply imagining that the person who controlled the religious environment of the insula's main residence would inevitably have controlled the religious environment of the insula's bakery). In light of this, we need to consider whether it is conceivable that a symbol of Jesus-devotion could have been placed upon the wall of the bakery within the Insula Arriana Polliana – as I have proposed in chapter 7 above.

Mazois and Monnier, for instance, thought that the two forms of devotion were oddly placed together – with Monnier calling them "irreconcilable" and Mazois calling the snake opposite the cross "an obscene image" from "an incomprehensible cult."[28] But this view of

---

27. On food production in the gardens of the Vesuvian towns, see especially Jashemski 1979.

things seems far off the mark. To demonstrate this, we will pose two central questions: First, why would someone want to place a cross of Jesus-devotion on the wall of the bakery? Second, would a tenant have been permitted to place such a feature on the wall of the rental property? As we will see, the two issues are interrelated.

The Cross, Protection, and the Deities

Is a cross of Jesus-devotion out of alignment with the bakery's densely polytheistic atmosphere, which itself was in complete accord with the atmosphere of the main residence of the Insula Arriana Polliana? We have already seen how some scholars have addressed that question. Others of influence have dealt with it in similar ways. Notice, for instance, how Thomas H. Dyer handled these issues in 1868:[29] "That Christians may have existed there [in Pompeii] is quite possible, but that they should have ventured to exhibit any public sign of their religion is in the highest degree improbable, as well as that they should have exhibited them in company with pagan emblems."

Here we are seeing assumption piled up on top of assumption. Dyer never explicitly states why it was "in the highest degree improbable" that Jesus-followers should exhibit any public sign of their religion. This is little more than assertion without foundation, based evidently on the assumption that Jesus-followers were always huddled away in fear of the persecuting authorities – an unfounded assumption, as we have already seen in chapter 5 above. But on what basis did Dyer assume that symbols of Jesus-devotion would not have been mixed with "pagan emblems"? He fails to explain.

In fact, however, the best answer to our question is not this: "The two forms of religious devotion are quite irreconcilable." Instead, it is this: "There is scope for placing these two forms of religious devotion alongside each other, in a variety of possibilities." Quite simply, if

---

28. Mazois 1824: vol. 2, 84: "l'image obscène, d'un culte incompréhensible."
29. Dyer 1875: 321. Similar objections are voiced by Baldi (1964: 39-40): the bas-relief faces a pagan painting and it is quite exposed to the public. He nonetheless thought, much like Mazois, that the bas-relief incorporated a crypto-Christian symbol; in Baldi's view, that cryptic symbol was hidden in the form of an axe.

the majority of religious artifacts within the bakery were expected to provide apotropaic protection in spaces of vulnerability, the same function is easily attributable to a cross of Jesus-devotion. That cross should be seen as adding the protective power of a nontraditional deity to the baker's shop. The bakery cross was an apotropaion at the shop's entryway, a symbol invoking the power of a new deity who was said to have overcome the forces of evil in his lifetime and defeated them through his resurrection after his death on a cross.

Was the baker's devotion to Jesus simply one component of a larger polytheistic package, or was his an exclusive allegiance to a single deity? We will never know, and either scenario is possible. If the cross in the bakery was a mark of Jesus-devotion (as demonstrated in chapter 7), that single finding does not permit a full inventory of the bakery's religious ethos. Perhaps the baker imagined the power of the crucified-but-resurrected deity worked in tandem with the traditional household deities represented by the snake on the wall opposite the cross, in a kind of "deity curtain" or "deity zap" against malicious invaders. In this scenario, the baker honored traditional Greco-Roman deities and added a new deity, Jesus Christ, to that panoply of deities.[30]

Or perhaps the cross was thought to represent the only true deity on guard, with the baker putting no confidence in the other religious features of the bakery. Those features might have remained on the wall from an earlier period in his religious journey or might have been inherited from an earlier tenancy (albeit one that postdated the earthquake, after which the premises seem to have been remodeled).[31] In scenarios of this kind, the baker's exclusive loyalty to his new deity

---

30. Ling (2009: 107) captures the ethos perfectly: the Greco-Roman world "encompassed a multiplicity of deities with different characters and different spheres of competence, and people would cultivate now one, now another, depending upon their personal preferences or upon the needs of the moment." See also Simon Price 2006: 12; Mitchell and van Neffelen 2010: 14. Compare syncretism found commonly in Pompeii, as outlined by Joanne Berry 2007: 208: "The House of the Gilded Cupids (VI.16.7) contained two aedicule lararia on opposite sides of its peristyle. One contained statuettes of . . . Jupiter, Juno and Minerva as the Capitoline triad, and Mercury and the Lares. The other, painted, lararium depicted Isis flanked by Harpocrates and Anubis to one side and Osiris to the other, and objects related to the cult of Isis such as the sistrum (rattle), revealing how both traditional and mystery gods could be venerated together." Part of the painted lararium appears in figure 7.8 above.
31. That residents inherited the artistry of earlier owners or tenants is one of the most assured results of Vesuvian studies. See, for instance, Oakes 2009: 32.

might have caused him to think of the bakery's other religious features in terms comparable to Paul's claim that "an idol is nothing in this world" (cf. 1 Corinthians 8:6; 1 Timothy 4:4–5) – that is, they are insignificant. Or perhaps the resurrected deity was the main deity of the bakery, with other religious paraphernalia being simply prudent forms of additional protection. Should we really expect Jesus-devotion in a rented bakery inevitably to require the tearing down of all (inherited?) pagan symbolism? Even Paul the apostle would probably have simply shrugged his shoulders if the workshops he rented happened to display paintings of idols or snakes or phallic symbols on their walls or at their entryways; in typical fashion, he would probably have used them simply as object lessons to promote the "good news" that he preached.[32]

Previous generations of scholars have exercised a notable failure of historical imagination in this regard. History indicates that the influx of Christianity into non-Christian contexts usually resulted in markedly syncretistic situations whereby indigenous and Christian commitments intertwine in a variety of configurations. Scholars of the Vesuvian towns, however, have tended to assume that Jesus-followers would (or should) have been wholly exclusive in their single-minded religious devotion.

This assumption seems to have emerged from scholars' own personal commitments. Mazois's own words suggest this since, for him, Christianity was the "new and pure religion" that contrasted completely with the "absurd superstitions of antiquity." No wonder he shows some unease with his conviction that the bakery cross was a Christian artifact; in his unrefined view, Christianity and paganism seem to have been differentiated, like oil and water, even in the earliest days of Christianity and in every indigenous situation, no matter how far removed from apostolic influence those situations might have been.

---

32. Much the same is envisaged in Hubbard 2010: 172, in an imagined situation: "Against the far wall was the lararium, which contained a small likeness of the genius, the guardian spirit, of Gaius Titius Justus, and was framed by two crested serpents. Since his baptism by Paulus [the apostle Paul], Gaius no longer maintained the shrine, but neither did he remove it. It was one thing to worship only one god; it was quite another to dismantle an altar."

The view that early Christianity was incompatible with the polytheism of its surroundings often derived from retrojecting nineteenth-century piety onto the first-century context. Nineteenth-century archaeology of Christian artifacts often served as an extension of Christian apologetics, and the archaeology of Christian antiquity was expected to verify the truthfulness of Christianity (i.e., the "pure religion"). It was not supposed to harvest ancient Jesus-devotion that looked like a variation on ancient forms of Greco-Roman superstition, especially so close to the city of Rome, the papal city. An artifact that showed "primitive believers" in what was deemed an "unfavorable" light was almost inevitably an artifact that must have been misinterpreted. Instead, the archaeology of Christian antiquity was expected to yoke together "the communion of saints" that transcends the centuries, enhancing "participation in the society of primitive believers."[33]

Here is how two historians exhibited this conviction in 1885 when they contrasted the art of the Christian catacombs in Rome and the art of pagan Pompeii. The catacombs (with their Christian monograms, anchors, palm branches, and crosses) testify to the principle "that even our furniture should be distinctively Christian"; by contrast, "[i]n Pompeii, one finds lamps and other vessels marked by heathenish devices, some of them gross and revolting."[34]

While the apostle Paul and other apostolic figures might well have appreciated the impulse to separate Christianity from "pagan" influences, the ancient reality was often much different – as Paul's letters themselves testify.[35] Syncretism, the mixing of religious traditions, was alive and well in the Greco-Roman world, and Christianity was not immune to it.[36] Ancient Jesus-devotion was

---

33. Snyder 2003: 6–7. Snyder exposes the theological assumptions of "the Roman school" of archaeology and the methodological errors that crept in as a consequence of those assumptions.
34. Roberts and Donaldson 1885: 297. On the rare occurrence of crosses within the catacombs, see Longenecker 2015: 81–86, 158, 179–83.
35. For instance, Jesus-followers in Corinth seem to have been making use of the services of prostitutes (many of whom would have been sex slaves; see 1 Corinthians 6:12–20), and reveling in sexual promiscuity "of a kind that even pagans do not tolerate" (1 Corinthians 5:1; see 5:1–13).
36. Bodel 2012: 251: In the first few centuries of the Common Era, the "persistence and tenacity of the popular veneration of household gods" is evidenced in the "vibrant polytheistic spirit that . . .

occasionally (perhaps frequently) adopted as another form of protection against the harsh realities of Greco-Roman life. Sometimes Jesus-devotion was simply seen as a means to increase a person's prospects (see Acts 8:9–24; 19:11–20); often, devotion to Jesus was not thought to impede one's devotion to other deities (see Revelation 2–3). In a dangerous world, it would often have been seen as prudent to add Jesus-devotion to the list of one's protecting deities.

That other forms of religious devotion were attested on the walls of the bakery, then, clearly cannot be used to exclude Jesus-devotion from the bakery. The same religious artifact can be used in a variety of different contexts, ranging from religious syncretism to religious exclusivism. Without other data suggesting one context or another, we cannot predetermine in advance how a religious symbol might have functioned in this regard. But this is precisely what happened when scholars excluded the possibility that a symbol of Jesus-devotion could have resided in the Pompeii bakery. They applied an exclusivist category to Jesus-devotion when other options are just as possible, especially in the early years of the Jesus-movement and in what might have amounted to a relatively insignificant setting in the growth of the early Jesus-movement.[37]

Have illegitimate assumptions of this kind played a part in bolstering the current consensus regarding the bakery artifact? That is hard to determine, but we find permutations of it running throughout the consensus view – not only in the early generations after Mazois (as in Dyer and Monnier) but much more recently as well. For instance, in 1970 Olivieri Farioli (echoing the view of Max Sulzberger from 1925) claimed that early Christianity had a disdain of idolatry and that a cross

---

long after the traditional forms of civic public worship had been abandoned, proved so difficult . . . to eradicate." This is evidenced in "patristic" denunciations of the "vibrant polytheistic spirit" among Christians; see Tertullian, *Apology* 13; *To the Heathen* 1.10; Arnobius of Sicca, *Against the Pagans* 3.41–42; Lactantius, *Epitome of the Divine Institutes* 28; *The Divine Institutes* 2.15. Syncretism sometimes marked out Jewish devotion as well; see, for instance, Hengel and Schwemer 1997: 161–67.

37. Bremmer (2014: 117) rightly notes the following: "At the time of Cumont [late nineteenth century] and long afterwards, the term 'syncretism' carried a pejorative sense and suggested a mixing of 'pure' Christianity or Roman religion with Oriental religious elements. Most scholars today are rather hesitant about using the term, as they have become increasingly aware that all religions constantly borrow elements from other religions or ideologies: there are no 'pure' religions."

on a wall would have offended Christian monotheistic sentiments.[38] Similarly, when deciding how to interpret the artifact on the wall of the Pompeii bakery, Antonio Varone made reference to "the horror of Saint Paul and the early Christians at the prospect of idolatry"; in light of that "horror" of worshiping objects, Varone deemed the artifact on the wall not to be a Christian cross.[39] For these scholars, not only are Christians to be monotheists ubiquitously, they are also to have shunned idolatry at each and every turn, and for that reason as well, the artifact on the wall of the bakery cannot be a Christian cross. This assessment, however, misses the point of the stucco cross in the bakery. Christian worship was not directed toward this cross. As an artifact of Jesus-devotion, it would have served an apotropaic function in warding off evil. There is nothing here about worshiping the cross.

Assessments of the bakery cross have been plagued by simplistic terms of reference that should never have gained the smallest foothold in the debate about Vesuvian artifacts. Those terms of reference are little other than dubious siblings to Bulwer-Lytton's mid-nineteenth-century moralisms about the voluptuous decadence of the pagan world in contrast to the blessed rise of pious Christians – as expressed in his popular novel *The Last Days of Pompeii*. If novelists have benefited from positioning Christians in stark opposition to their first-century environments, historians must be more subtle than that, since black-white contrasts often cover over a variety of intermediate grays. But in fact, simplistic terms of reference have helped to control the scholarly discourse, illegitimately shaping the consensus to some extent over much of the past two hundred years.

Evidently, then, scholars of the past have been thrown off balance by

---

38. Farioli 1970: 66, citing Sulzberger 1925: 341-42, 348. Farioli's argument on pp. 66-67 includes two further spurious claims: (1) that Christians would not have used the cross because of the horror associated with it, and (2) that the cross was not in circulation among Christians prior to Constantine.
39. Varone 1979: 33: "l'orrore di S. Paulo e dei primi Cristiani per l'idolatria," which Varone says results in "la automatica esclusione della rappresentazione di un oggetto da venerare." Lurking nearby Varone's interpretations is the issue of whether an interpretation is "in full accord with Paul's meditation on the cross" ("in piena linea con la meditazione paolina circa la croce"; 1979: 39.) Varone further supports his view about the bakery artifact by replicating the claim that the cross became a Christian symbol only after Constantine.

the simple way in which the question has been posed: "Did Christians live in Pompeii?" Christian identity was open to gradients of interpretation – as the exclusivist apostle Paul found out repeatedly (to his own frustration) when founding groups of Jesus-followers within urban contexts.[40] Consequently, the question should not initially be "Did Christians live in Pompeii?" Instead, at least in the first instance, the question should be couched in terms of whether "Jesus-devotion" can be traced within those towns, since that term can be employed to describe a variety of configurations in which worship of the resurrected deity may have taken hold.

In contrast to the consensus view, we have seen good reason to answer a slightly different question, "Was Jesus-devotion in Pompeii?" with a much different answer – "Yes." A cross of Jesus-devotion was completely at home in the religious atmosphere of both the bakery and the Insula Arriana Polliana itself. The purpose of that cross was to tap into the power of a resurrected deity and offer apotropaic protection at the entrance of the bakery. Up for debate, however, is whether this power was sought alongside the powers of the traditional household deities or in distinction from those inherited deities. But unlike archaeologists of the past, we should have no difficulty in conceiving of a scenario in which a cross of Jesus-devotion hung on the wall of a liminal-space entryway in Pompeii – an initiative completely at home within an ancient culture gripped by fear of suprahuman forces.

Tenancy, Ownership, and the Deities

If we assume (with most others) that the baker was a tenant within the bakery, we need to consider the extent to which a tenant might have influence in determining the religious symbolism of rented space. Is it imaginable that a tenant should have commissioned a stucco bas-relief artistic piece for the wall of a rented accommodation?

Quite simply, the answer is yes. While the rules of Roman lease law

---

40. Barclay (1992) rightly differentiates the reception of Paul's gospel in Thessalonica and in Corinth, contrasting the more "apocalyptic" appropriation of Paul's message in Thessalonica with the more "accommodated" appropriation of it in Corinth. Corinthian accommodation has been highlighted repeatedly; see, for instance, Briones 2013: 131–50.

ensured that the owner (i.e., Maius) would have considerable rights over his rental properties, it also ensured that the tenant had certain rights as well, including the right to enjoy the premises according to his or her own lifestyle preferences without overbearing predetermination by the landlord.[41] These matters were, of course, open to interpretation in any given instance. But the point is that there was a certain give-and-take to these things that, while frequently favoring the owner, did not render the tenant powerless in pursuing minimal adjustments within the rental property.

Although the addition of stucco bas-relief would have been a minimal adjustment to the property, the baker might nonetheless have initially sought permission from Maius's household manager (or better, Maius's enslaved agent Primus, as mentioned in CIL 4.138) to install the bas-relief within the bakery. It is not at all unimaginable that permission would have been granted. The baker might have explained that the bas-relief would entreat the favor of a powerful deity whose symbol and benefits were much like those of the goddess Isis.[42] In this scenario, the manager might have thought nothing of the prospect.[43] But if Primus had raised his eyebrows at the idea, a financial inducement might have helped to persuade the hesitant manager. And if there were concerns that a symbol of a nontraditional deity would be left on the wall at the end of the tenancy, a payment might have been made up front to cover the cost of removing the bas-relief and replacing it with fresh plaster once the baker vacated the premises – hardly a difficult scenario to envisage, and an easy task to perform.

Neither should we assume that Maius exercised complete control over the religious expressions within the bakery. Such would seem unusually excessive. Even in Greco-Roman master-slave relationships,

---

41. See Frier 1980: 181–83. Franklin (2001: 96) speaks about the possibility of residences being "painted to meet its renters' tastes"; Ling (2009: 143) notes that the "[d]etails of ownership and tenancy arrangements, doubtless as complex and varied as in most modern cities, are largely lost to us."
42. Perhaps this scenario illustrates the advantage of styling the cross with Ankh-like features. Such styling may have "neutralized" the symbol somewhat, thereby paving the way for a favorable reception of the baker's request to erect the stucco bas-relief.
43. Cf. Balch 2004: 43: "Worship of the foreign goddess Isis was popular in the luxurious houses of small-town Pompeii, which suggests that other foreign gods might also be welcome."

it was not inevitably the case that a master required his slaves to replicate his own religious convictions without remainder.[44] A slave within a household would have been required to participate in ceremonies of devotion to the household deities on the *Kalends*, *Ides*, and *Nones* of each month, and on other special occasions throughout the year; but beyond that, a slave's religious devotion was usually not a matter of much concern or interest, as long as it was not expressed in a fashion deemed subversive to the good of the household and society.[45] If absolute conformity of religious devotion was not necessary within households, that would be all the more the case for spaces rented to clients or others beyond the household.

***

Four assumptions inform the view that the bakery cross cannot be an artifact of Jesus-devotion.

1. The cross became a Christian symbol only in the time of Constantine and beyond.
2. Pre-Constantinian Christians were always persecuted; consequently, pre-Constantinian Christians would never have advertised their faith publicly.
3. Christians could not fathom placing their devotion alongside pagan superstition; therefore this cannot have been an artifact of Jesus-devotion.
4. Christians were opposed to idolatry, and since Christians would see a symbolic cross as a form of idolatry, this cannot be a Christian cross.

---

44. The imagery of household conversions depicted in Acts (16:11–15; 16:25–34; 18:5–8) should not lead us to think that all households were monolithic in their spiritual alignment. Even Paul's letter to Philemon suggests otherwise, with Philemon's household having within it a slave who was not a Jesus-follower before departing from Philemon's household (see Longenecker 2016a). For second- and early third-century evidence, see Osiek and Balch 1997: 191–92 Moreover, the situation in the Insula Arriana Polliana is different, since the bakery is rented (or owned?) by someone who may have been beyond the parameters of the household.
45. Compare Osiek and Balch 2007: 83, where they highlight the "religious independence of household members to pursue devotions beyond that of the household."

All four assumptions are problematic. The chain of logic supporting the consensus does not simply have one weak link in it; instead, it is composed solely of weak links. It is bewildering, then, that these assumptions have survived for so long as the foundations on which the consensus view is built. There are no other supports for the consensus on this artifact. Unless new arguments are mounted to bolster the floundering consensus, the best scholarship will allow the consensus to founder without launching rescue missions. In relation to this artifact, the consensus ship is going nowhere but down; there is nothing worthwhile to salvage from it.

By contrast, there are no practicalities that speak against seeing the artifact as a relic of Jesus-devotion. The baker in the southwest corner of the Insula Arriana Polliana had a stucco bas-relief cross placed on the wall of his bakery as an expression of his religious commitments and as an outworking of his concern to enhance the security of his household in an insecure world. That cross made perfectly good sense within the religious atmosphere of the bakery, and scholarly concerns about the inappropriateness of erecting a cross in the bakery's shop have proved unfounded at every turn. In short, there is no reason to short-circuit the findings of the previous chapter, in which it was seen that the least implausible interpretation of the bakery wall-cross is that it is, indeed, an artifact of first-century Jesus-devotion.

In 2008, Giovanni Liccardo claimed that "the existence of Christian communities in Pompeii . . . awaits the first indisputable and decisive evidence."[46] In fact, by the time his comments were published, the evidence had already been around for nearly two hundred years. Moreover, there is further evidence, as we will see in the remaining chapters. The question is no longer whether these data can sustain the weight of determining that Jesus-devotion was present in Pompeii; instead, the question is simply whether these data can be seen to dovetail with the Jesus-devotion that we already know to be have been present there. As we will see, when all the pieces fall into place,

---

46. Liccardo 2008: 149: "l'esistenza di comunita cristiane a Pompei e a Herculaneum prima del 79 attende prove indiscutibili e risolutive."

there are significant witnesses to first-century Jesus-devotion within the material record from Pompeii.

9

Jesus-Devotion in the Letters

In the 1950s, an artifact was discovered that had the potential to illustrate fairly conclusively that Jesus-devotion had resided within pre-eruption Pompeii. Unfortunately, the significance of that single artifact has been greatly undervalued since its discovery. A single graffito among more than eleven thousand Vesuvian graffiti, this artifact has rarely been discussed, and when it is discussed, it has been interpreted inadequately. This short chapter seeks to redress those deficiencies.

The Artifact

During the excavations of autumn 1955, a curious graffito (11 x 20 cm) was discovered on the wall of a residence in insula 1.13 (see figure 9.1).[1] It was readily recognizable as containing the letters *viv*, deriving

---

1. Regarding the find-spot of this artifact, della Corte (who was an eyewitness to the artifact and was the first to document its existence) identifies the find-spot within insula 2.3 (1958: 113), whereas Barnard lists the find-spot as being within insula 1.13 (1984: 25). Although placing things in the wrong insulae is not an uncommon practice in Vesuvian scholarship (see Laidlaw 2007: 631n3), that is probably not what we have here. In fact, both scholars are correct, in their own terms of reference. Della Corte was using an enumeration system for regions 1 and 2 that differed from the system adopted later. What della Corte called insula 2.3 was subsequently identified as insula 1.13. As late as 1979, Varone still placed this graffito in 2.3 (1979: 39). I have not been able to discover

145

from the Latin verb *vivere*, "to live."[2] Moreover, there is no dissent that the graffito conjoins a cross-shaped symbol directly below the *viv*-stem (with the *viv*-stem being reemphasized at the bottom with another V placed on the lower part of the vertical stave, or perhaps those are simply stray marks). The cross was either an equilateral cross or a body cross (see Varone's reconstruction of it in figure 9.1).[3]

Figure 9.1. The viv- graffito. CIL 4.10062

In his studies from 1979 and 1980 regarding the possibility that Christians were present in pre-eruption Pompeii, Antonio Varone found it intriguing that an incomplete form of the verb "to live"

where this graffito was discovered within insula 1.13. If it was discovered in 1955, it probably resided in any of the following locations, which were being excavated that year: 1.13.7, 1.13.8, 1.13.9, or 1.13.11.

2. The view that the top letters were simply two occurrences of the letter V is incorrectly asserted by Williams in Jensen, Lampe, Tabbernee, and Williams 2014: 423.

3. From Varone 1980: insert between pages 40 and 41. Della Corte (1958: 113, and figure 181 on page 183) depicted the graffito with an elongated stave below the transept arm (equating to a body cross rather than an equilateral cross). The interpretation offered here can apply to either formation equally well. (To get ahead of the argument by a paragraph or two, notice the slightly elongated stave below the transept arm of the *TI* ligature in the Eros ring of figure 9.3 below; if della Corte's depiction is to be preferred, we simply have an elongated *T* in this graffito.)

appears above the shape of a cross in this graffito. Together with a few other scholars who have considered this artifact, he referred to it as a *vivat* graffito. This builds on the view (held earlier by Matteo della Corte and others) that the graffito might be a Christian graffito that salutes the cross: *Viv(at) Crux*, or "Long live the cross."[4] Could this be evidence of a Christian presence in Pompeii? Varone declared the artifact too unstable to permit such a conclusion.[5]

Varone's agnosticism is poorly founded. This is because he, together with others before and after him, missed a singularly important point about the graffito. The key here is the ending of the verb. By supplying the letters *-at* as a missing verbal stem (*vivat*), Varone and others have failed to recognize that the stem's ending is supplied within the graffito. The two intersecting lines below the letters *viv* provide the verbal ending and therefore tell us something about the referent of the verb.

Inscriptions and other ancient artifacts frequently exhibit alphabetical ligatures, in which two (or more) letters are artistically joined together in some fashion. The cross in this graffito is precisely that – a ligature (and more). As noted in chapter 6 above, it was not uncommon for the letters *T* and *I* to be joined in a ligature, with the *I* resting on the horizontal arm of the *T* at its center. We have seen this formation already on the stamp ring of Aulus Vettius Restitutus (see figure 9.2). The same formation appears on other stamp rings from Pompeii as well, such as that of Lucius Brittius Eros, where the *T* and *I* of "Brittius" are formed in this manner (see figure 9.3).[6] With this in view, the form of *vivere* is not, in fact, incomplete, as Varone and others have imagined. Nor should the verbal form be referred to as *vivat*, as Varone and others have done. The verbal ending is housed within the shape of the cross. That ending is *-it*. Consequently, it is not right to say,

---

4. See this misreading, for instance, in della Corte, 1958: 113; Baldi 1964: 67; Varone 1979: 39; Varone 1980: 34–36; Barnard 1984: 25–26.
5. Varone (1979: 39) thinks the graffito could be either (1) a genuine faith affirmation of a Christian who understood the regenerative value of the cross or (2) a doodle.
6. For a ligature placing the *I* above the letter *N*, see the stamp ring of Gaius Stlaccius Epitynchanus (C. Stlacci Epitynachani) at the following website: www.pompeiiinpictures.com/pompeiiinpictures/R6/6 15 05.htm.

as Varone does, that "the sense of [the cross] drawn on a wall and in correlation with the inscription VIV is not clear." It is perfectly clear. What we have on the wall are five letters (two in ligature formation) that combine to form the word *vivit*, "he/she/it lives."[7]

Figure 9.2. The six final letters of the Restitutus stamp ring (in negative aspect), with the three occurrences of T working with other letters to form three ligatures (TI, TU, TI); see also figure 6.2.

Figure 9.3. The stamp ring of Eros (in negative aspect), with a cross-shaped ligature (from right to left: L.Brit Eros).

What would the purpose be of writing *vivit* on the wall of residence, and why would someone present a cross as a central feature within a *vivit* graffito? Is this graffito an obvious statement about someone in the residence, with an interesting combination of the final two letters? Is this about the householder? His manager? A slave? A lover? Did the same inscriber etch "he sleeps" on the wall next to his bedding, with

---

7. Varone (1979: 39): "Non si comprende infatti il senso di un tale marchio tracciato su una parete e in correlazione con la scritta 'VIV.'"

the final two letters of *dormit* forming a cross shape for no reason other than to adorn the word with an interesting design?

It is unlikely that this is a simple exercise in adorning the word *vivit* with an interesting shape in the final two letters. This is especially evident when it is recognized that a more interesting structure could have been constructed for the graffito by lining the first *I* of the stem *viv* directly above the second *I*, forming an extended ligature with a longer vertical line. In that construction, the crossbar of the *T* would occur with two occurrences of the *I* directly above it and the two occurrences of the letter *V* balanced on either side of the top of the vertical stroke. Evidently the inscriber was not interested simply in a cleverly devised form of the word *vivit* for its own sake.

What, then, does this graffito signify? It does not take great imagination to land on the answer. With its combination of a cross and the phrase "he lives," this graffito is unlikely to refer to anyone other than the crucified but resurrected deity – the same deity who is referenced in the bakery cross. Evidently a Jesus-follower saw more in a common ligature than a simple combination of two letters. Just as Jesus-followers elsewhere found a reference to the cross of Jesus in the "mark" of Ezekiel 9 (as noted in chapter 6 above), so too a Jesus-follower in Pompeii found a reference to the cross of Jesus in the ligature enabling him (or her?) to combine the letters *I* and *T*, and that ligature became the basis for the assertion of a theological claim: *vivit*.

This cross has not played much of a role in scholarly discourse since its discovery. Perhaps this is because scholars simply saw it as a strange oddity (*vivat crux*). As a consequence, the consensus view has sauntered along, undeterred. The time has come to leave the old ways behind, rooted as they were in a misperception of the internal workings of the important *vivit* artifact.

The Form and Function of the *Vivit* Cross

What can be said about the form of the cross in this graffito? Whether the letters *IT* formed a body cross (as della Corte depicted it) or an equilateral cross (as Varone depicted it), the *vivit* cross also references a *T* cross, with the letter *I* centered above the cross depicted in the letter *T*. Just as the *Epistle of Barnabas* interprets the shape of the cross in two different forms in close proximity (see chapter 5), so too the *vivit* cross seems to incorporate a T cross within a larger cross construction.

The *vivit* cross and the bakery cross testify to different formations of the cross within the material record of Pompeian Jesus-devotion. Beyond the Vesuvian context, witnesses prior to 120 demonstrate that the cross as a symbol of Christian devotion was being formed in three different ways: as a *T* cross, a body cross, and an equilateral cross (as I have demonstrated elsewhere and referenced in chapters 2 and 5 above).[8] Jesus-devotion in Pompeii already displays the early signs of such diversity (see also chapters 12 and 13 below).

We have seen that the *vivit* graffito is built on an *IT* ligature in which a Jesus-follower has seen new meaning. Might it also draw its significance from the "Jewish cross" discussed in chapter 6, referencing "the mark" of eschatological protection in Ezekiel 9:4-6? Since early Christianity emerged from the cradle of Judaism, the possibility that a Jewish influence lies behind a cross of Jesus-devotion cannot be ruled out (particularly if the *vivit* cross was equilateral in form). If this influence could ever be proved, we would be seeing the impact of Ezekiel 9 not only in Jewish texts (*Psalms of Solomon*; the *Damascus Document*) and artifacts (the Jerusalem ossuaries) but also in a text (Revelation) and an artifact (the *vivit* cross) of first-century Jesus-devotion.

Beyond its formation, what about its function? The *vivit* cross seems to have served an analogous purpose to the bakery cross – that is, both probably functioned to harness the protection of the crucified deity. Both the bakery cross and the *vivit* cross testify to the belief that a powerful deity had died and returned to life again, defeating the powerful forces of evil and the unassailable phenomenon of death – a prospect promised to this deity's devotees as well. With the residence

---

8. See further Longenecker 2015 (for instance, p. 70: "Differences in the shape of the cross were not to be avoided, since each distinct shape fostered different possibilities for theological discourse"; p. 170: "This variety of shapes allowed early Christian theologians scope for exploring the cross's multifaceted potential in terms of its symbolic value").

bearing the insignia of the cross of Jesus and embossed with a form of the verb "to live," forces of evil might well prefer to take their chances elsewhere, leaving the residents free from malicious meddling.

On another residential wall in Pompeii, someone etched his plea for divine assistance using words from Virgil's *Aeneid* (9.404): "You, goddess, present one, assist our work" (*tu Dea, tu pr(a)ese(ns), nostro succurre labor(i)*; *CIL* 4.2310k). As we have seen in chapter 8 above, another Pompeian exhorted the deity Hercules Callinicus to flourish within his residence in order to "take away all evil" from its premises.[9] By comparison and contrast, one Jesus-follower sought divine assistance from a different deity, placing his hopes for protection in a crucified deity who had been resurrected to a new and powerful life.

***

We have now registered two artifacts from Pompeii as crosses of Jesus-devotion. In chapters 11 through 13, further crosses from Pompeii will be registered. Prior to that, however, the Pompeian graffito that makes mention of "Christians" requires consideration, since that artifact will benefit the interpretation of the artifacts of subsequent chapters.

---

9. See chapter 8, footnote **15**. Note also that a Latin inscription of the Hebrew word *cherem* (probably *kerem*, the "vineyard" of Israel) was found in the entry vestibule of "the House of the Hebrews" (1.11.14), together with two five-pointed stars – probably for apotropaic protection within a Jewish household. (In Jewish traditions, the five-pointed star was associated with Solomon, whose wisdom enabled him to control magical powers.) On this artifact, see Giordano and Kahn 2001: 89–103.

10

Jesus-Devotion and the Inn

Prior to the eruption of Mount Vesuvius, someone in Pompeii wrote something about "Christians" in an informal inscription. But it is not clear what was being said in that inscription. This chapter outlines the discovery of the artifact and overviews previous attempts to interpret it, before offering a fresh interpretation.

The *Christianos* Inscription

In 1862, a faint charcoal inscription was found that seemed to contain the Latin word *Christianos* ("Christians" in accusative plural form; from *CIL* 4.679).[1] The inscription resided in a large Pompeii residence (7.11.11), with the ground floor alone comprising three thousand square feet of living space (excluding the kitchen, the leased apartments, and the gardens). Several small apartments were located upstairs as well. The house was probably overseen by a single person (rather than having been leased out to various parties), and probably served as a residential inn, with the owner making rented

---

1. Kiessling 1862. For a list of discussions regarding this inscription, see Weber's entry on *CIL* 4.679 in Weber et al. 2011: 1245–46.

accommodation available to travelers within his own extended house.[2] The entryway into the house from the street opens up almost immediately into its atrium, with the inscription being at the center of the atrium's western wall (see figure 10.1).

Figure 10.1. The plan of the House of the Christian Inscription (in darkest outline), with the arrow added to highlight the location of the inscription.

The first archaeologist to discuss the finding was Alfred Kiessling in the same year that the inscription was discovered. The charcoal had faded from view by 1864, the same year that Giovanni Battista de Rossi published a report about it.[3] In that report, de Rossi reproduced

---

2. See della Corte 1942: 73. Della Corte thought (1962: 27) that the building probably comprised one of the best residential hotels of the town.

Giulio Minervini's reconstruction of the six lines of characters that had been evident on the wall (Minervini himself having been an eyewitness to the inscription before it disappeared, together with Kiessling and Giuseppe Fiorelli). Figure 10.2 is Minervini's reconstruction of the characters on the wall.[4]

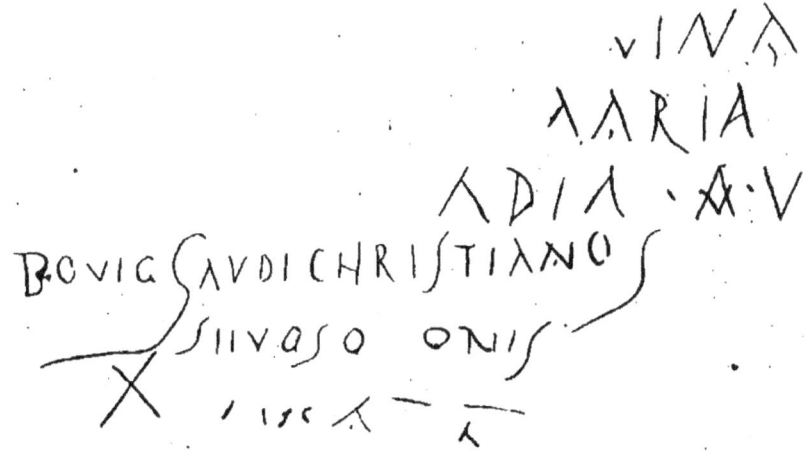

Figure 10.2. Minervini's depiction of the Christianos inscription.

Although the inscription was difficult to decipher, if there ever was a recognizable word in it, that word was *Christianos*.[5] Evidently someone within Pompeii made mention of Christians (see figure 10.3).[6] But can

---

3. Snyder (2003: 4) acclaims de Rossi as one of the two "real founders of the science of early Christian archaeology."
4. From de Rossi 1864: 71. According to Paul Berry, in the early 1990s a high-powered microscope scanned the location where the graffito had been. At a magnification level of 100, "carbon fragments lodged in the stucco texture" were still decipherable – the results being recorded by Berry in 1995: 25. It is hard to know what to make of this claim. It seems highly dubious. Berry also proposes (1995: 25-26, 28) that the graffito underwent two cleanings in which early misreadings of the graffito (for instance, Kiessling's reconstruction of the primary word as *Christiani*) were corrected by later readings (for instance, Minervini and de Rossi's reconstruction, *Christianos*). I have not been able to find this corroborated in either Kiessling or de Rossi. The process itself is not in dispute, however. John Clarke (2007: 132) recounts a similar series of events for another Pompeian artifact, which was open to misinterpretation after the first cleaning but whose second cleaning revealed it clearly.
5. Some have doubted whether even this much was ever clear. Beard (2008: 302) says that reading *Christianos* in the graffito "is almost certainly a figment of pious imagination" because the words "faded almost instantly." Better is de Rossi (1864: 72), who notes that the graffito contained "a clear mention of Christians" ("una chiara menzione de Cristiani"), despite having faded soon after its discovery. All three of the main eyewitnesses to the graffito (Fiorelli, Kiessling, and Minervini) were agreed that the graffito made reference to Christians.

we decipher the gist of the inscription's meaning? Some have thought we can.

Figure 10.3. The word Christianos as reconstructed by Minervini.

Previous Interpretations

Scholars often struggle to interpret the lines of faint ancient graffiti. When reading an inscribed squiggle on a wall, even the best of scholars have at times been forced to admit things like "*ultimae lineae quid sibi velint nescio,*" or "I don't know the meaning of the last line."[7] Regarding the *Christianos* inscription, it is not only the last line but the inscription as a whole that is problematic. Even knowing where the main inscription begins and ends is something of a feat in itself.

For this reason, the *Christianos* inscription has attracted several interpretations since its discovery. Kiessling, the first to propose an interpretation in print and one of three main eyewitnesses to the inscription, argued that line 4 probably read: *igni gaudi Christiani*, or "To the fire, with joy, O Christians!" Kiessling deemed all the other characters on the wall to be unstable (see his reconstruction in figure 10.5).[8]

---

6. Della Corte (1962: 27) speaks of the word "Maria" being "plainly visible" in the graffito, and argues that that name enhances its credentials as a Christian artifact. But the word is not "plainly visible," since the first letter may not be the letter M; others have suggested a V (*varia*) or an A. Even if it were the word "Maria," this would do little to increase the chances of it being a Christian artifact.
7. Zangemeister, from Schöne and Zangemeister 1871: 107.
8. Kiessling 1862: 92; see also de Rossi's discussion of Kiessling, 1864: 70.

ꝶ · VI GAVDI . . HRISTIANI
8 X̄ SICV . SO . . ORIIS

Figure 10.5: Kiessling's printed depiction of the inscription (lines 4 and 5).

Two years later, de Rossi proposed a different interpretation. Claiming that his interpretation drew on the insights of Minervini and Fiorelli, de Rossi claimed that line 4 of the inscription read *audi Christianos*.[9] He then coupled this reading of line 4 to some of the letters below the word *Christianos* on line 5, which Kiessling had not included in his interpretation. De Rossi reconstructed those lines in this way:

> *audi Christianos*
> *s[a]evos o[l]ores.*[10]

For de Rossi, the inscription (which seems to use the second-person singular form "listen" in order to address the readers generically) was simply: "Listen to the Christians, the cruel swans."[11] (See figure 10.6, depicting Zeus transformed into a swan, deceiving Leda in order to seduce her.) Although de Rossi notes that "we cannot clearly understand all the malice or the wit of this insult," if the first line seems to commend the Christians, the second inverts that by demeaning them.[12] Further, de Rossi imagined that this inscription might well link to others found in the same atrium, such as: *Mulus hic muscellas docuit*, "here a mule gives lessons to flies" (*CIL* 4.2016). For de Rossi, a Christian group may have met in the atrium of this residence. (Compare Acts 19:9–10, where Paul is depicted as teaching in the "lecture hall of Tyrannus" over a period of two years while

---

9. See de Rossi 1864: 70.
10. De Rossi 1864: 72. Note that if the third to the last letter is an R, then the E following it is formed by two vertical lines, a common inscriptional practice and one evidenced earlier on the same line of the graffito, as seen in Minervini's reconstruction.
11. The generic second-person singular appears in other Pompeii inscriptions, such as *CIL* 4.1939; see Milnor 2013: 124–26.
12. De Rossi 1864: 72 ("non possiamo chiaramente intendere tutta la malizia o l'arguzia di questa beffa").

in Ephesus.)[13] In these graffiti from the same atrium, the Christians and their leader bear the brunt of a biting sarcasm.[14] For de Rossi, Christians were based in Pompeii, and the *Christianos* inscription proved the point.

Figure 10.6. A Pompeii fresco depicting the seduction of Leda by the Greek deity Zeus, who had taken the form of a swan (MANN 27695).

In 1886, an unnamed author agreed, although he started his interpretation several letters earlier than de Rossi had done. In an article entitled "Monumental Evidences of Christianity," this author noted that the first letters of line 4 might best be taken as a ligature combining two letters – the letters *P* (as Kiessling thought) and *R*. This interpretation does justice to the reconstructions of both Kiessling and Minervini, each of whom depict an otherwise awkward appendage emerging from the first letter, which might well be explained by the

---

13. Philosophers too were known to give lectures in private homes and rented facilities.
14. De Rossi 1864.

conflation of the two letters sharing the same ligature stem. The consequence of this, argued the author, is that line 4 begins *"Pro vic. S."* or *"Pro vico sacro."* Accordingly, the full two-lined inscription was thought to include a reference to the Christians being "in front of the Sacred Street."[15] (For a Pompeian ligature combining an *R* with other letters, see figure 10.7.)

Figure 10.7. Left: A ligature in a tomb inscription (middle line); right: a close-up of the ligature.

In 1962 another interpretation was proposed by Margherita Guarducci. She too adopted the first letters of line 4 in her interpretation but read them differently and supplied two allegedly missing letters:

Bovios audi[t] Christianos
sevos o[s]ores.

This interpretation renders the meaning: "Bovios listens to the Christians, the cruel haters."[16] In this interpretation, the inscription chides not only Jesus-followers but also someone by the name of Bovios, who seems interested in what Christians have to say.[17]

---

15. Unlisted author 1886: 395. Together with my research assistants, I have searched extensively to discover who this author is; unfortunately, it would seem that only Sherlock Holmes can crack this case. Paul Berry (1995: 23) includes an extensive list of scholars who have discussed this artifact but fails to mention this unknown author.
16. Guarducci 1962. She took this graffito to malign Christians on the walls of what was, in effect, a drinking house that serviced the men who visited the brothel across the street (at 7.12.18–20) – with a backstory in which Christians denounced the practice of prostitution. (The brothel at 7.12.18–20 is "the *only* structure at Pompeii that unambiguously meets scholars' criteria for an ancient brothel" [Levine-Richardson 2011: 318–19]).
17. Some of its features weaken the attraction of this interpretation. Although the absence of the letter *T* falls within the scope of epigraphic practice, it would have been nice if the inscriber

An interpretation of a wholly different kind was proposed by William Romaine Newbold in 1926. Rather than bracketing off the sections of inscribed words and focusing only on a few words at the center of the inscription (as in the interpretations outlined above), Newbold argued that (1) the characters inscribed in all six lines are to be taken into account, and (2) all of the characters except for those forming the word *Christianos* are transliterations of Aramaic.[18] Newbold's proposed reconstruction of the Latin letters appear on the left, with his proposed Aramaic transliteration appearing on the right.[19]

vina	*bînâ*
aaria	*ahrâya*
rdia .a. v	*redîâ A. ûdhêk*
dec vigGav dichristianos	*be-gav dî Christianos*
siivoso onis	*seyyihbûsû enîs*
X ivc p. (?) p. (?)	*kishôk [p. p.?]*

According to Newbold, this renders the meaning: "A strange mind has driven 'A.' and he has pressed in among the Christians who make a man a prisoner as a laughing-stock [to the people of Pompeii?]." The name of the person who has "pressed in among the Christians" is not specified, being concealed by the abbreviation A.[20]

---

had noticed that leaving it out makes the verb imperative ("listen!") rather than indicative ("he listens"). Moreover, it is not at all clear that the start of the fourth line, purported to include the name "Bovios," includes two occurrences of the letter O.

18. Newbold 1926: 288–89. He argues that a total of five inscriptions from various places and times in the Greco-Roman world are nonsensical until they are transliterated from Latin to Aramaic: "Read as Latin these inscriptions make no sense, but if pronounced as Aramaic they would be . . . intelligible to any one who understood the language. . . . If the words be taken as Aramaic, the ideas attaching to them blend one with the other into coherent, logical sense." Newbold admits that going from Latin into Aramaic would pose "some difficulty" since "a number of Aramaic consonants either cannot be represented at all or are represented imperfectly by Latin or Greek letters, and the vowel sounds of the inscriptions differ slightly from those of the traditional pronunciation." But he claims that "any one, whether acquainted with Aramaic or not, who will compare with the text of the inscriptions the traditional pronunciation given below them, will be convinced that the resemblance between them is not a mere matter of accident." In this, he seems overly optimistic.

19. Newbold 1926: 292.

Another Possibility

None of the previously proposed interpretations of the *Christianos* inscription have commanded significant assent, and perhaps this disparity of views is simply the best we can expect for such an unstable inscriptional curiosity.[21] Nonetheless, although these inscribed characters elude interpretative certainties, one approach to them has yet to be considered. It operates on the supposition that at least two inscribers have contributed charcoal graffiti to the wall, with the second replying to the first.

There are plenty of examples of conversational banter within Pompeian graffiti. For instance, in *CIL* 4.8408, one inscriber wrote an optimistic sentiment: "Lovers, like bees, lead a honeyed life." Under this, someone else simply wrote "I wish." In *CIL* 4.1839, a first inscriber wrote "Agato, the slave of Herennius, prays to Venus," under which a second hand wrote "I pray that he'll die!" In *CIL* 4.346, a first inscriber urged his peers to vote for Marcus Cerrinius as a civic official, under which someone else wrote, "Some people love him; some are loved by him; I can't stand him."

A much fuller exchange between two rivals is found in *CIL* 4.8258–8259. Severus wrote the following: "Successus the weaver loves the barmaid of the inn, called Iris, who doesn't care for him, but he asks and she feels sorry for him. A rival wrote this. Farewell." Then Successus replied: "You're jealous, bursting out with that. Don't try

---

20. Elucidating the tone of the proposed reconstruction, Newbold offers this commentary (1926: 295): "A disturbance of mind imposed by magic from without destroys the victim's power of judgment and binds his will, so that he is forced to seek the magician's company and to believe his nonsense, thus virtually becoming his prisoner and a laughingstock to all that know him." Newbold considered the Aramaic character of the graffito to indicate that the one who was "captured" by the Christians might well have been a Jew. In Newbold's reconstruction, a Jewish Jesus-follower in Pompeii had experienced ostracism from other Jews who considered the local Christians to be the subject of derision within Pompeian society.
21. In my view, Newbold's interpretation carries the least force. It requires the first letter before *audi* in the fourth line to be a G, which does not seem at all likely (and which is problematic for Kiessling's interpretation as well). Moreover, it seems unlikely that the character X toward the start of the fifth line is meant to operate with the letters to the right on that same line. Similarly, Newbold wants us to imagine that imprecise transliterations within his proposal can be explained by loosely defined transliteration practices for first-century Aramaic vowels. Newbold's thesis is given a sympathetic hearing in Giordano and Kahn (2001: 84–88) but, noting its "numerous difficulties" (2001: 88), is ultimately rejected (2001: 88n25).

to muscle in on someone who's better-looking and is a wicked and charming man." Then Severus countered: "I have written and spoken. You love Iris, who doesn't care for you. Severus to Successus."[22]

Something similar may be evidenced within the *Christianos* inscription. The basis for this supposition comes from several divergences in epigraphic habits evidenced on the fourth and fifth inscribed lines.[23]

Take, for instance, the occurrences of the letter *S* on lines four and five. The tail of the final *S* of *Christianos* in line 4 is substantially elongated, dropping significantly below the other letters in the word. By contrast, the tail of the final *S* in line 5 (which ends a word whose meaning is disputed) is only slightly elongated in comparison to the two other occurrences of *S* on that line. The final *S* on line 5 and the final *S* of *Christianos* on line 4 are conspicuously different from each other. That difference is only enhanced if we take account of the final *S* prior to the word *audi* on line 4, which again is noticeably elongated. Accordingly, the occurrences of the final *S* on line 4 are noticeably different from the final *S* of line 5.

Further, if we assume with the inscription's earliest interpreters that the last letters of line 5 include the letter *R* (accepting the view of Kiessling, Minervini, Fiorelli, and de Rossi [so too Guarducci]) instead of accepting Newbold's later preference for the letter *N*, then we can contrast the *R* on line 5 with the *R* of *Christianos* on line 4. The two letters are composed completely differently (as evidenced in Minervini's reconstruction of the lettering). The *R* in *Christianos* has a rounded half-circle that touches the vertical line at the top and midpoint of the vertical line; the bottom right leg of the *R*, which is quite short, juts out at the midpoint of the vertical line. By contrast,

---

22. These inscriptions are commonly cited; they all appear in Varone 2002, respectively at 60, 27, 51, and 113–14. Lindsay (1960: 102) offers this example (although, as was his style, without citation of the inscription number): "Good luck to Liveius Regulus," with someone else adding "Good luck to you Regulus because you're a twerp" (although "twerp" is probably a sanitized substitute for the original wording).
23. For six other examples of the same phenomenon (in which handwriting differences are evident), see *CIL* 4.1893 and 4.1894, discussed in Varone 2002: 43–44; 4.581, discussed in Keegan 2014: 176; 4.1837 (five inscriptional hands), discussed in Keegan 2014: 268–69; 4.3494, discussed in Milnor 2014: 84–85; 4.5296, discussed in Milnor 2014: 199.

the alleged *R* in line 5 has none of these characteristics. There is no rounded half-circle; the midpoint of the vertical line is not approached by either of the strokes used to form the right side of the letter; and the bottom right leg of the *R* is elongated. Both are acceptable formations of the letter *R*, but the presence of two quite different formations of the letter *R* is a further indication that we might well have two inscriptional hands at work on the wall.

Further still, the angles of the fourth and fifth lines diverge somewhat from each other. In Minervini's reconstruction, line 4 rises as it moves to the right, whereas line 5 remains horizontal. This feature deviates from the preponderance of practice in Pompeian single-graffito epigraphy. Of course, multi-lined graffiti are not standard-bearers of horizontal precision, but neither is it normal for a graffito to diverge this conspicuously in its internal orientation. In Minervini's diagram, the letters in line 4 of the *Christianos* inscription incline almost consistently at a 5 degree angle, whereas the letters along line 5 rest along the 0 degree axis.[24]

While ancient inscriptions and graffiti are not hallmarks of epigraphic consistency, the assumption that we have only one hand at work in this instance is problematized by three significant differences between lines 4 and 5. If, for the moment, we follow de Rossi and delimit the characters to *audi Christianos, s[a]evos o[l]ores*, what emerges would seem to be two distinct graffiti. The first makes reference to Christians, and the second characterizes them as cruel in some fashion.[25]

Harder to decipher are the letters to the left of *audi Christianos* on line

---

24. This characteristic is not shared by Kiessling's line drawing (see Figure 11 in Guarducci 1962). I take Minervini's line drawing to be much superior in this regard. It is hard to imagine that Minervini sloppily allowed line 4 to rise 5 degrees in his line drawing, when in fact line 4 was horizontal in orientation, and it is not hard to imagine Kiessling simply transcribing the line in horizontal aspect, despite its upward incline.
25. The insult may have two other characteristics to consider. First, it is possible that the creator of the "cruel" graffiti intentionally omitted the "missing letter" in the second word of his two-word insult. Why? To activate the graffito's potential for demeaning the Christians in a humorous manner. Faced with a gap in the graffito, the reader (perhaps drinking buddies?) would have been forced to decide how to fill that gap. With the letters *L*, *R*, and *D* as viable alternatives, the perceptive reader has three legitimate ways of doing that: Christians can be liken to either *s[a]evos olores* ("cruel swans"), *s[a]evos osores* ("cruel haters"), or *s[a]evos odores* ("cruel odors," or "farts"). That the letter needed to be supplied by the reader is another example of

4. Are they part of the *audi Christianos* graffito? There is good reason for thinking so. As we have seen, the person who inscribed the final *S* of *Christianos* enjoyed elongating its height, as if drawing attention to it as the final letter of the word. Precisely the same characteristic marks out the letter preceding *audi*, which is significantly elongated above and below the preceding letters.

Two implications derive from this. First, the same hand composed the letters at the start of line 4 and the words *audi Christianos*. Second, the letter prior to *audi* was not a *G*, thereby ruling out the interpretations of Kiessling and Newbold.

If the letters at the start of line 4 partner with *audi Christianos* to comprise a single phrase, are those starting letters simply a poorly written formation of a man's name ("Bovios"), as Guarducci thought? Or are they a truncated form of *bovinos* (accusative plural of *bovinus*)? If that were the case, the whole of the fourth line might have been an uncomplimentary "listen to the bullish Christians," with another inscriber joining in the fun with a subsequent insult of his own underneath the *Christianos* graffito.

There is still another possibility, as noted by our unnamed author of 1886. He proposed that the first letter of line 4 should be (as Kiessling thought from the start) a *P* and, moreover, that it was not a single letter but a double-lettered ligature, *PR*. The reconstructions of Kiessling and Minervini can be interpreted as indicating the first letter to have a protruding appendage to the right of its midpoint. If this indicates a ligature with the shared letters *PR*, then the letters before *audi Christianos* form not the phrase *pro vici s.*, as the unnamed author proposed ("in front of the Sacred Street," which should really have

Pompeian inscriptional humor, since the letter *D* would easily have come readily to mind. (For other examples of inscriptional humor, see especially John Clarke 2007.)

Second, and the first point notwithstanding, the option of supplying the letter *S* has an added attraction over the other two options. That is, it allows the two-word graffito to have an almost balanced character in the repeating pattern of alternating consonants and vowels: *S E V O S O [S] O R E S*. With the exception of the third letters from left or right (the *V* and the *R*), the letters are balanced, with the partnered letters falling on either side of the midpoint (the middle *O*). Here again, the omission of a letter seems to have been intentional: if the word "cruel" had been spelled *saevos* instead of *sevos*, there would be no possibility of balance within the "cruel haters" option.

been written *pro vico s.*) but, instead, the phrase *pro vicis* (ablative plural of *vicus*, meaning "street," "district," or "neighborhood") – which translates as "on behalf of the districts."[26] This would enable us to recognize the whole of line 4 as part of the graffito, involving a laudatory endorsement of the Christians (paraphrased: "listening to the Christians would be good for the neighborhoods"), to which the insult (if that interpretation is correct) was subsequently added on line 5.

Does the graffito of line 4 extend further back into the lines above it? Minervini's reconstruction of the lettering on the wall suggests that the letters above line 4 were the products of yet another hand altogether. Because the letters of lines 1 through 3 are notably larger than those on line 4, it seems likely that the *Christianos* graffito began at line 4.

Regardless of how we interpret the various components of this tantalizing wall, a number of indicators point in the same direction regarding what we should be expecting from it. It would seem that at least two inscribers commented on Christians on lines 4 and 5, and at least one of those inscribers had something derogatory to say about them.

Summary Observations

Our findings in later chapters will allow us to add further clarification to this graffito (both chapters 11 and 13). But for now, we have seen enough to recognize that a wall of a residential inn may well have contained an inscriptional "conversation" of some kind, with the possibility that one conversation participant added something derogatory about Christians being "cruel" below the original graffito about *Christianos*. Whether or not Christians resided or discoursed within this particular residence, they were talked about within its walls in at least two graffiti.

---

26. For two ligatures involving the letter *P* (one of which incorporates five letters, including the letter *R*), see the stamp ring of Lucius Sepunius Symphronis here: www.pompeiiinpictures.com/pompeiiinpictures/R6/6 15 05.htm.

The *Christianos* graffito does not inevitably prove that Christians were local to the region of Pompeii. But because the bakery cross and the *vivit* cross have already provided evidence that Jesus-devotion was present within Pompeii, only historical flat-footedness would cause us to contend that the Christians referred to in this graffito were flung far afield from Pompeii. We are, then, in a much different position from August Mau and Karl Zangemeister, both of whom claimed that the Christians referenced in this graffito could not have been local since Tertullian said there were no Christians in Pompeii.[27] As we have seen, Tertullian's claim was motivated by theological apologetics and had no necessary underpinning historically. In light of the data assembled in the previous (and following) chapters, it is most likely that the Christians referenced in this graffito were locals who had just enough of a profile within the town to be mocked by at least one person and spoken of in some fashion by another. The graffiti on the wall of the inn testify that Christians must have had at least a modicum of public profile within the Vesuvian town.

We may never know whether "direct contact [with Christians] was made in the hotel itself," as one scholar has recently postulated.[28] But we can be fairly sure that the Jesus-devotees referred to in the graffito were not simply solitary individuals without a collective context in which to explore their devotion. It follows from the plural referent *Christianos* that Jesus-devotion had some kind of a corporate identity in public perceptions. Christians may not have been numerous or influential in Pompeii, but they had enough of a public profile to be teased by at least one of their peers. Although far overshadowed by the standard forms of Greco-Roman devotion, Jesus-devotion seems to have had a toehold in the social discourse of some of Pompeii's population.

---

27. Mau 1902: 18; Zangemeister in Mau and Zangemeister 1909: 461.
28. Adams 2013: 158. For my part, I do not postulate that the inn was a meeting place for Jesus-followers. All we know, if my reconstruction is correct, is that two people referenced them in graffiti in the inn.

11

Jesus-Devotion in Transactions

We have already seen that a few of Pompeii's walls testify to the presence of Jesus-devotion within that town. The primary artifact foregrounded in this present chapter adds another layer to our understanding of Jesus-devotion in that town and, in the process, opens up new possibilities for understanding the attraction of Jesus-devotion not only in Pompeii but elsewhere on the Italian peninsula as well. In fact, the primary artifact from Pompeii analyzed in this chapter has never been considered for its relevance to our issue. As we will see, that omission has been a glaring deficit. This artifact is not simply another piece of relevant Pompeian evidence; it also triangulates with data within and beyond Pompeii, thereby grounding this artifact of Jesus-devotion within a broader relational context.

The Meges Stamp Ring

Throughout the second half of the nineteenth century, Fausto and Felice Niccolini (and members of their extended family) produced a magnificent four-volume collection of intricate reproductions of Pompeian realia (*Le Case ed il Monumenti di Pompei*). As Richard Brilliant notes, the Niccolinis' beautiful and accurate drawings of Pompeian realia have "never [been] equaled in range of treatment nor in quality of illustration."[1]

Figure 11.1. Niccolini's collection of Pompeian keys (with some small defacement spots from paper deterioration).

Within the Niccolini collection appears a display featuring a variety of stamp rings alongside keys for unlocking doors and a lock mechanism (see figure 11.1). The items collected in this display are described as follows: "Different keys, a lock, and various stamp rings

1. Brilliant 1979: 145.

are collected in this figure."[2] Of these eleven items, the only one of interest here is the stamp ring toward the top left of the figure – a ring used by its owner to undertake business transactions. The front of that stamp ring is dominated by the five letters *MEGES* framed in a curved stamp, with the first two letters (the *M* and the initial *E*) formed as a shared-stem ligature (see figure 11.2).[3]

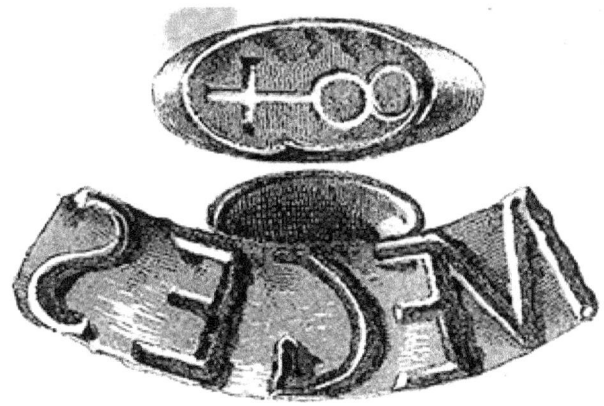

Figure 11.2. The stamp ring, depicting both the front stamp and the decoration on the back bezel.

It is the bezel on the back of this ring, with its curious engraving, that is of special interest (see figure 11.3). What might be displayed on the bezel, with its perpendicular lines and double circle? Does it depict a single object?

---

2. Niccolini and Niccolini 1862: vol. 2, part 2, no page number: "Diverse chiavi, una toppa e varie marche sono raccolti in questa tavola." He continues: "No. 1 chiave con cantena a barbazzale no. 2, 3, 4, 5, 6, y 7 diverse marche. No. 8, 9, 10 pezzi che si suppongono appartenere ad un istesso serrame. No. 11 altra chiave." The description is in Niccolini vol. 2, part 2, whereas the depiction of the artifacts themselves is in vol. 2, part 4. There is no indication of the find-spots for these items.
3. Perhaps the owner of this ring bore the name after a relatively minor character in Greek mythology – Meges Phyleides, known from Homer's *Iliad* and elsewhere as an able commander and fighter during the Trojan War.

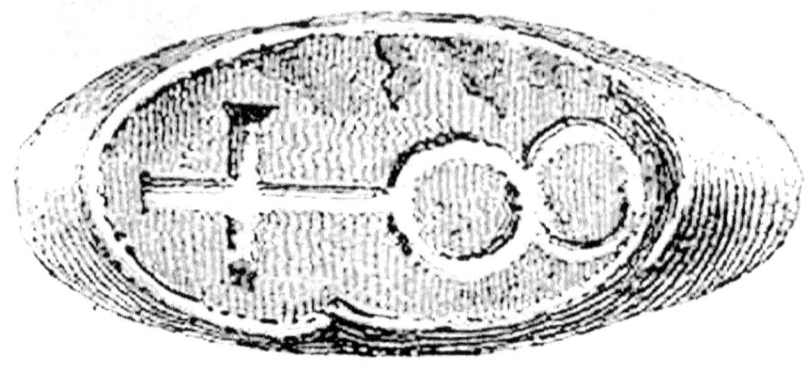

Figure 11.3. A close-up of Niccolini's display of the decoration on the back of the Meges stamp ring from Pompeii.

One aspect of the bezel's engraving has some semblance to ancient door keys. Keys from the Greco-Roman world frequently incorporated a circular base within their structure in order to permit them to be strung onto straps. In that regard, the central shaft and first circle of this ring have some semblance to ancient keys (see figure 11.4). Nonetheless, three features of this engraving are anomalous to the usual composition of Roman keys:

1. Roman keys did not have two matching appendages or "bits" straddling the key's central shaft at right angles; bits emerged from only one side of the central shaft, not two.[4]
2. Roman keys did not include the protrusion of the central shaft past the key bit; the bit delimited the length of the key's central shaft.
3. Roman keys did not have two rings at their base; they did not always have a ring at their end, but if they did, only one was necessary.[5]

4. The Roman key CA-64098 in the Menil Collection, Houston, has two protrusions very close to its base, but these were not the bits of the key (which is what the appendages would be in the Niccolini drawing if the engraving on the Meges ring depicted a key); instead, butting up against the circular base of the key, they seem only to have assisted with the turning of the key by giving leverage to the user. My thanks to Thomas Pace for pointing this out to me. On the issue of Roman locks and keys, see especially Pace 2014.
5. It might be that the outer ring represents a key strap onto which a circle-based ring was attached.

Evidently, then, the engraving displayed in the back bezel of this signet ring does not depict a key.

Figure 11.4. An ancient Roman key, not unlike those found in Pompeii and Herculaneum.

What other options might present themselves? It is tempting to imagine the engraving as depicting a caduceus – a short staff from which two intertwined snakes emerged, often in the form of an almost complete double circle (see figure 11.5). The caduceus marked its bearer as a herald of the deities. Although usually associated with Hermes, the caduceus was also frequently carried by Mercury who, among other things, was a deity of profit, trade, and merchants.

But this is unlikely, not least since points 1 and 2 exclude the possibility that this engraving depicts a key.

THE CROSSES OF POMPEII

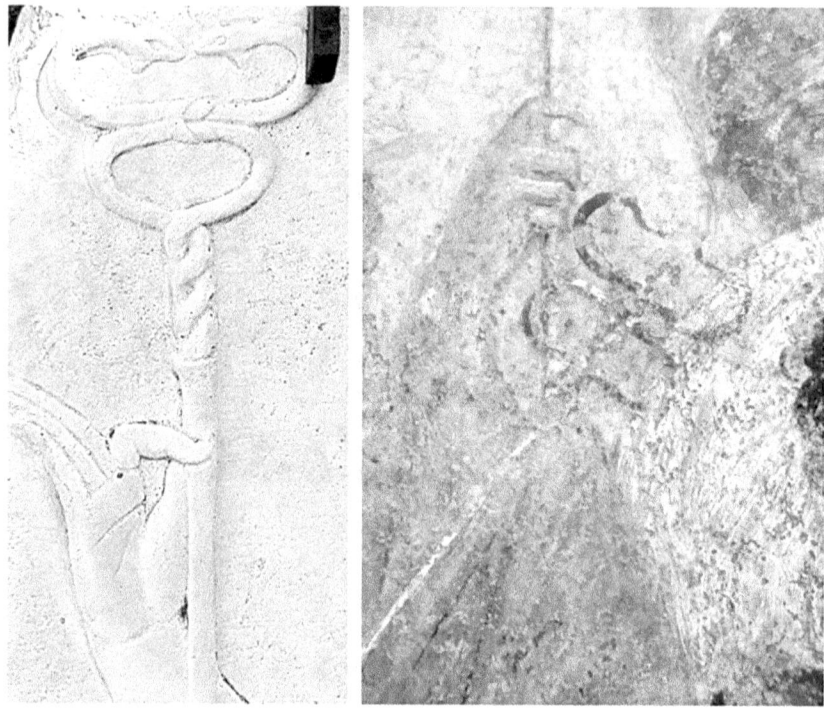

Figure 11.5. Left: a caduceus held by Mercury in the temple area of Herculaneum's seafront suburban district; right: a caduceus in a Pompeii fresco depicting Achilles and Agamemnon (MANN 9105).

But the caduceus does not help to interpret the symbolism of the Meges ring. Whenever a crossbar appears on a caduceus staff, the crossbar is regularly positioned near to the intertwined snakes, and therefore much closer to the top of the staff than the bottom (see Pompeian equivalents in figure 11.6). If the Meges ring depicted a caduceus, the crossbar should appear toward the top of the staff rather than the bottom. The interesting back bezel within the Meges stamp ring, then, does not depict a caduceus.

Figure 11.6. Two Pompeian examples of Mercury and his caduceus, with horizontal arms close to the snakes at the top of the stave (left from 1.8.8 and right from 7.4.48).

What else might this engraving represent within the ring's bezel? Perhaps a highly stylized Egyptian Ankh? Probably not. The elongated stave above the transept arms is not a feature of the Ankh, nor is the double circle.

Understanding the ring's insignia as a single object seems to get us nowhere. But the same is not the case if we take it to include two connected objects. Accordingly, the right side would seem to comprise a double-circled pattern, while the left side would seem to comprise a cross shape. Leaving aside the double-circle momentarily, I propose that the cross-shaped object in the bezel is an insignia of Jesus-devotion. No other option is as likely. It seems ill-suited as a representation of a mundane object. (No one would have hired a craftsman to carve a wall-bracket into a stamp ring, for instance.) If a symbol, the shape does not depict a double-headed axe (for the same reasons articulated in chapter 7 above), nor does it conform to the expected patterns of the Jewish eschatological cross, which would normally expect the appendages to be of the same length. It seems, then, that something else is going on within the insignia. The only live option is to recognize this ring as containing the same symbol of Jesus-devotion that we have already seen in chapters 7 through 9 above.

If this route is the only viable one open to us, it may not be coincidental that the cross in the signet ring conforms closely to the patterning of the cross on the wall of the Pompeii bakery. For both crosses, the bottom of the stave is the longest of the four parts. In the ring, the flaring at the end of the right transverse arm is also a stylistic match with the bakery cross. (For reasons of symmetry, there was probably meant to be flaring at the end of the left transverse arm as well; it shows signs of damage, however, which may have been made when the symbol was being carved into the ring, impeding the successful flaring of that arm.) These characteristics are already familiar within the database of Pompeian crosses of Jesus-devotion, in the case of the bakery cross.

There are differences between the two crosses, of course. The cross in the Meges ring has a proportionately longer upper stave, and it too was made to flare. Nonetheless the two are recognizable as sharing common features, to the extent that they are easily superimposed onto each other without damaging the compositional integrity of either, as in figure 11.7.

Figure 11.7. The bakery cross and the signet-ring cross superimposed onto each other.

The cruciform shape on the left of the Meges ring is best interpreted, then, as a stylized symbol representing a cross of Jesus-devotion. As noted in chapter 5 above, Christians in later centuries would go on to wear rings with the cross embedded in them. It was a way of marking themselves out as belonging to the deity of the cross and probably had apotropaic significance.[6] In the same way, this artifact probably gives evidence of a Jesus-follower in Pompeii who wore a ring with a symbol

---

6. See also Longenecker 2015: 86–92.

of a cross incised into the back of it, as a symbol of religious devotion, perhaps with an apotropaic function. If so, the ring's owner pegged his hopes on the one who had been empowered over death itself.

This ring gives us something that previous artifacts have not been able to supply – that is, an indicator regarding the character of its owner's Jesus-devotion. Although we cannot exclude a polytheistic religiosity, the owner of the Meges ring is clearly featuring the cross as a central symbol of his identity. If he aligned himself with other deities as well, it was his Jesus-devotion that he chose to highlight in a ring that served to identify him to others when adding his seal to business transactions.

The Symbolism of the Double Circle

One other aspect of the Meges stamp ring needs to be considered – that is, the double circle at the bottom of the cross. To modern eyes, this looks like the number 8 but, of course, the number 8 was written *VIII* in the Greco-Roman world. What might this double circle represent?

Ancient amulets are commonly found in the shape of a tightly coiled S, representing two snakes joined at the middle (see figure 11.8) – apotropaia that seek to tap into the power of Asclepius, the deity of healing. This is an unlikely candidate to explain the double circle in the Meges ring, however, not least since amulets of this kind almost always have noticeable openings where the snake heads are depicted.

What other options might there be for interpreting the double circle? One letter from the Oscan alphabet (equivalent to the Latin F) has some semblance to the double circle of the Meges ring (see figure 11.9[7]). The Oscan language had been the primary language of the indigenous Samnite tribes that populated the area prior to the Romanization of the territory in the early first century BCE (i.e., after the "Social War" of 91–88 BCE). Might this ring, then, foreground an Oscan letter? Perhaps it was the first letter of a Samnite name, with the owner highlighting his indigenous identity in this pro-Roman town.

---

7. British Museum, 1867.0508.76. This inscription reads: "Vibius Popidius, son of Vibius and chief magistrate, oversaw this work and officially approved it."

Perhaps this Jesus-follower prided his Oscan family heritage. Although this possibility cannot be excluded, I know of no Vesuvian artifacts that offer an analogous situation, and there is no evidence that Oscan heritage was undergoing a resurgence.[8] In fact, two other options are more viable.

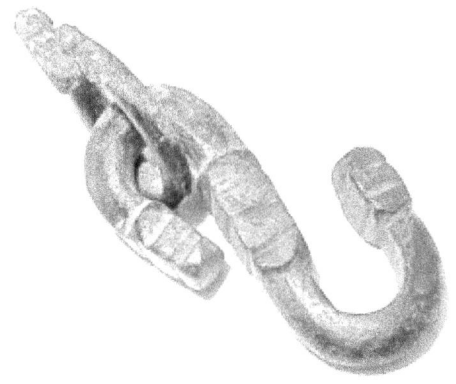

Figure 11.8. An ancient double-headed snake amulet.

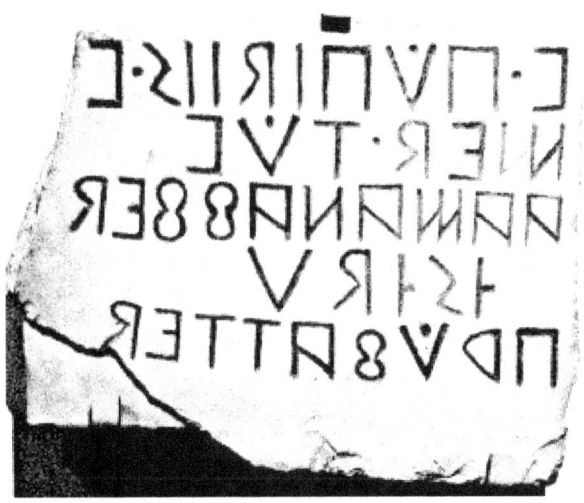

Figure 11.9. An Oscan inscription in Pompeii that dates to between 300 and 150 BCE.

8. On the dearth of Oscan inscriptions in Pompeii, see Milnor 2014: 18–19.

It is possible that the double circle signifies the number 1,000. Something similar to the double circle appears regularly in the wax tablets that record 137 business transactions in which the auctioneer-banker Caecilius Jucundus was involved. Used to represent the number M (= 1,000), the figure is formed like an X with the sides enclosed by rounded brackets (see figure 11.10[9]).

Figure 11.10. Three occurrences of the symbol for 1,000 in one of the transaction records of Caecilius Jucundus.

This is not quite what we see on the back bezel of the Meges ring, however. Although the editors of *CIL* used the reclining 8 to represent this numerical symbol in their transcriptions of the wax tablets, they make it clear in an editorial note that the figure used in the wax tablets themselves is not a reclining 8 but an enclosed X.[10]

Nonetheless, evidence from Pompeii might permit an interpretation in which the double circle represents the number 1,000. Two tombs beyond the Vesuvian Gate make the point by way of contrast. On a tomb dedicated to a woman named Septumia, mention is made of the fact that the town councilors paid two thousand sesterces for her funeral. The symbol used for the two occurrences of the number 1,000 matches the enclosed X of the business transactions of Jucundus. By contrast, however, another tomb outside the same gate is dedicated to Gaius Vestorius Priscus, who died at the age of twenty-two, having only just been elected as aedile. Again the town councilors paid two thousand sesterces for his funeral. On Priscus's tomb, however, the

9. From Mau and Zangemeister 1898: 313.
10. Mau and Zangemeister 1898: 453.

symbol used to represent 1,000 looks more like a double circle than an enclosed X. In view of the formations for the symbol 1,000 on the Priscus tomb (see figure 11.11), we cannot rule out the possibility that the double circle of the Meges ring represents the number 1,000.

Figure 11.11. The two formations of the symbol for 1,000, found twice in the Septumia tomb inscription (left) and twice on the Priscus tomb inscription (right).

Even if this is a possibility, it is not easy to imagine what a symbol for 1,000 would be doing on a ring of this kind. Moreover, arguably the double circle is at the wrong orientation if it is meant to symbolize 1,000; the cross is oriented vertically, and the number would be oriented at a ninety-degree angle to the cross. Furthermore, there is a more viable alternative, one that makes perfect sense within the context of the ring.

It is notable that the same double circle evident in the Meges ring appears in two Italian inscriptions that reference Christian identity in the pre-Constantinian period. One of those is the *Christianos* graffito from Pompeii. The fifth line on the wall in the House of the Christian Inscription begins with two characters: the double circle and a double-stroked character, X. Here, as in the Meges ring, the double circle is in vertical orientation (as opposed to horizontal orientation used to depict 1,000 in symbolic form). As we saw in chapter 10 above, Kiessling transcribed the graffito/graffiti with a double circle prominent at the start of the fifth line (see figure 11.12[11]):

---

11. Kiessling 1862: 92; see also de Rossi 1864: 70. Kiessling's line over the X might suggest the presence of a *nomen sacrum*, a sacred name – in this case "Christ." In fact, the line that appears over the X is simply the tail of the S from the line above, which Kiessling took (or better, mistook) to be a G.

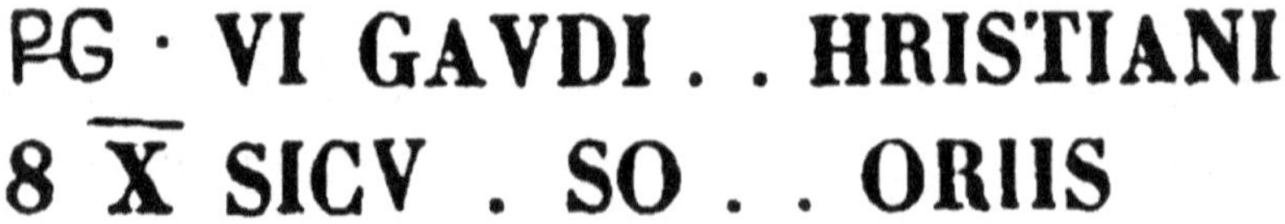

PG · VI GAVDI . . HRISTIANI
8 X̄ SICV . SO . . ORIIS

Figure 11.12. Kiessling's depiction of what he thought to be stable characters on the wall.

Here are the two pertinent forms as Varone depicts them (figure 11.13[12]):

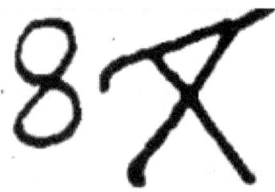

Figure 11.13. Varone's depiction of the two figures at the start of line 5 (with the tail of an S trailing down above the X).

Paul Berry presents the double circle in this way (figure 11.14[13]):

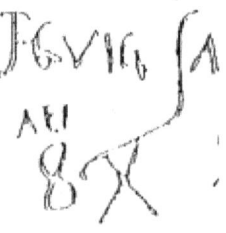

Figure 11.14. Paul Berry's depiction of the relevant characters.

---

12. Varone 1980: insert between pages 40 and 41.
13. From Paul Berry 1995: plate 9b.

There is, then, no scholarly dispute that the double circle and an *X* appeared a line below the *audi Christianos* graffito. Nonetheless, these two figures have fallen below the radar in scholarly discussion. Newbolt incorporated the *X* into his attempt at an Aramaic reconstruction of the graffito, but he is in the minority in seeking to make sense of anything before the first *S* in the last full line of characters. And no one has attempted to explain the double circle at the very start of that line. As Paul Berry notes, "the symbol has never been explained."[14] This is a notable weakness in all previous efforts to interpret the fourth and fifth lines. Perhaps the Meges ring gives us reason to look again at options for interpreting the double circle on the wall of the *Christianos* graffito. Can it simply be coincidence that the double circle appears alongside two of the few artifacts from Pompeii that pertain to the emergent Jesus-movement in that town?

The question gains further impetus from the fact that precisely the same double-circle symbol has been found among the group of Christian symbols from the Baths of Neptune in Ostia Antica – symbols already discussed in chapter 5 above. In that smorgasbord of pre-Constantinian symbols of Christian devotion, the double circle appears twice, once in simple outline form and once with the circles filled in (see figure 11.15[15]). Of course, these symbols were inscribed two hundred years or so after the eruption of Vesuvius. But when looking for analogies to the signet ring's double circle within the ancient material record, these two Christian symbols from Ostia provide the closest historical analogy, along with the double circle in Pompeii's *Christianos* graffito. That these symbols all appear in artifacts pertaining to Jesus-devotion makes the proposed connections relatively compelling. What we seem to be observing within the shoddy material record is a fragile line between two places on the Italian peninsula that testify to a short-lived appreciation of the double circle as a symbol of early Jesus-devotion. It is probably not simple coincidence that these three artifacts display a double circle and link

---

14. Paul Berry 1995: 25.
15. For explanations of the Christian symbols in this figure, see Longenecker 2015: 78n6.

to notably Christian features – the Christian cross in the Meges ring, the Christian symbols in the Ostian inscriptions, and the mention of *Christianos* in the graffito in the inn (see figure 11.16).

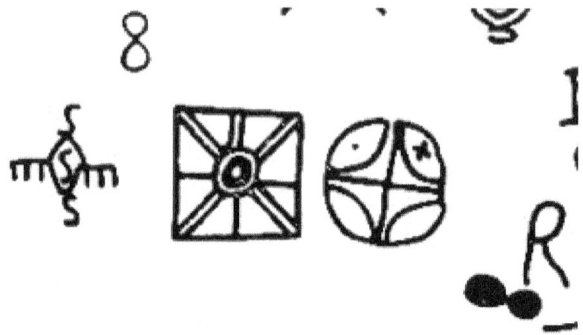

Figure 11.15. Christian symbols in Room 6 of the Baths of Neptune in Ostia, with two double circles.

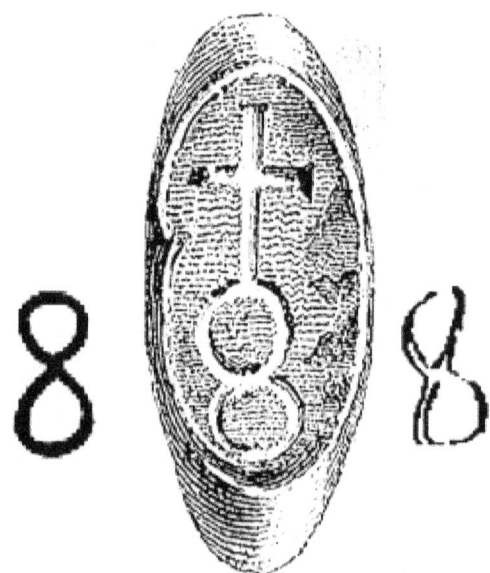

Figure 11.16. Three double circles from artifacts testifying to early Jesus-devotion (left to right: the inscription in the Baths of Neptune in Ostia, the Meges ring, and the Christianos graffito).

What was the symbolic significance of the double circle? It may not be irrelevant that this same symbol, placed on its side, would later go on to become the figure of infinity in mathematics and science. With its back-and-forth, in-and-out circular movements that foster a constant motion within its shape, perhaps the double-circled shape was conducive to the sense of a never-ending procession.

This interpretation, in fact, is supported by another feature of the *Christianos* graffito. Three small letters were found directly above the double circle of that graffito, on what might be called line 4.5. Fiorelli thought these small letters might be AET, and that they might be an abbreviation of *aetatis,* "with age." According to Fiorelli, this abbreviation might have referred to the age or price of wine available to customers in the inn, with the X of line 5 identifying the quantity to be ten.[16] This seems a rather strained interpretation. It requires us to believe that the three small letters of line 4.5 worked together with a much larger letter on line 5 below. Moreover, Fiorelli's interpretation makes no mention of the double circle that the small letters stand directly above.

The much more likely option is that the three letters of line 4.5 work together with the double circle that they stand directly above (rather than the X), and that they were not an abbreviation of *aetatis* but, instead, were formed as AEI. This is how they appear in Kiessling's line drawing of the object (as represented in Paul Berry's reconstruction in Figure 11.14).[17] It is not insignificant that those three letters correspond perfectly with the Greek word *aei* (ἀεί), which expresses time without limits — "to the end of time" or "always." Understood

---

16. Fiorelli 1873: 97.
17. Kiessling's line drawing is reproduced as Figure 11 in Guarducci 1962, and as Figure 2 in Wayment and Grey 2015. The argument of Wayment and Grey appeared too late for me to take account of here. Suffice it to say that I remain unconvinced by their attempt to reconstruct the *Christianos* graffito, for several reasons: Minervini's line drawing does not allow the inclusion of four letters in the space of line 5 that their argument requires; they take the third letter from the end of line 5 to be N, whereas the main eyewitnesses to the graffito thought it to be an R (as evidenced by de Rossi [informed by Minervini and Fiorelli] and by Kiessling's 1862 printed reproduction); the paleographic differences between lines 4 and 5 (as noted above) are not accounted for; important aspects of the graffito are left unexplained (the 8, the X, and the AEI). Even the word "Bovios" is extremely weak. Of course, any interpretation of this fragile graffito will have its weaknesses, but the proposal of Wayment and Grey includes too many to be compelling.

in this light, someone added this small word above the double circle in order to articulate its theological meaning — that is, what is being spoken about in the inscription pertains to "eternity." The double circle of the *Christianos* graffito, which to this point "has never been explained" in scholarly literature, is not some mundane figure. Instead, it is a theological symbol signaling the transcendence of ordinary time (as was the case with its appearance among the Ostian inscriptions).

Accordingly, the double circle below the cross on the Meges stamp ring seems to have symbolized eternal life. In this way, the Meges ring is comparable to the *vivit* cross, which embedded a form of the verb "to live" within its apotropaic symbolism of the cross. Like the *vivit* cross, the Meges ring probably incorporates a symbol of eternal life (the double circle) alongside its depiction of the cross.[18]

In this light, although the double circle would later reemerge among Christian inscriptions in Ostia's Baths of Neptune, the first evidence of its usage as a symbol of religious devotion (and perhaps one without much longevity ahead of it in the ancient world) is from Pompeii. From a stamp ring worn by a Jesus-follower and a charcoal graffito, we can conclude that some Jesus-followers in the shadow of Vesuvius found the double circle to encapsulate their conviction that eternal life was made available to the devotees of Jesus, the deity who had been crucified and whose devotees were known by the name "Christians." One Jesus-devotee, who evidently went by the name Meges, saw attraction in putting two symbols together within his stamp ring. The cross identifies the place of the deity's death; the double circle identifies the deity's eternal life (compare the double emphases of the

---

18. Here we might also consider whether the double insignia on this ring (the cross and a double circle), although not themselves forming a caduceus, may nonetheless have been devised to reference a caduceus. Perhaps Meges, a managerial slave who conducted business for his master and perhaps for himself (see chapter 15 below), devised his ring's symbol of Jesus-devotion to include a gesture to the caduceus that was frequently associated with the deity Mercury, a deity of trade, profit, and merchants. In this scenario, an advocate of Jesus-devotion has pegged his financial hopes not on Mercury but on the deity who died on a cross and rose to life – perhaps a metaphor for financial success. Just as a Jesus-follower in the Insula Arriana Polliana devised a cross that referenced the Ankh of Isis-devotion, and just as a Jesus-follower in 1.13 referenced a standard ligature formation in the *vivit* cross, so too the Meges ring may have referenced the caduceus in its formation.

JESUS-DEVOTION IN TRANSACTIONS

vivit cross, with the one who lives being the one whose identity is visually cruciform).

A parallel to this manner of referencing the story of salvation through religious imagery is found in three signet rings from the Vesuvian towns (one from Pompeii and two from Herculaneum). They depict a dove with an olive branch in its beak. These rings most likely reference the story of Noah and the flood (Genesis 6–9), a prominent story from the Hebrew Bible about salvation from destruction. These rings must have been worn by Jews (or possibly Jewish Christians).[19] In much the same way, the double imagery of the Meges stamp ring symbolizes a similar story of rescue, with each image referencing a central part of the Christian message about salvation from death to life.

The *Christianos* Graffito Revisited

These findings allow us to return to the *Christianos* graffito once again in order to shore up the best approach for interpreting it. The findings of chapter 10 above were not sufficient to determine the tone of the *audi Christianos* graffito. The fact that the double circle appears a line below *audi Christianos* and functioned as a symbol of Christian conviction helps to determine the register of the *audi Christianos* graffito as one of commendation, in which the benefits of Jesus-devotion were publicly registered on the wall. The double circle was adopted by Jesus-followers to encapsulate an aspect of their devotion – that is, it brings benefits "until the end of time." This is not part of the Latin insult that probably appears to the right on line 5; it looks more like a form of explanatory proclamation. We are now in position to recognize that the *Christianos* inscription was not, in fact, written *about* Christians; instead, it was written *by* a Christian.[20]

---

19. See Varone 1980: insert between pages 40 and 41. Notice too that images of doves with olive branches in their beaks appear in the Christian catacombs of Rome; see Brettman 1985: 22–23. On the popularity of the dove (often with an olive branch) within early Christian imagery, see Snyder 2003: 38–41. The ring from Pompeii depicting a fish probably belonged to someone who marketed fish, rather than being the Christian sign of the *ichthus* fish.
20. It is commonly thought that "Christians" was originally a derogatory term used by non-Christians against Jesus-followers. In this instance, however, it is used as a term of self-identification by Jesus-followers themselves. Perhaps the shift from denigration to self-identification had already happened by the time of this graffito.

If the *Christianos* graffito was proclamatory in some fashion, two further consequences are evident. First, certain options can be excluded regarding the difficult letters to the left of *audi* on line 4. It is often thought that they must have enhanced a demeaning tone. But as a form of proclamation, the *audi Christianos* graffito probably did not read "listen to the bovine Christians!" Nor did it demean "Bovios" for listening to them (*Bovios audi[t] Christianos*). Whatever the first letters of the line meant, they were not part of an insult. The insult begins halfway along the fifth line, when someone may have written something about Christians being cruel. (Notice too that the inscriber tucked that comment tidily between the two occurrences of the elongated letter *S* in the original graffito on line 4 about listening to the Christians.)

Second, there remains one further feature on the wall in the House of the Christian Inscription that has yet to be interpreted but now easily falls into place – that is, the X that resides on the wall to the right of the symbolic double circle (see figure 11.17). In light of its association with the Christian symbol of the double circle, the likely option is that the X is not a stray figure without significance, nor does it represent the Roman numeral ten.[21] Instead, it may well represent a Greek word (like the word *aei*) that begins with the letter X, or *chi* – that is, *Christos*, the Greek word from which the Latin *Christianos* ultimately derives.[22] In this case, the beginning of the fifth line of the graffito encapsulates the conviction that eternal life (represented by the double circle) comes through Christ (represented by the X).[23]

---

21. It is possible that the X was a reclining Jewish cross of eschatological protection, ultimately rooted in Ezekiel 9 (as noted in chapter 6 above). Since none of the other crosses from Pompeii are formed as reclining crosses, however, other interpretative options would seem more likely. (The only possible reclining cross is the street cross 16, discussed in chapters 12 and 13 below. I take its reclining orientation to be incidental, however.)
22. On the presence of Greek among Latin inscriptions, see Milnor 2014: 222–23, especially note 49. As Bagnall notes (2011: 142), inscriptional data frequently demonstrates an overlapping of languages, which were all eligible as "parts of bilingual or multilingual communication and recording systems." Moreover, he observes that "some individuals switched easily, even playfully, between [the languages]," and suggests that "the disciplinary boundaries usually constructed on the basis of ancient languages serve our studies poorly" (143). In light of this, it is not surprising to find a Greek *chi* representing *Christos* in a Latin graffito concerning *Christianos*. The presence of what may be a three-letter Greek word above the double circle (*aei*) adds further weight to this.
23. It is interesting to note here della Corte's interpretation of a Pompeian graffito *XIDO*, which he

The two symbols just below the *audi Christianos* graffito reinforce each other and capture in a nutshell the basic convictions of simple Jesus-devotion, doing so in a fashion that parallels the symbolism of the *vivit* cross.

Figure 11.17. The two figures at the start of line 5, as recorded by Kiessling, Varone, and Berry respectively.

***

Several artifacts have been brought together in this chapter in a fashion that enables new insights to emerge from their interrelationship. Chief among them is the Meges stamp ring, which has never been incorporated into previous considerations of whether Jesus-devotion is evidenced within the Vesuvian towns. This artifact enables us to pivot out beyond discussion of crosses on walls and into further evidential terrain. The fact that previous discussions about Jesus-devotion in the Vesuvian towns have been restricted primarily to two crosses found on walls in Herculaneum and Pompeii has meant that the "wall-bracket" theory has managed to become the unquestioned consensus view. But when the database extends to other wall crosses that clearly have nothing to do with wall-brackets (i.e., the *vivit* cross) and to crosses that have nothing to do with walls (the Meges ring), the frame of reference that previously determined scholarly discourse on the matter is shown yet again to require radical revision. By means of this stamp ring, we have accessed new dimensions of Jesus-devotion in the Vesuvian towns. Instead of data lying inertly in

takes to be a christological claim: "X (= *Christus*), I(*esus*), Do(*minus*)" (1958: 136). In his favor, the graffito is otherwise nonsensical.

isolation, we have seen interconnections between artifacts that shed a glimmer of light on Jesus-devotion not only in Pompeii itself but elsewhere on the Italian peninsula as well.

Our survey of Jesus-devotion within Vesuvian realia is not yet over, however. Instead, we move to murkier terrain – the streets of Pompeii, where we find further, albeit supplemental, evidence.

PART IV

The Supplemental Evidence

"Like a society in the collective grip of
some obsessive-compulsive disorder,
afraid of stepping on the cracks in the pavement,
every point of contact with the divine
was governed by precise and immutable rules."
(Butterworth and Laurence, *Pompeii* [2005], 21)

"It is a fallacy that
incomplete data cannot be used
in the explanation of archaeological phenomena."
(Laurence, *Roman Pompeii* [1994], 6)

12

Crossing the Streets

We have seen plenty of reasons to abandon the popular line, "There may have been Christians in Pompeii but we have no material evidence to suggest as much." In fact, we do have evidence – the *vivit* cross, the bakery cross, and the Meges-ring cross, together with the *Christianos* graffito. These artifacts, the primary evidence in our case, require us to overturn the current consensus regarding Jesus-devotion in Pompeii.

The same may be true for the artifacts discussed in this chapter and the next. These artifacts, which will serve to supplement the primary evidence, have never entered the discussion regarding the possibility of Jesus-devotion in Pompeii. In fact, with one exception, they have never been mentioned within Pompeian scholarship. As we will see, this represents a serious lacuna in discourse about the ancient site. The next two chapters, then, push the boat out a bit further, taking us into uncharted waters where new currents come into effect.

Symbols on the Streets

Visitors to Pompeii are so enamored by the remarkable sights all around them that they usually do not spend much time looking at what lies near their feet. But sometimes treasures are missed as a consequence. The streets of Pompeii were not simply access routes to get from one location to another; at times, they were used as surfaces upon which to place a symbol or a message.

Most of these messages are clear to the eye. An example of this is the inscription carved onto two curbstones at the northwest corner of insula 9.4 – where two important traffic arteries meet (the north-south street Via Stabiana/del Vesuvio and the east-west street Via della Fortuna/di Nola). This inscription commemorates the date when the pavements of the burgeoning town were first laid (see figure 12.1).[1]

Figure 12.1. An inscription on a Pompeii curbstone.

Another example of using street stones to communicate and/or embed symbols involves the ubiquitous phallic symbol, which makes its way even onto a paving stone of a Pompeii street. Unless a tour guide draws attention to it, only a small fraction of people would notice

1. The inscription reads EX.K.QUI, "from the first day of July." The month of July was called Quinctuilus prior to 44 BCE, when it was changed to Iulius in honor of Julius Caesar. See Mau 1902: 228. A similar inscription reads K.Q (July 1) in the paving of Vico Storto; see Marriott 1895: 87. For similar incisions in curbstones and other stone, see Saliou 1999, especially figures 33–39 and 42.

the phallic symbol that some pre-eruption resident chiseled (in bas-relief) into a paving stone along Via dell'Abbondanza; most would simply step right on or over it (see figure 12.2).

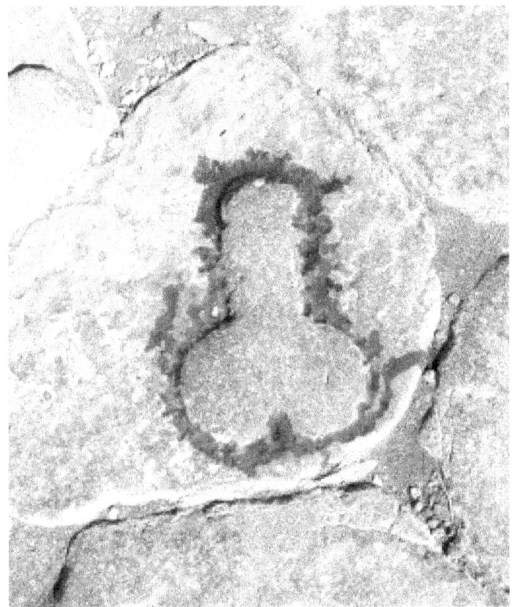

Figure 12.2. A phallic symbol on a street paving stone on Via dell'Abbondanza, with water added to highlight the symbol.

Even if the symbol is clear to the eye (once the artifact is noticed), the purpose of this symbol is less clear. Was the phallus relief simply another attempt to ensure that good fortune thrived in the neighborhood – making it an apotropaion that deflected the invasion of evil? Or did it serve as an advertisement, pointing to the location of a brothel for the benefit of newcomers to the town?[2] Or were both functions operating simultaneously? Regardless of how we might answer these questions, the point is simply that the streets of Pompeii were occasionally used to inscribe symbols or messages of some sort.

2. This interpretation is advocated by Laurence 1994: 75. In 2005, however, Butterworth and Laurence held this view: phalluses of this kind "have been taken as signposts to the red-light districts, but are more likely to have been intended to ward off the evil eye."

Figure 12.3. White inserts between paving stones outside the Temple of Apollo on Via Marina.

Another example of visual messaging within stone can be found on the street that connects the Forum and the Marine Gate. At the top of that steep street that channels traffic from the Marine Gate up to the Forum and its temples, small white marble inserts were placed in the gaps between the large stone slabs (see figure 12.3). These artistic adornments greeted those who entered the town from the Marine Gate, lying between the temple of Apollo and the temple of Venus. Perhaps functioning somewhat like the proverbial red carpet, these street visuals may have enhanced the sense of that it is good to arrive in Pompeii. Or they may have played a part in promoting a sense of the town's opulence. Or, since they lay between two of its oldest temples, they may have promoted a sense of the town's long-standing piety. Regardless of how we interpret them, it is clear that the paving stones in this region were used to communicate a message to those who walked on them.

Having registered examples of symbols and communication carved into the stones of Pompeii's streets, we can now examine nearly twenty further incisions that depict an equilateral cross. Could these marks have been incised by Jesus-devotees prior to the eruption of Mount Vesuvius? If so, what would their function have been?

An Inventory of Paving-Stone Marks

Two neighborhoods within the sprawling town of Pompeii have curious marks on the top of some of the hard-wearing lava stones that paved their streets. These marks can be found by the ordinary tourist even today, although some of them are more evident to the eye than others. In 1895, the British anthropologist H. P. Fitzgerald Marriott made a comment about ancient marks on Pompeii stones – a comment that is increasingly pertinent with each day that passes and with each tourist who walks along Pompeii's streets. He said: "Some of these marks can only be found easily in the morning, others at midday, and others in the evening, according to the direction from which the sun strikes them."[3] While he was speaking about marks in general, Marriott's comments easily apply in particular to the marks discussed in this chapter and the next. Small equilateral crosses appear on ten paving stones in the streets of region 6, and another eight appear along Via Stabiana, the main street that virtually cuts the town in half along a northwest-to-southeast axis (see figure 12.4). These curious marks require close consideration.

---

3. Marriott 1895: 62.

THE CROSSES OF POMPEII

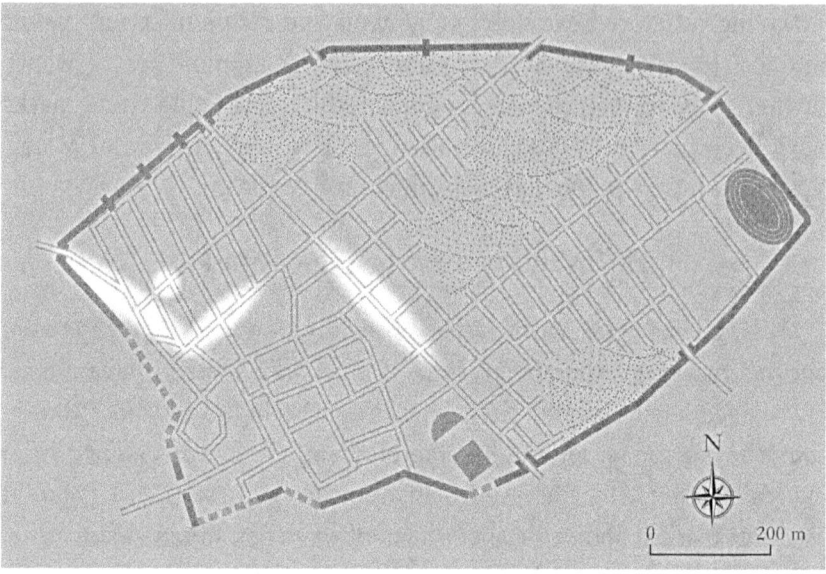

Figure 12.4. The highlighted areas are the find-spots of two groups of cross-shaped marks incised into Pompeii's street paving stones.

To assist in ease of reference, these crosses will be labeled numerically and located in relation to the modern street names. Figure 12.5 displays the ten crosses in the streets of region 6. Figure 12.6 locates those numbered crosses on a map of region 6, while figure 12.7 identifies the modern names of the pertinent streets (for later reference in this discussion). Similarly, figure 12.8 displays the eight crosses along Via Stabiana (known as Via Pompeiana in antiquity), between regions 7 and 9. Figure 12.9 locates those numbered crosses on a map, and figure 12.10 identifies the modern names of the pertinent streets (for later reference in this discussion). (Further discussion of the location of these marks, together with photos of their surroundings, is found in the appendix of this book.)

CROSSING THE STREETS

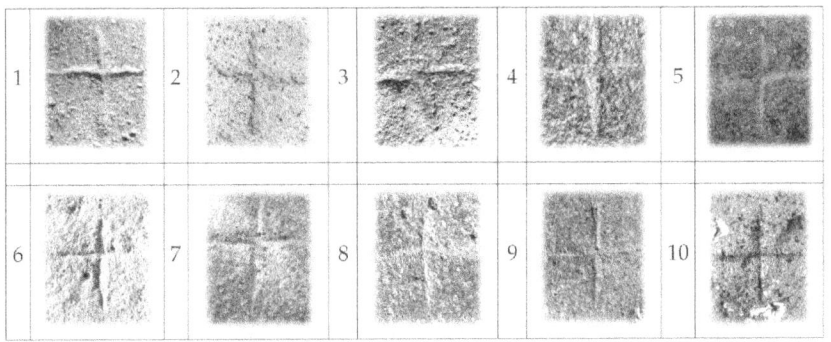

Figure 12.5. The paving-stone crosses of region 6, numbered.

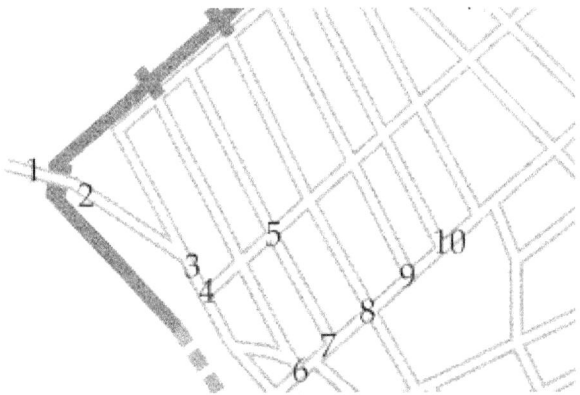

Figure 12.6. The location of the ten street crosses of region 6.

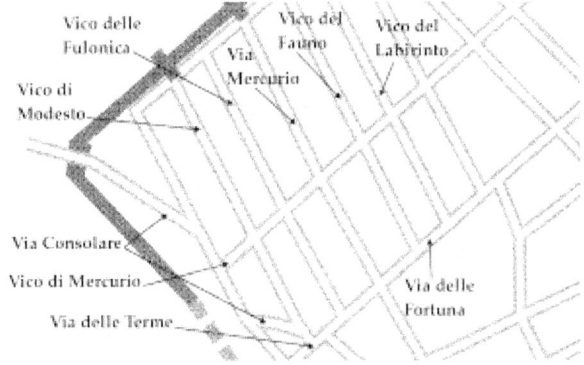

Figure 12.7. The modern street names relevant to the ten street crosses of region 6.

THE CROSSES OF POMPEII

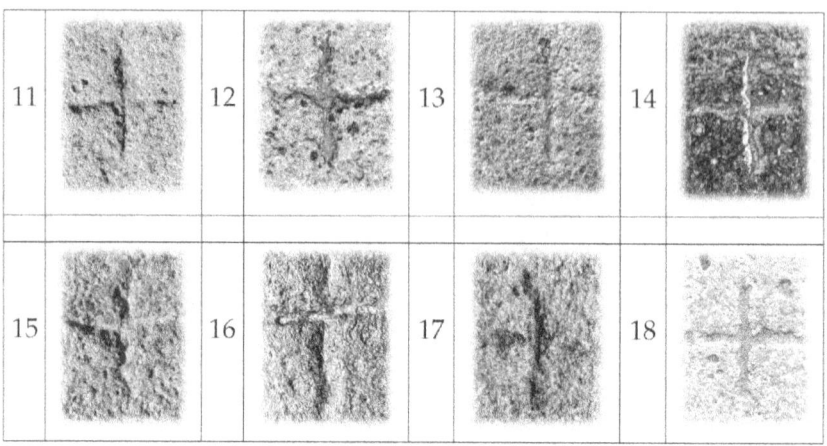

Figure 12.8. The paving-stone crosses along Via Stabiana, numbered.

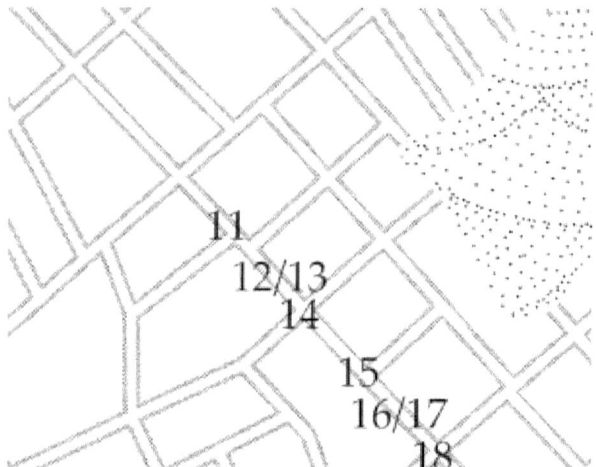

Figure 12.9. The location of the ten street crosses of region 6.

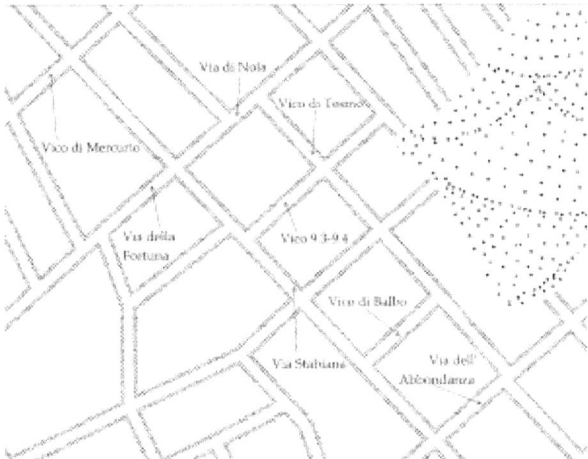

Figure 12.10. The modern street names relevant to the eight street crosses along Via Stabiana.

While eleven of these cross markings appear at street intersections and border insulae, seven others are placed at entrances of one kind or another. For instance, the Herculaneum Gate (known as Porta Saliniensis in antiquity) is the site of cross 1, which sits in the middle of the right-hand side of the road when entering the town; if a line were drawn across the two sides of the exterior archway of the gate, cross 1 would be almost directly in the line's path (see figure 12.11[4] for an artist's depiction of the Herculaneum Gate as approached from outside the town). Cross 2 seems to be partnered with cross 1, being placed just after the gate complex ends (as one moves into the town), so that crosses 1 and 2 straddle the outer and inner parts of the Herculaneum Gate, respectively. Cross 3 appears outside a small workshop at 6.17.22, with one arm pointing directly into the entryway of the workshop.[5] Cross 12 appears on a paving stone in front of 9.3.1–2, a shop front associated with a residential dyer's business; the right arm of the cross points directly into the entryway of this workshop. Cross 13 appears on a paving stone directly in front of the main entrance to 9.3.5, the

---

4. From Gell and Gandy 1852: plate 13.
5. My thanks to Natalie Webb for spotting cross 3.

impressive House of Lucretius (9.3.5/24); the right arm of the cross points directly into the entryway of this house. Two crosses appear on paving stones near to each other in front of 9.1.12; these marks, crosses 16 and 17, are approximately two feet apart, having been incised on neighboring paving stones. They are incised at different angles, one of them pointing directly into the entryway of the residence.

Figure 12.11. A nineteenth-century depiction of the Herculaneum Gate, looking into the town.

Whether at intersections or at entryways, none of the marks were found in an area where the paving stones have undergone modern disturbance or replacement. They all reside on stones in a street layout undisturbed since ancient carts carved well-defined wheel ruts into the stones. All of the eighteen paving stones are embedded in their first-century paving network.

These may not have been the only cross-shaped marks evident on Pompeian paving stones. Some of the town's paving stones may have been removed or displaced, and still others were not accessible to me. I have been able to study at least four-fifths of Pompeii's paved streets and intersections, and have spent many hours with eyes surveying long tracts of the town's paved streets.[6] (Many of the smaller streets in regions 1 and 2 were unpaved in 79.) But if it is not possible to claim that the crosses listed here are a complete record of the Pompeian paving-stone cross marks, they are nonetheless a significant record deserving of consideration as to their interpretative significance.

The eighteen paving-stone cross marks are notably similar. They share an equilateral pattern and are incised into their paving stones to roughly the same depth (allowing for slight differences, not least due to differences in wear).[7] Generally speaking, the cross marks in region 6 are slightly larger than the ones along Via Stabiana (see figure 12.12 for dimensions of the eighteen street crosses). In region 6, the crosses are usually 5.5 to 9 centimeters in diameter (although crosses 5 and 8 are smaller than that, and cross 2 is larger); the crosses along Via Stabiana are usually 4 to 5.5 centimeters in diameter (except for cross 18, which is larger).[8] The cross marks almost always share the orientation of the street that they reside on, so that one axis follows the angle of the street (with cross 16 being the only real exception, although consider cross 6 below). Since the streets of region 6 generally lie along a different angle from the angle of Via Stabiana, the eighteen crosses from the two neighborhoods do not share a common point of reference – whether that be Mount Vesuvius, a celestial body in the sky at the spring equinox, or whatever. Their orientation is usually determined simply by the angle of the streets into which they are embedded.

---

6. Sometimes this involved resorting to the old-fashioned method of brushing off layers of dirt with a broom. If there are any further paving-stones marks of this kind in the ancient town, I have not been able to see them. Presumably such marks were not viewable because they have been disturbed from their original positions (rare), have been paved with modern materials (rare), have been screened off from public access (rare), or have been covered by excessive amounts of sand (occasional).
7. On sunny days, the sun's angle might enhance one axis of the cross marks (i.e., vertical or horizontal) at one time of the day and the other axis at another time. The north arm of cross 3 is very weak, no matter the time of day. Its visibility is enhanced with a dab of water, an angled light (e.g., flashlight), or both.
8. My thanks to Stephanie Peek for spotting cross 18. Crosses 2 and 18 share some similarities that cause them to stand out from the others. They are deeper and larger than the others and required much greater effort to be produced. See, however, the dimensions of crosses 9 and 10 as well.

	Height (cm)	Width (cm)
Cross 1	8.2	8.2
Cross 2	11.0	10.2
Cross 3	8.5	7.9
Cross 4	6.4	6.4
Cross 5	5.5	5.0
Cross 6	8.6	8.7
Cross 7	8.7	7.1
Cross 8	6.1	5.9
Cross 9	9.4	9.4
Cross 10	9.4	7.9
Cross 11	5.9	5.4
Cross 12	5.4	4.8
Cross 13	5.2	5.2
Cross 14	4.3	4.3
Cross 15	4.2	4.2
Cross 16	4.9	3.2
Cross 17	3.8	3.7
Cross 18	9.4	10.2

Figure 12.12. The dimensions of the eighteen paving-stone crosses (2.54 centimeters = 1 inch).

(Note: Four months after sending this book to press, while enjoying my fifth visit to Pompeii in two and a half years, I found another mark of precisely the same kind as the ones introduced in this chapter. The December sun was low in the sky, allowing the contours to stand out in ways that had not been evident in earlier visits to Pompeii. Since this mark is precisely like the others discussed here, the total number of marks of this kind rises to nineteen. Frustratingly, this nineteenth mark, embedded on a paving stone along Via Stabiana, lies between marks 13 and 14. Residing three residential entrances south of mark 13, it would seem to operate in relation to either 9.3.8 to the east or 7.2.3 to the west. I include discussion of this mark in the appendix of this book, and I introduce it at a few points in the discussions of chapters 13 through 15. It does not carry any further weight, however, since it arrived too late to be a part of the main discussions. The omission of this mark is of little consequence to the overall argument, and fits comfortably within it.)

Dating the Paving-Stone Crosses

In light of the similarities shared by these individual street crosses, it would seem reasonable to interpret them as being related to one another in some fashion, although grouped in two different districts of the ancient town. Of course, if someone searched with a dose of diligence, without too much effort she could find insignificant cross-shaped scratches or imperfections in Pompeii's street stones – unintentional, coincidental accidents of human or natural history. But the marks registered above are of a different order altogether. These are not simply stone imperfections or indentations that happen to form perpendicular lines by chance. They are intentionally inscribed and systematically placed as part of an intricate web, with each of the parts organically related to other parts in some fashion.

But if intention stands behind them, whose intention? Are these marks ancient incisions, or have they appeared more recently, after the volcanic material was removed from Pompeii's streets?

Our first impulse must be to imagine that these crosses are not ancient marks. But if they are modern, the most likely possibility (as others have suggested to me) is that they are survey points chiseled into the ancient paving-stones by modern archaeologists who chose to mark their survey triangulation locations permanently into the paving stones and utilized a cross shape to do so – evidently standing their survey tripods directly above the mark.

In this scenario, the cross marks would likely have been carved at some point after the mid-1850s. A quick survey of Pompeii maps illustrates why. A map from 1817 shows that only crosses 1 through

5 had been uncovered at that point.⁹ A map of the excavations up to 1831 show that crosses 10 through 18 were still buried under volcanic ash in that year.¹⁰ The same is true for a map published in 1852.¹¹ A map published in 1857 shows that Via Stabiana had only recently been excavated to the point that permitted all these crosses to be incised.¹² In fact, the residence at 9.1.12 had only been excavated in 1856. Consequently, if these marks were incised by archaeologists at similar times in the two neighborhoods, that might have occurred in the five-year period between the mid-1850s and 1860, the latter being the date when Giuseppe Fiorelli became influential at the site (although he had been a powerful presence on the site even prior to 1860).¹³ Fiorelli's significance is important here, so a word about his contributions is necessary.

The inspector of excavations at Pompeii from 1860 to 1863 and the Director of Pompeii and the National Archaeological Museum of Naples from 1863 to 1875, Fiorelli is lauded as the one who introduced a new era in the excavation of the town, especially after the demise of the Bourbon dynasty and the unification of Italy in 1861. If his predecessors all too often tended to treat the town's remains as treasures to be raided (usually for the enhancement of the Bourbon dynasty), Fiorelli treated them as treasures to be preserved.¹⁴ Considering the context of artifacts to be just as important as the artifacts themselves, Fiorelli "brought order to the continuing archaeological enterprise at Pompeii" by imposing "systematic controls over the acquisition, recording, classification, and publication of information gathered from the excavations."¹⁵

---

9. See Gell and Gandy 1852: 11.
10. Clarke 1831: map pullout. See also the map of 1826 in Cooke 1827, vol. 1: 70.
11. See Zahn 1852.
12. See Joanne Berry 2007: 51. Whereas the Herculaneum Gate was excavated in the 1760s and region 6 was excavated roughly between 1806 and 1815, Via Stabiana itself was progressively excavated in a southerly direction between the mid-1840s and the mid-1850s.
13. From 1858 to 1860, Fiorelli constructed his scale model of Pompeii (1: 350), which can still be seen in the National Archaeological Museum in Naples.
14. In this, he was largely reflecting the spirit of his day. Compare Bahn 2012: 11: "It was really only in the early to mid-nineteenth century that archaeology took over from antiquarianism, in the sense of aspiring to be systematic and scientific about the vestiges of the past."
15. Brilliant 1979: 104–5.

Part of this "ordering" of the archaeological processes included the undertaking of surveys within the town in order to pin down its internal dimensions. True to his scientific spirit, Fiorelli compiled a map showing the position of the survey triangulation points throughout the town in its 1872 configuration. But when those survey points are compared with the positions of the paving-stone marks, they correlate at only three locations – that is, at crosses 8, 14, and 18 (see figure 12.13[16]). Even those points, however, were only minor survey points for Fiorelli, with most other points attracting more triangulation lines. None of the other fifteen crosses appear at survey points. The streets of Pompeii give no evidence that Fiorelli's surveyors chiseled crosses into paving stones at other survey points; even the main triangulation points (e.g., northeastern corner of the Forum) show no indication that chiseling cross marks into street stones was the practice of the day. Evidently, such rash measures were not deemed necessary in the surveying overseen by Fiorelli during the 1860s and early 1870s.

In fact, there is little reason to imagine such measures ever to have been deemed necessary, whether before or after Fiorelli. The incising of crosses onto paving stones to serve as survey points would be a classic example of archaeological buffoonery.[17] Even if we imagine these paving-stone crosses to have been incised by clownishly rogue survey teams, surely even they could have left their mark in a much more efficient fashion. These paving-stone crosses were usually incised to a much larger size than would have been necessary for a simple survey point. Moreover, the crosses frequently show signs of

---

16. Fiorelli 1873: appendix.
17. Other possible explanations are similarly found wanting. Both the Insula Arriana Polliana and the House of the Faun were hit by allied bombs on November 9, 1943, so perhaps the five crosses connecting these two sites had something to do with the reconstruction efforts after that damage. (Bombs damaged properties in insula 6.6 at entryways 1, 5, 6, 7, 10, 10a, and 11, and in insula 6.12 at entryway 5.) But there was bomb damage elsewhere in the town where similar crosses are not found, and crosses are found where there was no bomb damage. Alternatively, the Anglo-American Project in Pompeii worked in region 6 in the late twentieth century and early in the twenty-first century, including the area around the Herculaneum Gate. But their efforts are focused on uncovering the history of Insula 1 in that region, and they have never gone near the other paving-stone crosses; nor would we expect such second-rate measures from a project of this kind. Precisely the same can be said of the Via Consolare Project, operating since 2005 through the San Francisco State Pompeii Internship Program.

significant incisional effort – with some of the marks being composed of at least five separate incisions (for instance, crosses 7 and 10). For the larger crosses (such as cross 2 and cross 18), even more effort was required. For archaeological surveyors to have spent the time and energy chiseling out multistroked elongated incisions in the hard volcanic stone of an ancient site is hardly a feasible scenario.

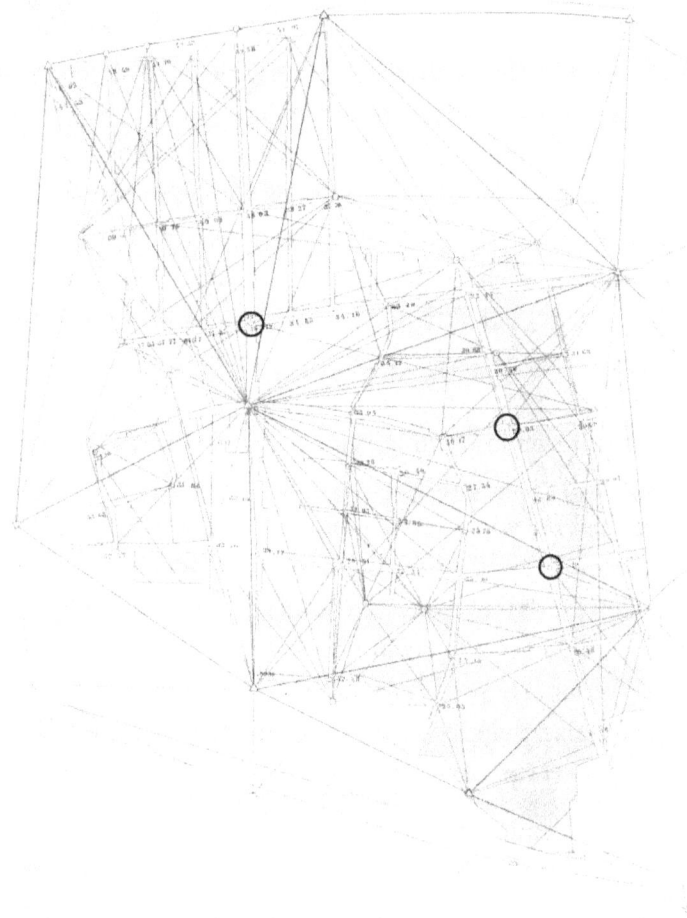

Figure 12.13. Circles highlight the three locations where paving-stone cross marks correspond with minor triangulation points on Fiorelli's plan.

Archaeological surveyors simply do not require such time-consuming and invasive markers in order to perform their surveys. The standard method of establishing a survey point in paving stones is simply to insert a large-headed metal nail (often with a metal washer) between paving stones. It is a straightforward method that requires minimal effort and takes only seconds to execute; with a few strokes of a hammer, the task is done. Moreover, this method of securing survey reference points does no damage to the ancient site.

Survey benchmarks of this kind are often evident between Pompeii's paving stones even today, having been left there by surveyors of the past. In fact, a benchmark nail is embedded next to the very same paving stone onto which cross 6 was incised (see figure 12.14), and the same is true for cross 14. Other paving stones that bear cross marks lie a few feet away from other survey nails (for instance, crosses 4, 7, and 11; see figure 12.15). Clearly, the archaeologists who drove those nails did not think it prudent to use the cross marks on those paving stones as their survey benchmarks; instead of referencing those ready-made marks, they chose the standard practice of inserting nails between the paving stones. The reverse process is even harder to imagine: surveyors chiseling out crosses instead of using survey nails left by previous survey teams. And if we are going to imagine surveyors chiseling cross marks in the street stones, we have to imagine them chiseling out crosses 16 and 17 only two feet away from each other, incising a survey marker in one stone, then incising a nearly identical survey marker in the neighboring stone. Such scenarios are almost unimaginable.[18]

---

18. When I passed by cross mark 14 in December 2015, a survey team was surveying the area. One of their instruments had been placed directly above the metal benchmark inserted between the paving stones about one foot away from mark 14. When chatting with one of the surveyors, I asked about the age of the benchmark. "About sixty years old," he estimated. He explained that there was a more modern survey system in place, but survey teams often continue to use the older system. I then showed him mark 14 in the paving stone, he said, "I have never seen that." When I asked whether it could have been a survey benchmark from the nineteenth century, he said, "I don't think so. Probably its Roman." Really? "Yes, definitely Roman." I wrote down our conversation minutes later, and have recounted the surveyor's words verbatim. For photos demonstrating the relationship of mark 14 to the survey team's use of the metal benchmark, see the appendix to this book.

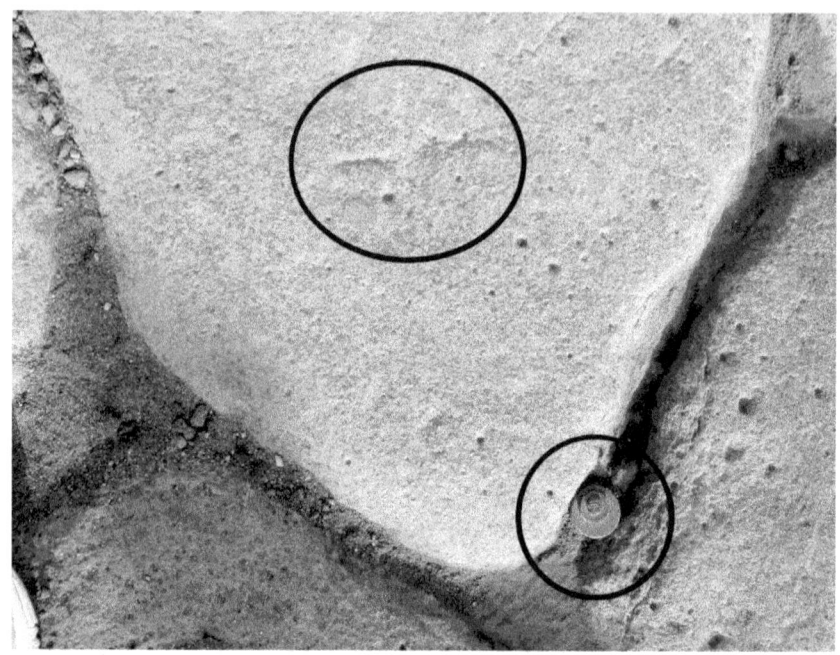

Figure 12.14. The proximity of cross 6 and a modern survey marker.

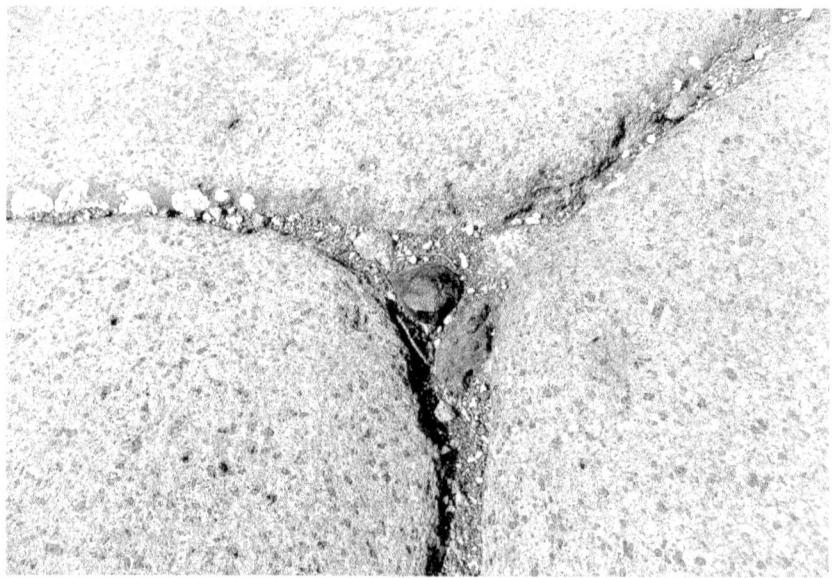

Figure 12.15. An old survey marker about a meter away from cross 11.

Could these marks have been incised by archaeologists for something other than survey reference points? At times, archaeologists extended long boards from an external wall into the streets in order to prop up those walls.[19] Boards serving this function, however, were jammed into crevasses between paving stones rather than secured by anything, and certainly they were not secured in the paving stones by tiny indented marks.[20]

If it is difficult to imagine these marks being incised by modern archaeologists (within a five-year window of the late 1850s), three factors suggest that they had already been incised when Vesuvius erupted in 79 (with other factors corroborating this conclusion in chapter 13 below).

First, Marriott noticed one of these crosses in his 1895 publication entitled *Facts about Pompei: Its Masons' Marks, Town Walls, Houses, and Portraits*.[21] Marriott noticed that a cross mark had been incised into a stone outside insula 9.1 on Via Stabiana – in which case, he was speaking of either cross 16 or cross 17. In fact, he was probably referring to cross 16, since he depicted the mark as appearing like an X against the angle of the street, which is true of cross 16 but not cross 17. Moreover, his drawing of the incision comes fairly close to cross 16 (see figure 12.16[22]). But what is notable about Marriott's interpretation is that he considered cross 16 to derive from the ancient town. This nineteenth-century scholar did not think that cross 16 was a recent, nineteenth-century intrusion onto ancient stone; in particular, he did not consider it to be a survey marker incised by a nineteenth-century survey team. In his view, it was a mark incised by someone from the Greco-Roman world. Marriott interpreted cross 16 simply to be an ancient stonemason's mark. When the full inventory of eighteen cross marks is in view, however, it is obvious that they cannot be mason's marks, which would have resulted in a completely random

---

19. Examples of this are evident in Varone and Stefani 2009: 119, 145, 396–97.
20. For the edge of a board having been jammed between paving stones, see Varone and Stefani 2009: 119.
21. Marriott 1895: 85.
22. Left image: From Marriott 1895: 85.

pattern, as various stones were placed throughout the town. Clearly the cross marks do resemble other ancient marks on stone (such as the six-pointed figure created from three intersecting lines in the drain stone outside the House of Julius Polybius), and in that sense these crosses are rightly interpreted as ancient marks.[23] But these marks are far too regular to be explained simply as the residual mark of an ancient mason. When the database is thought to comprise only one or two crosses, such a theory could perhaps be surmised – as was the case with Marriott. But when the whole network of cross marks is in view, a systematic explanation is required. Accordingly, three things are evident from Marriott's discussion: (1) Marriott was wrong about cross 16 being a mason's mark; (2) Marriott never imagined that cross 16 was a modern surveyor's mark (such techniques evidently being unknown to him); and (3) Marriott understood cross 16 to be a first-century mark.

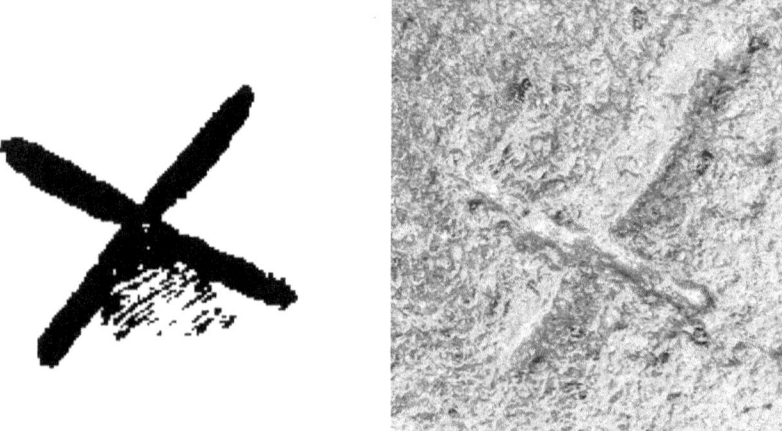

Figure 12.16. Left: Marriott's depiction of the reclining cross outside 9.1.12; right: a photo of cross 16.

---

23. For the mark incised into the drain stone, see http://pompeiiinpictures.com/pompeiiinpictures/R9/9 13 03 p1.htm.

Second, of the eighteen marks, cross 4 is probably the most disguised, having less depth than most other marks. This is probably due to the inevitable wear caused by traffic. Such wearing was unlikely to have been caused by modern tourist footfall. Cross 4 is the only one of the eighteen that sits squarely within a rut created by cart traffic going in and out of Vico di Mercurio (see figure 12.17). If this gives it some protection against modern footfall, cross 4 was not protected from ancient cart wheels. The wearing of cross 4 probably derives from ancient cart traffic within region 6. This serves to suggest that these cross marks belong to the ancient rather than modern world.

Figure 12.17. The placement of cross 4 within the wheel rut created by ancient carts.

The third factor that places these crosses in the ancient world comes not from where a cross was placed but where it was not placed. Cross 11 stands at an insula boundary or street intersection, and each of the intersections to the south of that cross enjoy the placement of other crosses (crosses 14, 15, and 18), with one exception: between crosses 11 and 12 (see figure 12.18). Precisely the absence of a cross mark at that intersection may well suggest that these crosses date to a time eighteen hundred years prior to Fiorelli's directorship. To understand the point, we need to reconstruct the events that heavily influenced the character of this neighborhood in the last twenty years of the town's life.

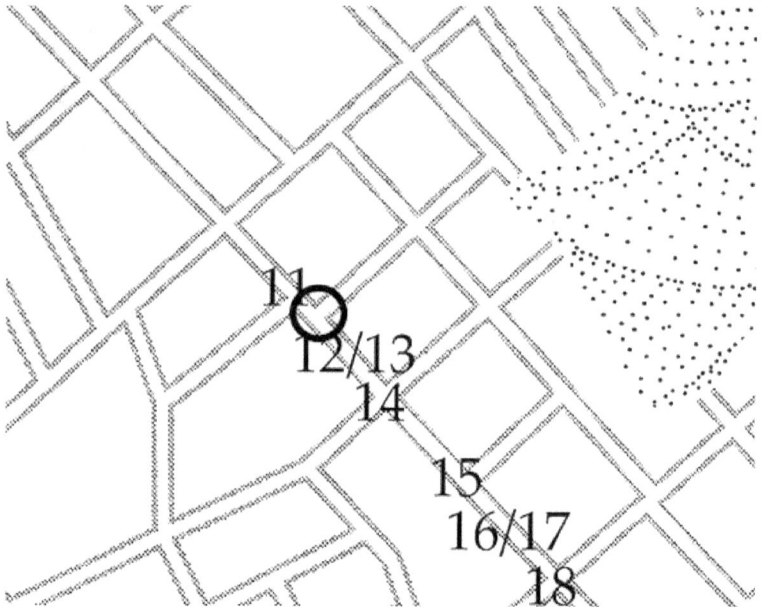

Figure 12.18. The absence of a cross at Vico 9.3–9.4 (highlighted by a circle).

When an earthquake hit the region in the year 62 or 63, the town of Pompeii incurred heavy damage. In the wake of that quake, the town initiated the building of a new bathing complex. Those baths, now known as the Central Baths, replaced an entire insula, taking over the whole of insula 9.4 (the southeast corner of the intersection at Via

Stabiana and Via di Nola, northeast of cross 11). In fact, the baths were built to a larger footprint than the footprint of the former insula. As a consequence, the Central Baths (which had not yet been opened by the time of the eruption) extended some way into the streets that bounded its eastern and southern sides.

This caused each of those streets to be vastly diminished in their functionality as access routes – Vico di Tesmo on the east (see figure 12.19) and, on the south, Vico 9.3–9.4 (it remains unnamed). The point is especially relevant to the southern street, Vico 9.3–9.4. As Eric Poehler notes regarding that street, "when the footprint of the Central baths overtook a portion of this street's space, it became unusable."[24] His point pertains to cart traffic, as evidenced by the fact that curb stones were added to block the street off from Via Stabiana, preventing vehicular access into the street (see figure 12.20). Of course, there would have remained some pedestrian traffic along that route. But because the functionality of Vico 9.3–9.4 was greatly reduced by the encroachment of the Central Baths, for all intents and purposes that route no longer served as a fully functioning street but simply as glorified passageway.[25]

The implication of this for our study is simple and significant. If a modern surveyor were intent on marking insular boundaries throughout this section of Via Stabiana, he would probably have included one where Via Stabiana meets Vico 9.3–9.4 – that is, between cross 11 and cross 12. That intersection marks the boundary of the residences and shops of insula 9.3 and the Central Baths of insula 9.4. But no cross mark appears at that point. This suggests that the Via Stabiana crosses were probably not incised by a modern archaeologist marking insulae boundaries. Conversely, if an ancient resident were putting marks on major intersections for some reason, this is an

24. Poehler 2005: 4.
25. The passageway allowed access to the back of the Central Baths (which were still under construction at the time of the eruption) and to residences 9.3.23 and 9.3.25, as well as 9.3.24, which was the back entrance to 9.3.5. That these glorified passageways (Vico 9.3–9.4 and Vico di Tesmo) lessened in their utility after the construction of the Central Baths may find confirmation from the fact that a graffito was found on the exterior wall between 9.5.19 and 9.5.20 in Vicolo di Tesmo stating that "Secundus and Primigenia meet here" (*CIL* 4.5358; see Varone 2002: 46). Then as now, lovers seek out fairly secluded sites to enjoy each other's company.

intersection that he might decide to omit in the aftermath of the earthquake, since this junction no longer acted as a significant intersection in the final years of the town's life.

Figure 12.19. The encroachment of the Central Baths onto Vico di Tesmo to the east of the baths.

The absence of a cross mark at this particular point, then, adds additional weight to the likelihood that the cross marks are, in fact, ancient incisions. Furthermore, since the minimization of Vico 9.3–9.4 took place several years after the earthquake of the early 60s, the cross marks along Via Stabiana probably derive from the final ten years of the town's life, when the roads around the Central Baths were being reworked and rerouted (as Poehler has convincingly argued; see chapter 13 below, where another feature points to the same period for the Via Stabiana cross marks).[26]

---

26. There is a chance that a cross mark was attempted where Vico 9.3-9.4 meets Via Stabiana. A scar on a paving stone at that location might indicate an unsuccessful attempt at placing a cross mark at that point (in Via Stabiana). If it is a failed attempt to incise a mark, it falls precisely where a cross mark would be expected, in the explanation set out in chapter 13 below. However, since we might imagine the failed attempt to have resulted in the production of another cross mark on

Figure 12.20. The curbstones added to prevent cart access into Vico 9.3–9.4 from Via Stabiana (with a modern "keep out" sign coincidentally reinforcing the ancient intention).

If these cross marks along Via Stabiana were incised in the decade or so before the eruption of Vesuvius, what are the options for interpreting them in terms derived from the first century? Moreover, why have they not been part of the scholarly discourse regarding the ancient site's artifacts? These questions will be addressed in chapter 13. There we will see further evidence suggesting a first-century date for these paving-stone marks. Moreover, we will see reasons why these ancient marks have been absent from the archaeological inventory of Vesuvian artifacts. Initially, however, our first task will be to consider the two most likely interpretations as to the function of these curious cross marks within their original, first-century context.

the same stone, and since no other mark of that kind is evident, I take it that this is not a failed attempt at incising a cross mark and, consequently, I do not include this scar in the inventory of cross marks.

13

Jesus-Devotion in the Streets

Andrew Wallace-Hadrill has noted the "nightmare of omissions" that plagues the modern archaeological study of the Vesuvian towns: "Each generation discovers with horror the extent to which information has been ignored, neglected, destroyed, and (the most wanton damage of all) left unreported and unpublished."[1] The cross marks that were incised into paving stones in the last ten years of the town's existence seem to fit most of these categories: "ignored, neglected, . . . left unreported and unpublished." Fortunately, the one category that does not apply to these marks is "destroyed," since these neglected first-century artifacts still remain emblazoned on the streets for any tourist to appreciate today.

Two things are needed at this point in our study. First, we need a theory that explains the function of these paving-stone marks, both systematically and in terms derived from the ancient world. Second, we need to consider why these ancient marks have failed to capture the scholarly attention that they deserve. Both issues are explored in this chapter.

---

1. Wallace-Hadrill 1994: 65.

Paving-Stone Marks for Ancient Street Traffic?

Seeking to arrive at a systematic explanation for the function of the paving-stone marks, we need first to consider whether they might have played a role in the traffic system of the ancient town. Note, for instance, that cross 1 is situated toward the right-hand side of the entrance through the Herculaneum Gate into the town, just as ancient Roman traffic traveled on the right-hand side of the road when the streets were broad enough to handle two-directional traffic.[2] As an ancient mark, it might be that the inscriber of cross 1 was cognizant of ancient traffic flow into the town and, accordingly, located that cross on the right-hand side of the entrance. The ancient person who incised this street cross may have assumed that its purpose had something to do with entering the town. (If so, this would support the view that cross 1 is ancient, not modern. Traffic flow in modern Italy was on the left-hand side of the road until the late nineteenth and early twentieth century.)[3]

Other street crosses appear in places where a one-way street system seems to have been in effect. While two-way cart traffic could easily be facilitated along the wider routes of the town, the same was not the case for many of the narrower streets. For this reason, as Eric Poehler has demonstrated, a traffic system had been devised for certain areas of the town.[4] This was especially required in the aftermath of the construction of the Central Baths. As noted in chapter 12 above, those baths encroached on the streets immediately to the east and south.

---

2. On traffic passage, see Poehler 2003. So too Butterworth and Laurence 2005: 128.
3. The World Standards organization (www.worldstandards.eu/cars/driving-on-the-left/) states the following: "In Italy the practice of driving on the right first began in the late 1890s. The first Italian Highway Code, issued on 30 June 1912, stated that all vehicles had to drive on the right. Cities with a tram network, however, could retain left-hand driving if they placed warning signs at their city borders. The 1923 decree is a bit stricter, but Rome and the northern cities of Milan, Turin and Genoa could still keep left until further orders from the Ministry of Public Works. By the mid-1920s, right-hand driving finally became standard throughout the country. Rome made the change on the 1 of March 1925 and Milan on 3 August 1926."
4. Poehler 2005; 2006. See also Kaiser 2011: 72–73; Roberts 2013: 46. The question of how this traffic system was monitored and controlled has received various answers, including the notion that a directional pamphlet was produced for cart drivers to follow. In my estimate, the traffic system must have been patrolled by a handful of civic slaves placed at key points within the system. Perhaps as few as four civic slaves placed at main artery intersections could have provided sufficient monitoring for the areas most affected by the building of the Central Baths.

Most significant in this regard was the width reduction of Vico di Terme. That street had previously accepted a sizable portion of southbound traffic from the major east-west artery (Via di Nola). This function was no longer viable, however, once the Central Baths encroached across its prior footprint. This one adjustment to Vico di Terme had a dramatic effect on the traffic flow at two separate parts of the town – along Via Stabiana to the south and the streets of region 6 to the west, with route directions being changed as a consequence:

1. Vico di Mercurio north of Via della Fortuna/Via di Nola was changed from being an eastbound to a westbound access route (see figure 13.1);
2. Vico di Terme, which had previously facilitated southbound traffic, became largely unusable to facilitate heavy cart traffic except at its most southerly point. There it switched from having been a southbound artery to being a northbound artery for one block. Northbound traffic along the southern end of Vico di Terme would then access Via Stabiana by way of a left turn onto Vico di Balbo before turning right onto Via Stabiana one block north of Via dell'Abbondanza (see figure 13.2[5]).

---

5. In figure 13.2 I have followed Poehler's reconstruction in all regards except one. I do not share his view that, after the construction of the Central Baths, Via Stabiana was merely a southgoing street along the west of 9.1, while Via dell'Abbondanza was merely an eastgoing street along the south of 9.1. While Vico di Balbo (between 9.1 and 9.2) changed from an eastbound to a westbound street at that point, this does not necessarily suggest that the west and south of 9.1 became unidirectional. The width of those streets at that point would suggest otherwise. The same conclusion is suggested by the awkwardness of Poehler's reconstruction in relation to traffic flowing north along Via Stabiana from the Stabian Gate at the south of the town. Instead of simply following along Via Stabiana north of Via dell'Abbondanza, that traffic would have to turn east along Via dell'Abbondanza for one block, then turn north along Vico di Tesmo for one block, then turn west along Vico di Balbo for one block, before finally turning north again along Via Stabiana. That scenario makes very little sense. Consequently, in figure 13.2, I have incorporated bidirectional arrows to the west and south of 9.1.

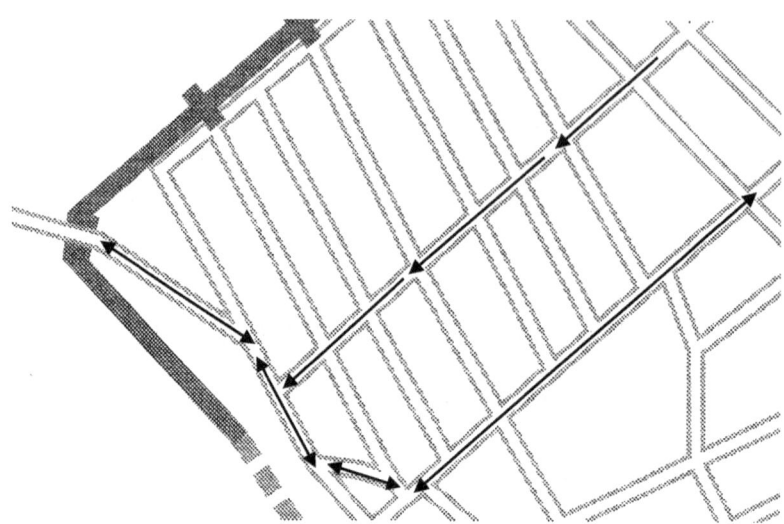

Figure 13.1. The main traffic flow in region 6 after the construction of the Central Baths (perhaps in the late 60s or early 70s), with Vico di Mercurio becoming a westbound route after having been an eastbound route previously.

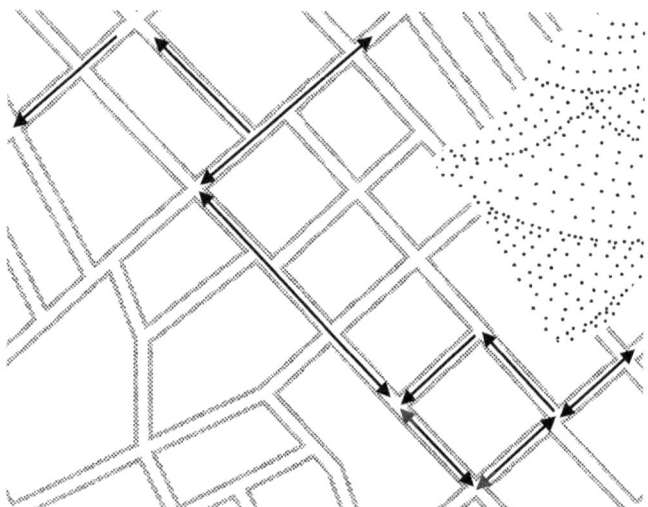

Figure 13.2. Traffic flow along Via Stabiana after the construction of the Central Baths (perhaps in the late 60s or early 70s), with Vico di Terme becoming a northbound route for one block north of Via dell'Abbondanza.

The impact of the Central Baths on the traffic routes within Pompeii is intriguing, since the two areas of traffic most affected are precisely the areas where the two groups of cross marks reside. Perhaps the cross marks on paving stones in these two neighborhoods had something to do with the reworking of the traffic system in the aftermath of the construction of the Central Baths. But how might that have been the case? Did they aid the flow of traffic in some fashion? Are they directional markers?

While scenarios of this kind need to be given due consideration, they ultimately fail to provide a satisfying solution, for at least three reasons.[6] First, these marks are really quite small and indistinct, and would not be well suited to perform a function in this regard.

Second, some of the marks appear in places where they would not be necessary. For instance, they would not have been necessary at locations where a directional change is not possible; there are, however, various locations where crosses appear in precisely such unnecessary circumstances.[7] Further, the presence of two markers, instead of just one, outside 9.1.12 would be wholly superfluous to requirements. Moreover, we might imagine that directional markers would not be necessary when a two-way road met a two-way road; this is, however, precisely what we find in at least three instances.[8]

Third, crosses do not appear in places where they should ideally have appeared. We would expect directional markers to be placed where Via dell'Abbondanza meets Vico di Tesmo, for instance. This is because (as Poehler notes) some of the traffic intending to turn north off Via dell'Abbondanza could have moved along Vico di Tesmo for a

---

6. Note Poehler's email message to me in response to my email asking whether he had taken note of the paving-stone cross marks in his research on traffic flow in region 6 and along Via Stabiana. His email reply of October 29, 2013, states that he was not cognizant of those marks, which consequently played no role in his conclusions about traffic flow. Note, also, his assurances that the marks were not incised by him and his team: "We always used nails in between the stones."
7. These include crosses 1 and 2 at the Herculaneum Gate, cross 3 at the entryway into 6.17.22, cross 12 at the entryway into 9.3.1–2, cross 13 at the entryway into 9.3.5, and crosses 16 and 17 at the entryway into 9.1.12 – as well as the late-noticed cross 19 at the entryway into 9.3.8 or 7.2.3.
8. At cross 6, where Via Consolare meets Via delle Terme; at cross 8, where Via di Mercurio meets Via delle Terme; and at cross 18, where Via Stabiana meets Via dell'Abbondanza.

block, before turning left along Vico di Balbo, and then turning right onto Via Stabiana. Instead, no mark appears at that point.

In essence, then, there is little reason to think that the paving-stone marks performed a function with regard to traffic flow. They appear where they should not have appeared and they do not appear where they should have appeared. The possibility that these marks were traffic signals takes us up a dead-end street.

Symbols on Stone?

If the paving-stone cross marks did not assist with first-century traffic congestion, there are not many other viable options left for us to consider. Instead of a mundane function, they must have served a more symbolic function. They do not conform to the pattern of the Egyptian Ankh. They were not incised by malicious opponents of Christians seeking to mark where Christians lived, as if to target them and disadvantage them among their peers (since the majority of them do not operate in relation to residential entrances). Being equilateral crosses, it is conceivable that they derive from a Jewish influence, being indebted to the symbolism of Ezekiel 9:4–6.[9] But the most viable option, and one that is not at odds with the possibility of a Jewish influence, is that these small marks derive from Jesus-devotion.

As with other Pompeian cross artifacts, this seems to be the least implausible interpretation. We have already seen evidence that Jesus-devotion resided within Pompeii and utilized cruciform shapes to capture its main symbolic image. And, in fact, cross 6 lies directly outside the bakery in which the Pompeian wall-cross was found (see figure 13.3). This is a most important feature of the region 6 marks. Their placement suggests that the Insula Arriana Polliana was the center point around which these crosses gravitate. They either blanketed that insula (largely the effect of crosses 4 through 7) or spiraled off from cross 6, with one arm pivoting off toward the

---

9. Here we might compare the case of a gentile from the second century CE whose contacts with Judaism provided him knowledge of curses within the Hebrew Bible (e.g., Deuteronomy 28:22, 28) that he incorporated into his list of curses (*IG* 12.9, 955, 1179).

northwest (crosses 1 through 4) and another pivoting off to the east (crosses 7 through 10). The placement of these crosses, then, focuses our attention on the Insula Arriana Polliana, and specifically on its southwestern tip. This is significant because it was precisely at that point that the stylized cross of Jesus-devotion resided on the wall of the bakery. With this in view, there is good reason to link an artifact from the main data set (i.e., the bakery cross) to the street crosses in the supplemental data set.

Figure 13.3. The paving stone on which a cross was etched (highlighted in the foreground by water marks) with the bakery in the Insula Arriana Polliana directly behind it and the cross (not to scale) placed on the wall where it was originally discovered.

Being symbols of Jesus-devotion, what was the function of these street crosses? As Kristina Milnor rightly notes, the locations of ancient incisions into Pompeii's materiality is frequently part and parcel of the function of those incisions.[10] This is likely to have been the case for these artifacts of Jesus-devotion. That is not to say, however, that these incisions served as directional markers to guide Jesus-followers to places of worship – as if they were early precursors to a GPS navigation system.[11] It is much more likely that these incisions performed a similar function to the bakery cross and the *vivit* cross – that is, they were intended as a form of protection against the invasive forces of evil. This function would account for their placement both at street intersections and at entryways into residences and workshops. Precisely these places were frequently adorned with representations of deities, ancestral spirits, and the phallus – protective suprahuman sentries and bringers of good fortune. As John Clarke notes, "[n]umerous altars to the protector-deities of the crossroads ... attest to the common belief that individuals needed protection from evil forces lurking out in the open."[12]

Take, for instance, cross 1 at the Herculaneum Gate – the closest town gate to the bakery in the Insula Arriana Polliana, with only a two- or three-minute walk separating the two locations. This seems to have been one of the busiest gates of the town, linking Pompeii to Herculaneum, Puteoli, Neapolis, and the coastal route to the north and to Rome. Suspicion about newcomers was a common fear in the ancient world, since travelers might wield the evil eye, tapping into the power of suprahuman spirits in order to bolster their prospects. Enhancing the apotropaic protection at the Herculaneum Gate would not have been thought of as a futile gesture to the first-century imagination.

---

10. Milnor 2014: 14: "where they [inscriptions] were found is often as much a part of their meaning as what they say."
11. Note Meeks's point (1983: 29): "When a stranger arrived in a city, ... he knew, or could easily learn, where to find immigrants and temporary residents from his own country or ethnos and practitioners of his own trade."
12. John Clarke 2007: 64.

Figure 13.4. Looking into Pompeii through the Herculaneum Gate (a view from the early nineteenth century). Mazois 1824: vol. 1, plate II.

Moreover, immediately beyond the Herculaneum Gate lay a high concentration of tombs of the dead.[13] As Joanne Berry notes, the popular view in the Greco-Roman world was that "the spirits of the dead could do harm to the living unless appeased," which is "why the dead were buried outside the boundaries of the towns, and why families performed regular ceremonies at their household tombs."[14]

13. The other gate with a high concentration of tombs was the Nuceria Gate in the south of the town. Other town gates attracted relatively few tombs. On Pompeii's tombs, see especially Campbell 2015. The ashes of the deceased were usually placed in urns that were accessed through tubes (which were placed in the ground next to *columellae* markers if the urn was buried, or were embedded within structures if the urn was kept within a tomb). These tubes allowed regular sustenance to be passed to the deceased in order to keep its spirit content. The remains of civic leaders were buried in prominent tombs, which included seat tombs that permitted passers-by to rest and perhaps to contemplate the contributions of the deceased to the well-being of the urban center (e.g., Eumachia, Mamia, etc.). Both of these features (feeding tubes and seat tombs) helped to demystify the otherwise ominous tomb areas, as did the inclusion of residences and shops in the region north of the Herculaneum Gate.
14. Berry 2007: 92. In this regard, notice especially the tomb of Gnaeus Vibrius Saturninus (HGW [=Herculaneum Gate Western tombs] 23), which is almost wholly taken up by a triclinium, allowing the family to dine in the presence of his "departed" spirit. *Jubilees* 22:16–17 labels the gentile nations as "unclean," listing a variety of reasons for this estimate, including that they "offer their sacrifices to the dead and they worship evil spirits, and they eat over the graves" of their departed.

Accordingly, someone with a typical first-century mind-set would not have thought that an apotropaic device was out of place at Pompeii's Herculaneum Gate, with town's impressive gates serving to reinforce the "clear symbolic division" between the tombs of the dead beyond and the realm of the living within.[15] In this context, the person who incised cross 1 might have hoped that any malicious spirits seeking to enter the town through the Herculaneum Gate would be disarmed by the apotropaic cross (just as others sought to disarm malevolent spirits in the tomb area by offering sacrifices to the benevolent spirits of the neighborhood, as noted in figure 8.1 above). Fearsome spirits might enter the town of their own accord or by way of human agents (entering primarily on the right hand side) who were spirit possessed or could wield the evil eye. The cross was incised on the right hand side of the passage through the Herculaneum Gate in the hope of preventing these forms of evil from entering the town and subsequently taking the path of least resistance into the heart of the town, which led directly in front of the bakery in the Insula Arriana Polliana. Cross 1 was probably incised to have an apotropaic effect on cart traffic in particular, while cross 2 was incised to act apotropaically on pedestrian traffic, since the two crosses seem aligned specifically in relation to the two entrances (cart and pedestrian).

A passage from the *Testament of Solomon* captures the sense of dread that accompanied tombs, where evil spirits lurked. One spirit is allowed to speak for itself in this ancient text – a third-century Christian text that develops an earlier Jewish text from about the first century. The demonic spirit, identifying itself as "a lecherous spirit of a giant man who died in a massacre in the age of giants," explains its strategy this way (17:1–3):

> My home is in inaccessible places. My activity is this: I seat myself near dead men in the tombs and at midnight I assume the form of the dead; if I seize anyone, I immediately kill him with the sword. If I should not be able to kill him, I cause him to be possessed by a demon and to gnaw his own flesh to pieces and the saliva of his jowls to flow down.

---

15. Laurence 1994: 138.

In ancient (and not so ancient) mythologies, a concentration of tombs just outside the town walls could easily be seen as ominous. This association of spirits and tombs is evident also in other ancient texts. The demoniac in Mark 5, for instance, is said to have lived among tombs (Mark 5:2–3), and daimons are linked to tombs in magical literature.[16]

Moreover, the *Testament of Solomon* points to the way in which the mark of the cross was perceived by pre-Constantinian Jesus-followers as having apotropaic power against evil spirits. After the evil spirit explains its strategy, Solomon forces him to reveal the spiritual power by which the spirit can be thwarted. The spirit explains in this way: "He who is about to return (as) Savior [= Jesus] thwarts me. If his mark is written on (one's) forehead, it thwarts me, and because I am afraid of it, I quickly turn and flee from him. This is the sign of the cross."

Along similar lines, six of the ten crosses in region 6 are easily recognizable as having served an apotropaic role in relation to the Insula Arriana Polliana. The closest town gate is the first line of defense, with crosses 1 and 2 placed there. Beyond cross 3 (which seems to function in relation to 6.17.22), two crosses protect intersections leading to the back of the insula (cross 4 to the west and cross 5 to the east).[17] Another two crosses provide the insula with a forward apotropaic curtain (crosses 6 and 7). Accordingly, crosses 4 through 7 seem to encase the Insula Arriana Polliana rather snugly within an apotropaic blanket or force field, with concentrated assistance from the apotropaic cross hanging prominently on the bakery wall and two other crosses on duty at the nearest entrance into the town.

At this point, it is interesting to note that, with the exception of cross 16, cross 6 is unusual in that its angle is not in alignment with the insula that it borders. It does not share the ninety-degree angle of the

---

16. See, for instance, Daniel and Maltomini 1990: 1.19, 2.35–36.
17. There is a bottleneck in Via Consolare south of cross 4 and north of cross 6, suggesting that some cart traffic would have proceeded eastward along the back of Insula Arriana Polliana precisely where cross 4 is placed – at least during the time when that street was an eastbound route; see below.

insula's outer walls. If it had, it would be angled to point along Via delle Terme at the south of the insula. Instead, if the arm of cross 6 pointing eastward along Via delle Terme were extended, it would collide with the Insula Arriana Polliana, rather than extending further along the street. Its orientation differentiates cross 6 from almost all the other paving stone crosses.

The explanation for the relatively anomalous orientation of cross 6 derives from the cross's intended function as an apotropaic device. The only arm of cross 6 that aligns with a street is the one that points midway into Via Consolare (see figure 13.5 and figure 13.6). In other words, the orientation of cross 6 betrays the fact that its incisor's frame of reference regarding the potential invasion of evil was to the northwest – precisely along the route where crosses 1 and 2 were incised. The orientation of cross 6 is in close alignment with the crosses bounding the Herculaneum Gate. An apotropaic function seems to explain, then, not only the placement of these street crosses but also the exceptional angle at which cross 6 was incised.

Figure 13.5. The perfect orientation of cross 6 toward the northwest (left) and its awkward orientation toward the northeast (right).

JESUS-DEVOTION IN THE STREETS

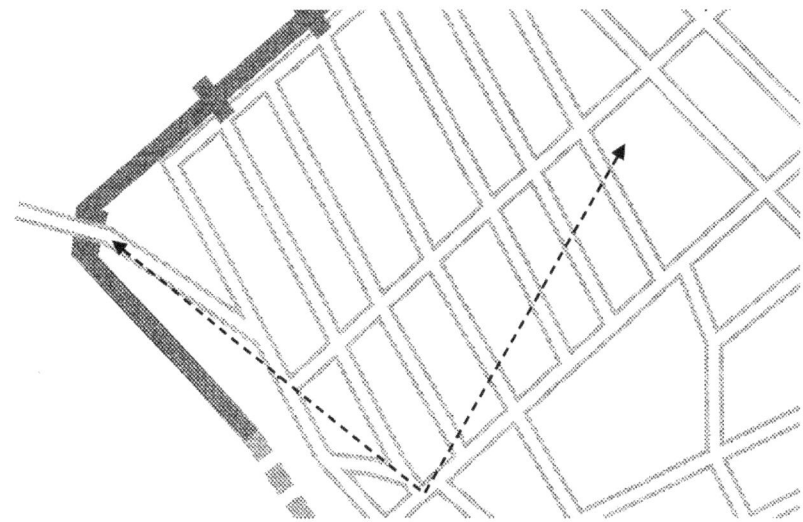

Figure 13.6. The orientation of cross 6 toward the northwest, in close alignment with the crosses at the Herculaneum Gate.

Figure 13.7. An 1820s painting depicting the Insula Arriana Polliana (far right) and the streets to the west of it, with Via Consolare to the left and Vico di Modesto toward the center-right (by William Bernard Cooke). From Cooke 1827: vol. 2, plate 3.

What about crosses 8 through 10 – the three crosses that tail off along Via della Fortuna? Perhaps they extended to a point where further Jesus-devotees resided – in this case, insula 6.12, the House of the Faun. Perhaps Jesus-devotees were among the household slaves or menial workers of that household, or within one of the insula's five front shops rented out for business.[18] In either case, the two crosses in the front of insula 6.12 (crosses 9 and 10) might correspond to the two in front of the Insula Arriana Polliana (crosses 6 and 7), with an additional cross incised into the one intervening intersection (cross 8) in an effort to forge a single apotropaic curtain in front of those two insulae.[19] Or perhaps the addition of cross 8 signals the presence of Jesus-devotion within insula 6.8 or insula 6.10.[20]

Another scenario may also pertain to the crosses to the east of insula 6.6. Crosses 8 through 10 might extend the protection of a beneficent deity along the frontage of one or more of Pompeii's *vici* – neighborhoods or divisions into which the town had been divided. Just as Rome was divided into divisions, so too was this Vesuvian town. Pompeii demonstrates how a Roman urban center "developed and controlled religious cult [sic] at the level of the city's subdivisions, with a series of shrines set up at crossroads" and "a board of *magistri* for each ward (*vicus*) of the city."[21] Approximately three dozen shrines of this kind were erected at crossroads throughout Pompeii, functioning

---

18. A sistrum, or ritual rattle that was shaken in the worship of Isis, was found within the slave quarters of the House of the Faun, testifying to a slave's advocacy of a "mystery religion" within that household. Perhaps Jesus-devotion was also present in the same territory of the house. Or, as Balch intimates regarding houses intrigued by the Isis cult (2004: 41): "These households were open to a foreign, eastern religion from Egypt, perhaps then also to one from Israel?" For discussion of the shops lining the front of the House of the Faun, see Hoffmann and de Vos 1994: 80–82.
19. At the time of the eruption, the streets to the east and north of the House of the Faun had only just been repaved or were in the process of being repaved (see Poehler 2005: 4). While there is no reason to expect crosses necessarily to have been placed at those points, the recent repaving around the House of the Faun may be part of the equation.
20. Let us imagine for a moment that Jesus-devotion may have had some relationship to insula 6.8, the neighbor of insula 6.6. That might have taken one of two forms. First, insula 6.8 may have housed a Jesus-follower (or Jesus-followers) in one of its residences. Second, Jesus-followers may have met within its premises on occasion. The dining room in the House of the Tragic Poet (6.8.5), for instance, is ideally suited as a rental premise for associations to dine together. With this and other options in view, cross 8 may have served any number of functions and cannot be used to positively locate Jesus-devotees within insula 6.8.
21. Small 2007: 189.

JESUS-DEVOTION IN THE STREETS

as places of devotion to the respective deities and *lares* that oversaw the various districts.²² Inscriptions adjoining the shrines sometimes listed those who were responsible for donating the shrines, citing those benefactors as "the *magistri* of the neighborhood and of the crossroads" (*CIL* 4.60). It might be that the cross marks that stretch through region 6 were placed along the boundaries of districts, in imitation of the shrines that honored the district's guardian deities and *lares*, enhancing the prospects of the district's inhabitants.²³

What about crosses 11 through 18, incised in paving stones along Via Stabiana? Presumably, they were incised for similar reasons – that is, to enhance apotropaic protection in the area. Certain premises seem to have been targeted as benefitting from the apotropaic protection of the resurrected deity. A stretch of roadway along Via Stabiana was protected by cross apotropaia at intersections to the north (cross 11) and south ends (cross 18), together with other intersection crosses along the way (crosses 14 and 15). Within that hive of crosses were residences where, it seems, some Jesus-devotees must have resided. This includes the premises at 9.3.1–2 (protected by cross 12), at 9.3.5 (protected by cross 13), and at 9.1.12 (protected by crosses 16 and 17). (Note: The late inclusion of cross 19, mentioned in chapter 12, adds the shop at 9.3.8 or the bakery of 7.2.3 to this list as well.)

It is interesting to note that the crosses along Via Stabiana were incised into the paving stones of a neighborhood that is densely populated with street altars to the protective deities and spirits of the neighborhood. For instance, in precisely the same intersection where cross 15 resides, a public shrine was built into the southwestern exterior wall of 9.2 (see figure 13.8).²⁴ Moreover, in precisely the same intersection where cross 14 resides, a sizable triple-arched public shrine was built into the northwestern corner of 9.2, engulfing even

---

22. In fact, crossroads often included shrines to Augustus (or his *genius*), so that he was worshiped there along with the *lares* of the area. See, for instance, Welch 2007: 557; Laurence 1994: 40–42.
23. We know of the existence of at least four different districts (and there would have been others beyond these as well): the districts of the Forenses (near the Forum), the Campanienses (near the Nola Gate), the Salinienses (near the Herculaneum or Salt Gate), and the Urbulanenses (near the Sarno Gate).
24. See Fiorelli 1875: 142.

the Via Stabiana sidewalk within its boundaries (see figure 13.9). At the back of 9.2 along both the west and east sides of Vicolo di Tesmo were two other public shrines. Several entrances in the neighborhood were protected by phalluses built into nearby exterior walls (including 9.2.6, 9.2.7, and 9.1.13). This was clearly a neighborhood that was heavily fortified in the war against malevolent spirits. Evidently a Jesus-devotee (perhaps with other Jesus-followers in tow) imagined that crosses of Jesus-devotion would not go amiss in this area, enhancing the protective defenses in a neighborhood where such defenses were thought to be especially necessary.

Figure 13.8. The wall shrine on the exterior wall at the southwest corner of 9.2, close to cross 15.

Figure 13.9. The public shrine at the northwest corner of 9.2, close to cross 14.

We have seen, then, that there is a systematic pattern to these incisions, and that pattern best corresponds with an ancient view of space, malevolent spirits, and protection. The practice has an interesting parallel in the story of King Ahaz in the Jewish Scriptures. Depicted as a shameful king of the people of Judah, he is said to have raided the implements used for sacrifice in the Jerusalem temple and, closing up the doors of that temple, he "made himself altars in every street corner of Jerusalem" (2 Chronicles 28:24).[25] Seeking to shift the spiritual tectonic plates of his kingdom, King Ahaz commandeered street intersections as prime places to introduce new spiritual powers that he hoped would enhance his political power.

This story, although depicting a time preceding the Greco-Roman world, nonetheless reveals something of the ancient mind-set regarding street intersections. Unlike their mundane function in Westernized societies, in the ancient world street intersections lent themselves to spiritual warfare. To control the street intersections

---

25. The translation is the New International Version. The Hebrew of the Masoretic text reads: בִּירוּשָׁלַ͏ִם בְּכָל־פִּנָּה; the Greek Septuagint reads ἐν πάσῃ γωνίᾳ ἐν Ιερουσαλημ.

was to influence the welfare and well-being of those within the neighborhood.

This is why Greco-Roman crossroads were frequently adorned with shrines to the deities and benevolent forces (in particular, the *lares* of that particular place).[26] In popular first-century imagination, "daimonia and spirits ... haunted the crossroads of every Roman street"; this was a variation on the view held "throughout the Roman world" that "the intersection of two roads was ... the gathering place of spirits (*daemones*) of the underworld."[27] Like entryways and gates, the intersection of roads and even smaller streets were points of liminality – thin spaces where human life was vulnerable to the invasion of suprahuman spiritual forces and therefore required protective rituals or shrines.[28] One deity, Hecate, was particularly known for protecting crossroads (along with doorways and gates). She was thought to guide people through liminal and transitional places, protecting them from malicious spirits at those places and beyond (even accompanying human souls as they left their bodies and traveled through the spiritual realm back to their place of rightful abode).[29] First-century historian Plutarch notes that meals were often held at crossroads in honor of Hecate and other apotropaioi – that is, the deities whose role was to keep evil away from the area.[30]

Precisely this sort of thing was happening within Pompeii. So it has been said, "Like the houses, the streets in Pompeii belonged to the gods."[31] Or as Joanne Berry notes, the shrines in the crossroads of Pompeii "appear to have marked the different districts of the town and were dedicated to the guardian gods (*Lares compitales*) of each district."[32] As a variation on a common Greco-Roman theme, protective crosses that channeled the benevolent power of a resurrected deity

---

26. On crossroad shrines, see Small 2007: 184, 189.
27. Hubbard 2010: 17 and 25.
28. See especially Johnston 1991; also Palmer 1974: 112–20.
29. See again Johnston 1991. On Hecate, see Plutarch, *Regum et imperatorum apophthegmata* 193–94; Ovid, *Fasti* 1.141–43; Virgil, *Aeneid* 4.609–10.
30. Plutarch, *Quaestionum convivialum* 708–9. See also his *Quaestiones romanae et graecae* 290d; and Johnston 1991.
31. Etienne 1992: 125.
32. Berry 2007: 198.

were placed at street intersections in two Pompeian neighborhoods, calling on the guarding spirit of that deity to benefit those neighborhoods. Since they were not shrines, the crosses at street intersections functioned more like apotropaia that expunged evil and enhanced the security of the neighborhood.

We cannot assume that all Jesus-devotees in Pompeii sought to influence the spiritual dynamics of neighborhoods by incising crosses on street stones. (The Jesus-devotees protected by the *vivit* cross in 1.13 seem not to have copied the practice.) Nonetheless, Jesus-devotees in region 6 and along Via Stabiana seem to have utilized the cross as a means of enhancing their own security and, evidently, the security of their neighborhoods. If they had sought to bolster only their own security systems, a cross on the wall at liminal points within their own residences might have been sufficient. Perhaps, then, the paving-stone crosses served a dual and intertwined purpose of enhancing the security of their own residences and of the neighborhoods to which they belonged.

If this was the case, these people seem not to be huddling together in covert, disengaged cells. Their posture toward their contemporaries seems more in line with the apostle Paul's advice that Christians should "do good to one another and to all" (1 Thessalonians 5:15), or the Petrine author's command to "do good" (1 Peter 2:12, 20; 3:11, 16–17; 4:19) and to be a "blessing" within their indigenous contexts, actively seeking the welfare of their neighbors (1 Peter 3:9).[33]

The Return of the *Christianos* Graffito

At this point we can make a small aside in order to consider once again the *Christianos* graffito in light of these street incisions. The point is not their proximity to each other, although *Christianos* was inscribed in a residence only one street to the west of the Christian crosses on Via Stabiana (see figure 13.10). The point is that the person who inscribed *audi Christianos* on the wall of 7.11.11/14 may have been referencing

---

33. See, for instance, Shaw 2014.

the enhancement of neighborhood security in the first letters of the *Christianos* graffito.

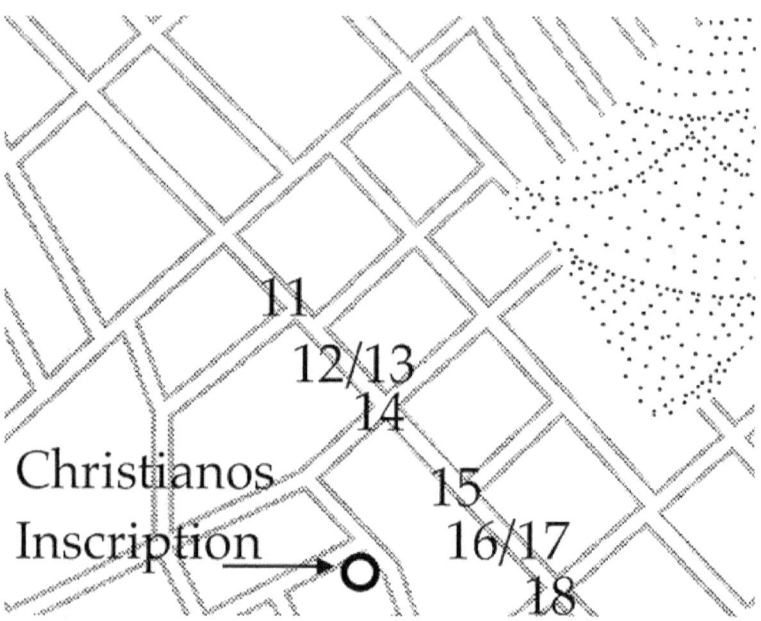

Figure 13.10. The eight crosses along Via Stabiana shown in close proximity to the *Christianos* graffito at 7.11.11/14.

We noted in chapter 10 above that the letters at the start of line 4 may originally have read *pro vicis*, "for the benefit of the districts" – an interpretation that, while not wholly compelling, is as good as any other on offer and, more importantly, does justice to the depiction of the graffito offered by two of the eyewitnesses to the artifact (Kiessling and Minervini). Against the backdrop of Pompeii's various districts, the *Christianos* graffito may include the recognition, or may advertise the conviction, that Christians in Pompeii sought to benefit the districts in which they were embedded.[34] This would give us a consistent reading of both the wall's inscriptional conversation and the street crosses. Prior to the addition of an insult about Christians being cruel (on the

---

34. Notably, this coheres well with the results of chapter 11, where we noted that the double circle at the start of line 5 gives the *audi Christianos* graffito a somewhat proclamatory tone.

right side of line 5), an inscriber urged that the Christian message should be heeded in order to benefit the districts of Pompeii (the whole of line 4) – benefits that derive from the beneficence of their deity, Christ, who gives eternal life (the apparent meaning of the double circle on the left of line 5).

These might be indications that Jesus-followers in Pompeii were like most other residents of Pompeii, in having "a close affinity to their neighborhood or *vicus*."[35] Jesus-followers might have been conscripting their crucified deity to serve in ways that approximated the function of the *lares* of a particular location – the protective spirits that were thought to safeguard certain domains (e.g., a residence, a district, etc.). Georges Dumézil's comment about the function of the *lares* (or here, the singular *lar*) within the Greco-Roman worldview helpfully illustrates the point: "whatever his place may be, the *Lar* is called upon to protect all the human beings in it, and men concern him as dwellers in or users of his domain."[36] Perhaps the crucified but resurrected deity was being called on to function in much the same way as the *lares* of the district.

It seems that the Jesus-devotees who incised crosses at strategic points in the streets of Pompeii imagined that resurrection power would envelop their earthly lives so that the forces of evil would not prevail against them in the places where they resided and worked. With these same incisions, they may also have sought to enhance the welfare of the town and its inhabitants by means of invoking that same protective power for the benefit of the districts in which they lived. It is possible that the *Christianos* graffito refers directly to that initiative.[37]

Crosses of Jesus-Devotion?

Here we can ask the inevitable question: Can these crosses be symbolic, perhaps even apotropaic, without any Christian dimension? Could they

---

35. Laurence 1994: 50.
36. Dumézil 1996: 342.
37. It needs to be noted that the identity of the street crosses as artifacts of first-century Jesus-devotion is in no way reliant on this interpretation of the *Christianos* graffito. The two are detachable, even if they nicely dovetail.

simply have reflected a common belief that the formation of two perpendicular lines in roughly equilateral relationship could be used as a protective device, without being attached to a particular set of religious beliefs (i.e., Christian) beyond that general sense?

That view is not adopted here. This is because the material record of Pompeii has already yielded evidence in which Jesus-devotion includes an apotropaic dimension and does so in relation to cruciform symbols. This is especially true for the *vivit* and the bakery crosses. And that the street crosses in region 6 encircle the Insula Arriana Polliana, where the Christian cross was prominently displayed, is a fact that should not be underestimated. Beyond that, we have seen that both the Meges ring and the *Christianos* graffito include a pre-Constantinian symbol that testifies to the Christian belief in eternal life. Further, as we have seen in chapters 5 and 6 above, evidence from the late first and early second century illustrates that Jesus-followers were already conceptualizing the cross as a theological symbol of protection by and identification with the Judeo-Christian deity (for example, the authors of the Johannine apocalypse and the *Epistle of Barnabas*). And further evidence from before the middle of the second century demonstrates that Christians were already embedding crosses into material realia for purposes of Christian identity and eschatological protection by the Judeo-Christian deity (for example, the author of 5 Ezra).

Accordingly, to postulate that the Pompeii street crosses have apotropaic significance but are not themselves symbols of Christian apotropaic interest would be analogous to using a drill to embed a nail; it just does not work that way, and if you work that approach too long, you end up making a real mess of everything.

It might be possible, of course, to suggest that the street crosses testify to Jewish interest in protection, without any Jesus-devotion in view. This would make them analogous to the equilateral lines found prominently displayed on some Jewish ossuaries in Jerusalem from the first century BCE/CE, in elaboration of the "mark" of protection mentioned in Ezekiel 9:4–6. But while a Jewish influence may not be an unlikely influence on some of the Pompeii crosses, it does not sufficiently explain all of the data. In fact, most of the artifacts in the main database cannot be sufficiently explained simply on the basis of a non-Christian interpretation of Ezekiel 9:4–6. Neither the bakery cross nor the cross in the Meges ring conforms to the expected shape of the "mark" of Ezekiel 9. The *vivit* cross may have conformed to the expected shape (if we are right in following Varone's diagram of it), but the coupling of life and cross motifs within it seems to be a sibling to the coupling of the same within the Meges ring, with its strong connections to other artifacts that reference Jesus-devotion (that is, the double circles of the *Christianos* graffito and the Ostia inscriptions). Accordingly, the full data cannot be interpreted without reference to Jesus-devotion. If there is a Jewish influence behind the adoption of the cross as a symbol of apotropaic protection among Jesus-followers in Pompeii, that is perfectly in keeping with the fact that the early Jesus-movement emerged from within the broad umbrella of Early Judaism. If it could be established that Ezekiel 9 had influenced the depiction of some Pompeian crosses, that would be an instance of Jesus-followers employing the rich resources of Jewish Scripture and tradition to articulate their theological worldview. Accordingly, to speak of a possible Jewish influence is not to deny that the street crosses were themselves the product of Jesus-devotion, and vice versa.[38]

The Issue of Waste

One further aspect of the street crosses needs to be considered. Does their position in the streets jeopardize the claim that they were incised as apotropaia of Jesus-devotion? After all, it is commonly imagined (aided, no doubt, by the efforts of sensationalistic tour guides) that the streets of Pompeii were awash with the defecation of humans and

---

38. As demonstrated in chapter 6 above, the same passage from Ezekiel would go on to influence Christian reflection on the signet ring of Israel's deity that affords protection to Jesus-followers (i.e., Revelation 7:2–3; cf. 9:4) and encourage Christians to mark the graves of the dead with the sign of the cross (5 *Ezra* 2:23). With those Jewish-Christian reflections emerging from the years 95 and 140 or so, the equilateral crosses of Pompeii might testify to the existence of a Jewish-Christian interpretation of the Ezekiel passage already in existence by the mid- to late 60s and popping up in subsequent generations of Christian reflection.

animals, and that the large stepping stones placed at street intersections (and elsewhere, although they are not evident at all in region 2) enabled people to move through the town without soaking their feet in excrement and filth (see figure 13.11). Are we really to imagine that these apotropaic crosses were incised in stones that were perpetually covered with layers of waste?

Figure 13.11. Stepping stones in the streets of Pompeii.

There are two dimensions to this issue: (1) waste in the streets of Pompeii, and (2) the nature of apotropaic effectiveness. Regarding the first, there are two sides to the coin regarding waste in the streets of Pompeii. It is without question that waste products were not absent from the streets of Pompeii. Along with by-products from businesses (e.g., bakeries, butchers, etc.), waste from residences and workshops would inevitably have been emptied in the streets. And sometimes particular places became favored spots for human defecation. One graffito near the Vesuvian Gate reads "Shitter, may everything turn out okay, so that you can leave this place" (*CIL* 4.6641). Elsewhere, another reads "Shitter beware of evil, or if you neglect this [and defecate anyway], Jupiter will be angry with you" (*CIL* 4.7716).³⁹ Obviously not all the human waste of Pompeii ended up in convenient places.⁴⁰ And clearly, the streets of ancient Pompeii fell far short of the standards of cleanliness evident in the tourist site today. To some extent and at different concentrations throughout the town, brews of waste concoction were not foreign to the streets of Pompeii.

Nonetheless, it also needs to be recognized that the objections of locals to the practice of defecating on the streets are understandable in light of the fact that Pompeii had other ways of taking care of most of its human waste. The streets of Pompeii were sunk deep and built wide not in order to contain the excrement of the town's human and animal population but to serve as runoff channels for the torrential rains that occasionally fall on the town. On those rainy days, huge basalt slabs (found primarily at intersections) functioned as stepping stones, enabling people to move through the town without having to traverse through the deep rain water that coursed through the streets.⁴¹

Pompeian streets were not, in fact, oozing septic tanks on the move.⁴² One of the most striking things about the Vesuvian towns is their sanitation system. Technology had long been in place that enabled proudly Roman towns to boast of a good level of sanitation.⁴³ This was true of Pompeii and its sister town Herculaneum as well, where most human excrement fell through downpipes into underground cesspits and (in a few sectors of the town) into sewers.⁴⁴

---

39. Two other graffiti with the simple message "Shitter beware of evil" (*CIL* 4.2, 4.7715) were also found in the same location – that is, in the alleyway between insulae 3.4 and 3.5. Interestingly, all of them are written in huge letters, the two shorter graffiti being roughly one meter (just over a yard) in height and covering about ten meters (eleven yards) of alleyway wall, the longer graffiti being smaller in height but about seven meters (seven and a half yards) in width.
40. So Koloski-Ostrow, 2015: 12: "many people were still using alleys or urban corners for their needs, others were probably more blatantly urinating against convenient building facades, and some had slaves with chamber pots."
41. So, for instance, Lessing and Varone 1995: 19.
42. Contra Ling 2009: 148: "[Pompeii's streets] were frequently deep in mire, and for the convenience of pedestrians there were regular crossing points formed by stepping stones."
43. Underground sanitation systems that moved human excrement to the sea have also been found in villages on the Orkney Islands dating to the third century BCE.
44. Jesus is remembered as saying that "whatever goes into the mouth enters the stomach and goes out into the sewer" (Matthew 15:17; cf. Mark 7:19). The imagery would have been perfectly understandable in a Romanized urban center like Pompeii (although "cesspit" would have done even better).

Many downpipes can still be seen throughout the town today – as in the Insula Arriana Polliana itself (for instance, in the wall at entryway 6.6.19, in the wall shared by 6.6.21 and 6.6.22, and in the wall shared by 6.6.22 and 6.6.23). As Paul Roberts notes, "[r]emarkably, almost every home in Pompeii has evidence of at least one latrine somewhere in its structure."[45] Moreover, public toilets permitting various users at one time were provided within the various baths dotted around the town of Pompeii – i.e., the Stabian, Suburban, Republican, Central (still unfinished at the time of the eruption), and Forum Baths. Public latrines could also be accessed in the Grand Palaestra, the theater, the Forum (adjacent to the granary), and even in the Praedia of Julia Felix (constructed in barrel-vaulted fashion). With good reason, then, Gemma Jansen sums up the situation noting that Pompeii "had several large and small public toilets and nearly every household had its own private one."[46] Or as Anna Olga Koloski-Ostrow notes, "Pompeii's sewer system demonstrates remarkable sophistication in water management."[47]

Further, much the same is evidenced in Rome, which Pompeii sought to imitate. The aediles of Rome were charged with ensuring that the streets of the city were kept in an acceptable fashion, and those whose premises bounded the streets were required to play a role in that process (CIL 1.593.20–55).[48] Suetonius tells us, for instance, that when Vespasian was aedile of Rome, "Gaius Caesar, incensed at his neglect of his duty of cleaning the streets, ordered that he be covered with mud, which the soldiers accordingly heaped into the bosom of his purple-bordered toga" (*Vespasianus* 5.3). Much the same seems to have been happening in Pompeii. The aediles of Pompeii were elected annually to oversee the upkeep of "the streets, and the sacred and public buildings" (see *CIL* 4.222; 10.885, 886, 890, 901).[49] Street cleaning

---

45. Roberts 2013: 261; see also Hobson 2009: 48. Roberts also notes that "the same high incidence of latrines has been confirmed by recent research in Herculaneum."
46. Jansen 2007: 262. Koloski-Ostrow agrees (2015: 5): "Pompeii had at least ten relief stations that appear to have been open to the public," with numerous latrines in private residences. As for private toilets, she notes (2015: 32–33) that "virtually every house in both Pompeii and Herculaneum had its own private toilet." See also Koloski-Ostrow 2007.
47. Koloski-Ostrow 2015: 76.
48. See, for instance, Wallace-Hadrill 2008: 300.

(perhaps by civic slaves under the aediles' direction, and by residents charged with the duty of street upkeep) would have included, among other things, removing animal excrement and, of course, some human waste as well. But street-cleaning initiatives within Pompeii would not have involved shoveling up the excrement of most of the human population; that excrement was largely in the sewers and cesspits below the town. So Jansen states the matter quite simply when noting that in Pompeii "excreta were disposed of in cesspits, and rainwater was carried away by the streets."[50]

This point is illustrated by other features of Pompeii's streets. Except in times of torrential rain, the streets were obviously used for cart access (as testified to by the deep wheel-cart grooves). The streets were also regularly used for pedestrian access.[51] This is seen in the lowered steps that were frequently carved into curbstones directly in front of residences, permitting easier access from the street onto the pavements – as is the case in front of the main residence in the Insula Arriana Polliana (see figure 13.12). Evidently people regularly stepped from the side pavements into the streets and vice versa – including residents and visitors to the most opulent of Pompeian houses. Moreover, we must imagine, as Alan Kaiser has noted, that shopkeepers would have exploited the sidewalks "for the display of their wares," causing people to walk "in the path of carts rather than on the sidewalks."[52] Further still, the marble inserts between the street stones in front of the temples to Apollo and Venus (as noted in

---

49. Martin 1990: 19: "Slaves owned by municipalities were used for many tasks, some of which were menial, such as collecting garbage, keeping the city clean, or building and maintaining roads." Ultimately, the oversight of this responsibility fell to the junior aediles. Roberts 2013: 48: "it was the responsibility of the magistrates to keep the city tidy and functioning well."
50. Jansen 2007: 264; see also 257, 262–63. Further, see Jansen 2000; Koga 1992. Cesspit waste was frequently harvested as fertilizer and sold to farmers, as evidenced by the Herculaneum inscription *CIL* 4.10606.
51. Contra Laurence 2008: 87.
52. Kaiser 2011: 95. He also notes that "the volume of cart traffic must have been small because few Romans could afford a cart and few locations within Pompeii offer facilities for storing them" (96). This is a corrective to imagining carts everywhere, but clearly carts were an essential part of the life of the city, and the adjective "small" is an underestimation. Kaiser is right to note, however, that the "transportation of goods by donkey or porter may have been attractive when loads were not too great" (96).

chapter 12 above) would have been added in poor judgment if Pompeii's streets were swollen with sewage runoff.

Figure 13.12. The lowered step cut into the curbstone directly in front of the entrance to the main residence of the Insula Arriana Polliana.

While it is true that Pompeian streets were not paradigms of cleanliness by twenty-first-century standards, human waste would have assaulted the nose far more than the eye, with many of the smells percolating up from below rather than issuing from festering feces on every street. Accordingly, there is little reason to think that these eighteen street crosses would have been consistently hidden from view. While it was inevitable that they would have been covered over occasionally, they would also have been exposed with some regularity. An interested party could easily have made sure of that, involving only periodic visits to the paving stones with a brush in hand.

The second aspect to consider in this regard is the nature of apotropaic devices. These small crosses in the streets may not have needed to be completely visible at all times in order to carry out their intended function. Apotropaic devices did not need to be perpetually visible to the human eye in order to perform their intended function. For instance, if a man's toga temporarily covered his serpent ring that enlisted the spiritual protection of Asclepius (see figure 13.13), that did not give malevolent spirits a moment of opportunity to strike. Or if the sleeve of a young girl's winter cloak extended past the protective phallic charm that her father gave her to wear on her charm bracelet (see figure 13.14; see also figure 11.8) or extended past the serpent bracelet around her wrist (see figure 13.15), she was not made vulnerable by that fact. Or if the phallic symbol in the street in front of 7.13.3 was temporarily covered by waste of some kind, there is little reason to think that panic would have ensued, in fear that the protective spirits had suddenly desisted from their benevolent function. The ancient mind did not imagine apotropaic devices to function in that fashion.

Figure 13.13. A serpent ring (date and provenance unknown).

Figure 13.14. A phallic charm (date and provenance unknown).

Figure 13.15. A serpent bracelet (date and provenance unknown).

So too, the cross-shaped patterns etched in street stones would have been perceived by those who incised them as imbibed with spiritual power regardless of whether they were perpetually visible. The apotropaic crosses were in operation whether or not they were temporarily unseen (as in the hours of darkness). These incisions on street stones would have been ill suited for any task that required them to be visible at all times – a requirement that did not apply to apotropaia.

For these reasons, the fact that these crosses were in Pompeii's streets is in no way detrimental to their apotropaic character. Their incisors knew that the crosses were there, and that fact alone helped to foster their sense of security, regardless of whether those crosses were always visible. Just knowing that small crosses of power were out in the streets near their residences evidently gave them comfort in a world where spiritual forces were always to be feared.

The Lacuna in Scholarly Discussion

Most artifacts of significance from the Greco-Roman world are subject to more than one interpretative possibility, and there is little reason to think that things might be different for the crosses found on the streets of Pompeii. Nonetheless, it is not at all apparent that interpreting the street crosses as expressions of Jesus-devotion is illegitimate. In fact, they seem to operate as siblings to the bakery cross on the one hand (not least in view of their proximity) and to the *vivit* cross on the other (due to their simple compositional form) – both of which are best recognized as artifacts of Jesus-devotion that served as protective and enhancing symbols. The claim would be beyond belief except for the fact that all other options are even less likely candidates for explaining the data satisfactorily.

But if this is the case, it is curious that these first-century crosses have not been included in previous rounds of scholarly discussion regarding the Pompeian material remains. What can explain that serious omission?

Several scenarios need to be considered in this regard. First, it seems that these first-century crosses have simply been overlooked. Anecdotal evidence might help to make the point. When discussing these cross marks with prominent Pompeii scholars, I have yet to encounter one who has seen the street crosses prior to our conversation about them. That is fair enough, since these small incisions are very hard to notice. The point is, however, that these marks have failed to come to the attention of scholars. This even includes scholars whose research has focused on the regions and, in fact, the very streets where those crosses have been inscribed. Apparently these small marks have simply not been noticed by those with the best-trained eyes.[53]

This anecdotal evidence couples well with Marriott's observations in the late nineteenth century. While Marriott noticed what we have called cross 16, he failed to notice cross 17, which lies only two feet away from cross 16 on a neighboring stone. This confirms his own comments about how hard it can be to recognize ancient marks in ancient stone.

A second scenario may also go some way toward explaining the failure of scholarly discourse regarding these marks in the streets. While it is true that these marks have been overlooked, on the occasion when one of them was noticed, it was also misidentified. The point concerns Marriott's 1895 discussion of cross 16. Although he depicted and described cross 16 correctly, Marriott claimed that it resided outside 9.1.8. But there are no cross marks in the street outside 9.1.8; in fact, cross 16 sits four doors away, at the entryway to 9.1.12.[54]

This error may look relatively insignificant, but it might have contributed somewhat to the neglect of the street crosses in scholarly discourse. Here's why. In 1909, the eminent archaeologist August Mau included in his supplement to volume four of *Corpus Inscriptionum Latinarum* an inventory of what he considered to be all the ancient marks incised into Pompeian stone – an inventory that serves as the gold standard for stone marks pertinent to the study of the Vesuvian towns. It is clear that Mau knew of Marriott's claim that a cross resides outside insula 9.1.8 on Via Stabiana (although it actually resided at 9.1.12). We know this because in 1895 Mau reviewed Marriott's book

---

53. See, for instance, the comment said to me by a surveyor, as recounted in chapter 12, footnote 18.
54. It is unlikely that Marriott was using a different enumeration system when he listed cross 16 as residing outside 9.1.8. Both 9.1.8 and 9.1.12 appear on Emil Presuhn's map of 1877, and both share characteristics that link them to the enumeration system that is still used today. So, in Presuhn's map, 9.1.8 appears across from a narrowed section of Via Stabiana, and 9.1.12 appears to the south of that narrowed section of street – in precise conformity the positioning of these two residences in today's enumeration system. The same enumeration system that Presuhn used also appears in Henry Thédenat's map of 1906. Accordingly, with maps on both sides of Marriott (temporally speaking) testifying to the use of the same enumeration system used today, there is no reason to think that Marriott was using a different enumeration system. He seems simply to have been mistaken.

in which cross 16 was listed as an ancient mark.⁵⁵ But cross 16 was not included in Mau's inventory of 1909. It is quite possible that Mau omitted the mark from his inventory because, looking for it outside 9.1.8 (in conjunction with Marriott's claim), he failed to find it there. Marriott's error may have had an unfortunate knock-on effect, with the result that the one paving stone cross that had been noticed prior to Mau's inventory of 1909 failed to get a foothold in that premier catalogue of Vesuvian realia.

Another scenario is also possible, however. Rather than a scholar's misidentification leading to the omission of cross 16 from Mau's inventory, it might be that Mau knew of cross 16 (outside 9.1.12) and decided not to include it because he did not think it was an artifact from the Greco-Roman world. If it looked to Mau like a Christian symbol, for instance, it would not have been allowed to pass through his interpretative filter. As noted in chapter 3 above, Mau did not believe that Christians populated the Vesuvian towns prior to the eruption of Vesuvius. It is important to recall why he held this view: because Tertullian had said that Christians did not reside in the Vesuvian towns.⁵⁶ (As we noted in chapter 2, Tertullian's claim was theologically motivated, driven by the needs of his apologetic interest in defending the legitimacy of Christianity.) In this scenario, if Mau had known of cross 16 (as pointed out by Marriott), found it outside 9.1.12 (despite Marriott), and interpreted it as a Christian symbol (unlike Marriott), he would have dated it to a posteruption context, since (as Tertullian stated) there were no Christians in Pompeii.

In this scenario, Mau might be seen as a victim of the interpretative deficiencies of his day – deficiencies already explored in earlier chapters of this book. Of course, the *vivit* cross would not be discovered until nearly fifty years after Mau's death in 1909, so not all of the interpretative deficiencies of his day can be attributed to assumptions poorly founded. And a systematic study of the eighteen paving-stone crosses considered above had not been undertaken prior to Mau's

---

55. See Mau 1895.
56. Mau 1902: 18.

inventory of 1909, so he cannot be held responsible for not knowing a study that would emerge more than a hundred years after his own inventory. Nonetheless, the point is that the interpretative ethos of his day may inevitably have left Mau without an adequate interpretative context in which to place ancient artifacts of this kind. Or as Milnor says in another regard, fresh ways of analyzing Pompeian evidence at times reveals how "certain disciplinary structures" inherited from the past prevented the material evidence from being interpreted in the most compelling fashion.[57]

In one way or another, then, the pieces of the puzzle fall into place to help explain the scholarly lacuna regarding Pompeii's street crosses. Mau, the august gatekeeper who drew up the inventory for future generations to consider, filtered the data through a defective perspective – a defect caused either by misinformation (i.e., Marriott's incorrect labeling of the location of cross 16), by poor judgment (i.e., adopting Tertullian as the final arbitrator of the matter), or by the interpretative deficiencies of his day. As a consequence, the paving-stone cross marks have eluded even the best-trained eyes. In a sense, those best-trained eyes have been trained by the best archaeologists of the past not to notice marks of this kind. When those marks are noticed, those best-trained eyes are trained to interpret them as anything but marks of first-century Jesus-devotion (for instance, "they must be survey markers").

Perhaps it is time to rethink whether we have inherited too much baggage from the best of the past. Rethinking that issue will cause us to repopulate the inventory of the ancient realia of Pompeii, and to do so in a fashion unencumbered by interpretations that derive to a significant extent from ill-founded claims of the past and about the past.

---

57. Milnor 2014: 224.

PART V

And So

"[A]s happens not infrequently in Pompeian studies,
errors have crept into the scholarly record
which persist as one generation of scholars
repeats incorrect information provided by the last."
(Milnor, *Graffiti and the Literary Landscape in Roman Pompeii* [2014], 15)

"Even the least philosophical of tourists visiting these sites
cannot quite escape unfashionable reflections
about good and evil,
and how they often come together."
(Grant, *Cities of Vesuvius* [1971], 7)

14

Belief and Skepticism

In *The Sign of Four* (1890), Sir Arthur Conan Doyle has his protagonist Sherlock Holmes make the following statement: "When you have eliminated the impossible, whatever remains, however improbable, must be the truth."

In the chapters above, five different types of evidence have been considered – the primary data in part 3 and supplemental data in part 4. When implausible interpretations are excluded from consideration, these artifact types (whether primary or supplemental) are best interpreted as first-century relics of Jesus-devotion in the town of Pompeii. In the order of consideration, these artifacts are:

1. the cross in the bakery of the Insula Arriana Polliana;
2. the *vivit* cross in insula 1.13;
3. the *Christianos* graffito of 7.11.11/14;
4. the Meges stamp-ring cross, along with a symbol of eternal life; and
5. the eighteen paving-stone crosses studied in chapters 12 and 13, with a nineteenth (cross 19) being added late in the research for this project.

In previous discussions of whether Christians resided in Pompeii, scholars have tended to do well simply to get as far as considering artifacts 1 and 3; on rare occasions, artifact 2 has been registered as a potential candidate, but without much cognizance of its import. I am unaware of any discussions of number 4. The same is true for the crosses in artifact type 5 (although Marriott discussed one of these crosses, albeit without considering the possibility of Jesus-devotion).

A word about the relationship of the primary and supplemental data sets is in order here. Placing the artifacts in a list, as I have done above, has the danger of eroding the distinction between primary and supplemental evidence. The primary data set carries the main argumentative force in the case for Jesus-devotion in the shadow of Vesuvius; the supplemental data set can be decoupled from the case without diminishing the force of the primary evidence. Nonetheless, we have also seen how the two kinds of evidence nicely nestle together, with the apotropaic street crosses of region 6 (i.e., part of the supplemental data set) converging around insula 6.6 and pivoting around the southwest corner of the insula – precisely the place where an apotropaic cross of Jesus-devotion resided on a bakery wall (i.e., part of the primary data set). So while the two types of evidence can be divorced from each other, they nonetheless make ideal partners.

It is also significant that these artifacts cross-reference each other in terms of their formation and/or function.

- The apotropaic function of the bakery cross overlaps with the same function for the *vivit* cross, the street crosses, and probably the cross in the Meges ring (thereby linking artifact types 1, 2, 4, and 5 above).

- The expanding edges of the bakery cross (in probable imitation of the Ankh) is shared also with the Meges stamp-ring cross (thereby linking artifact types 1 and 4).

- The double-circled "8" appears in three types of artifacts, all of which reference Jesus-devotion: the *Christianos* graffito, the Meges stamp ring, and Christian inscriptions from Ostia (thereby linking artifact types 3 and 4 with Christian inscriptions beyond the

Pompeian database, thereby providing an external interpretative control).

- As noted, the paving-stone crosses in region 6 seem to encircle the Insula Arriana Polliana, whose premises included a bakery in which a stucco cross hung in display (thereby linking artifact types 1 and 5).
- If the *vivit* cross was more like an equilateral cross than a body cross (as in Varone's drawn diagram), it conforms in its formation with the paving-stone crosses (thereby linking artifact types 2 and 5). Conversely, if it was more like a body cross than an equilateral cross, then it conforms in that regard with the bakery cross and the cross in the Meges stamp ring (thereby linking artifact types 1 and 2).

Not one of the artifact types is excluded from this cross-referencing phenomenon, whether drawn from the primary or supplemental data sets. We can move from one cross to any other cross through either a shared function or a shared form. And at one point, we can move beyond the Pompeian data (to Ostian data), thereby providing an external control on the interpretation of the Vesuvian realia.

Evidently, then, Jesus-followers not only shared a common interest in the cross as a symbol of their religious devotion (or one aspect of their devotion) but shared ideas about how to represent that symbol and how to put it to use. Jesus-followers residing in different parts of Pompeii seem to have been cognizant of one another and conversant with one another, feeding off one another's insights in exploration of their devotion to a crucified deity who, having been raised to life, brings life to his followers. This gives us a window into the interconnectedness of their lives. No wonder they could be known collectively as *Christianos*.

If we know that they were grouped together under the label "Christians," we also know where some of them lived. The *vivit* cross places Jesus-devotion in insula 1.13, while the bakery cross places it in the bakery at 6.6.17/20–21. We do not know the residence of the Jesus-follower who seems to have been known by the name Meges.

If the supplemental evidence is taken into account, it would seem that Jesus-devotion also resided in several other places throughout regions 6 and 9:

- street cross 3 places it in the small workshop and residence at 6.17.22;
- street cross 12 places it at a dyer's workshop and residence at 9.3.1–2;
- street cross 13 places it within the residence at 9.3.5;
- street crosses 16 and 17 place it within the residence at 9.1.12;
- street cross 19 places it either in the small workshop and residence at 9.3.8 or at the bakery and residence at 7.2.3.

While less evident, it is also possible that Jesus-devotion resided within the House of the Faun at 6.12.2 or in one of its outlying units (in view of street crosses 9 and 10).

Other artifacts that are sometimes suggested as indicators of Jesus-devotion in Pompeii have not been considered in this survey, since they do not enjoy a viable plausibility rating.[1] Undoubtedly there must be other cruciform-shaped objects among the realia of Pompeii, and it would be foolish to imagine that they too should automatically be included within the database of Pompeian Jesus-devotion on that basis. The case would need to be made afresh for each artifact individually, with the interpretative default being cautious skepticism unless the data tilt noticeably in favor of inclusion within the evidential database of Jesus-devotion within Pompeii.

To date, that evidential database consists of the bakery cross, the *vivit* cross, the *Christianos* graffito, the Meges stamp ring, and eighteen street crosses. With those twenty-two artifacts, the database of Christian artifacts from Pompeii outstrips the database demonstrating the presence of Jews within Pompeii. A graffito with the Jewish name "Martha" (*CIL* 4.5244, from 9.8.7), a charcoal graffito mentioning "Sodom and Gomorrah" (*CIL* 4.4976, from 9.1.26), a man whose

---

1. Some of these artifacts are listed above; see footnote 2 in chapter 3.

cognomen was Iudaicus (*CIL* 4.6990, from 6.16.30; see also 4.9757), one ring depicting a dove with an olive branch in its mouth, and a fresco of the wise judgment of Solomon in 1 Kings 3 (from 8.5.24, although the relevance of this painting for this issue is rightly disputed; see figure 14.1) – these are the most reliable data demonstrating that, as one scholar states, "Jews are well attested at Pompeii."[2] If the Jewish presence within Pompeii can be described as "well attested," by analogy the same claim can be made about the presence of Jesus-devotion in that same location. No longer can we say that even if there were Jesus-followers in Pompeii, "they have left (and indeed at this early date they could have left) no tangible trace that we can recognize."[3] To the contrary, they have left tangible traces, and we have been able to recognize nearly two dozen of them.

---

2. Small 2007: 195. Other proposed data are less secure. Amphorae marked *garum castum* might well have signaled "kosher garum" for a Jewish population (*CIL* 4.2569, 2611, 5660–62), but there are other options that make that identification problematic; see Curtis 2012. The attempt to reconstruct Hebrew names from Latin equivalents, as is frequently attempted by Giordano and Kahn 2001, is often spurious. Note, however, that the name "Maria" (*CIL* 4.1507, 4.1840, 1.7866, and 1.8224), which is frequently said simply to be the feminine form of Marius, might at times reflect Jewish origins instead. Mau (1902: 18) rightly made the point this way: "[The notion that Maria] is not the Hebrew name, but the feminine form of the Roman name Marius, is far astray. It appears in a list of female slaves who were working in a weaver's establishment, Vitalis, Florentina, Amaryllis, Januaria, Heracla, Maria, Lalage, Damalis, Doris. The Marian family was represented at Pompeii, but the Roman name Maria could not have been given to a slave." Mau concluded that "we have here a Jewish name." Other Jewish names might include *Iesus* (*CIL* 4.4287) and *Ieshua* (*CIL* 4.8010).
   Josephus tells us of two people who died in the eruption of Vesuvius, and at least one had Jewish identity or heritage (*Jewish Antiquities* 20:141–44). It is sometimes thought that the two who died in the eruption are Drusilla, a sister of Herod Agrippa, and her husband Felix, once a procurator of Judea. (According to Acts 23:12–24:27, Felix was the procurator who heard Paul's defense in Jerusalem and conversed with him "very often"; Acts 24:26.) But the one who died in the eruption is referred to as a "young man" and his wife, and it is unlikely that this descriptor could be used to describe Felix. The alternative, which makes better sense in the context, is that the two who were killed were the son of Felix and Drusilla, named Agrippa, together with his unnamed wife. Either way, someone with Jewish heritage died in the eruption, by the name of either Drusilla or Agrippa. My thanks to Mike Parsons for pointing out the likelihood of the Agrippa scenario. See Hornik and Parsons 2016: ad loc.
3. Ward-Perkins and Claridge 1976: 61 = 1978: 86.

Figure 14.1. The wise judgment of Solomon, from 8.5.24 (MANN 113197).

Accordingly, a notable list of artifacts shifts the burden of proof onto those who would continue to claim that "there is no firm evidence" of Jesus-devotion in the Vesuvian towns.[4] Thus far in the twenty-first century, only one lone voice has contested the consensus view. Recall this estimate from 2007:

> The evidence for Christianity in Pompeii and Herculaneum is of uneven value, and has been much debated, but when the more dubious arguments are discounted there remains a residue of archaeological documentation which should leave no doubt that there were Christians in Pompeii before the eruption.[5]

If the claim that "Christians were in Pompeii before the eruption" could be made in 2007, prior to the consideration of a much fuller inventory of relevant artifacts, it would seem all the more pertinent now. Since we do, in fact, have "a residue of archaeological documentation which should leave no doubt that there were Christians in Pompeii before the eruption," it is no longer an option to continue parroting out-of-date views on this matter, even if they once formed the consensus. To do so would simply be an exercise in replicating "group-think" mentality, based ultimately on romantic notions of the pristinely exclusivist nature of early Christianity (notions that ironically come to their fullest expression in the novelistic tradition of Pompeian fiction), rather than dealing with the hard realia of the historical record.

What then are we to make of the fact that the long-established

---

4. Ling 2009: 114.
5. Small 2007: 194.

consensus has held sway for such a long time? An analogy provides a way into that matter. On November 5, 2008, Queen Elizabeth visited the London School of Economics, where Professor Luis Garciano offered her an overview of the economic downturn that was to engulf most of the Western world in a financial tailspin for the next five years or more. Having been told about the various factors that had been building up for years prior to the economic catastrophe, the Queen asked Professor Garciano a simple question: "If these things were so large, how come everyone missed it?" In reply, Garciano told the Queen: "At every stage, someone was relying on somebody else and everyone thought they were doing the right thing."[6]

We might ask a similarly worded question: "If the historical record tilts the balance of probability toward the view that Jesus-devotion was present in Pompeii, how has the alternative view been able to command the consensus? How come everyone missed it?"

There is no grand conspiracy to be unmasked here. Scholars have been acting in accord with what they thought was "the right thing" – that is, they have gone where they thought the evidence had taken them. But it is also true that a certain amount of "passing on of the consensus view" (or in Garciano's words, "relying on somebody else") has taken place. There is obvious force in Thomas Kuhn's famous estimate that a scholarly consensus (i.e., a "disciplinary matrix" or "paradigm") "governs, in the first instance, not a subject matter but rather a group of practitioners."[7] This is, of course, inevitable. It is the way that scholarship progresses, and the way that advancement in intellectual history takes place. But occasionally that process of scholarly "governance" requires a shake-up, a reassessment of the situation. This is necessary when data makes a consensus problematic – either (1) old data previously moved to the periphery of a discipline's field of vision is brought back into the light and interpreted in accord

---

6. This was cited in the British newspapers on November 5, 2008. See also Zingales 2012: first paragraph of chapter 6 [no pagination].
7. Kuhn 1970: 180. Compare Max Planck's observation (cited by Kuhn 1970: 150): "A scientific truth does not triumph by convincing its opponents and making them see the light, but rather because its opponents die and a new generation grows up that is familiar with it."

with better interpretative principles, or (2) fresh data is introduced to a discipline's field of vision. The preceding chapters have shown the need for such a reassessment of the consensus, with both old and new data being placed "in a new system of relations with one another by giving them a different framework" of interpretation.[8]

The last days of Pompeii are as close as we can get within the pre-Constantinian age to the freedom of expression enjoyed by Christians in the Constantinian era. Perhaps those days also give us a foreshadowing of things to come in the Constantinian age, with the cross serving as a symbol of power against forces (here, spiritual; there, political) that were deemed to be detrimental to well-being.

Against this case, of course, some will prefer to keep repeating old mantras in support of the old consensus. "The cross wasn't a Christian symbol until the fourth century, so there can't be any Christian crosses in Pompeii." "Christians were in constant fear for their lives and would never have advertised their faith, so there can't be any Christian crosses in Pompeii." "Christian faith could not have appeared in a pagan context, so the bakery bas-relief stucco panel was a shelf holder." To perpetuate such refrains, however, would be to err with the doctrinaire, to prefer traditional dogma (albeit academic dogma) over the databases of pertinent evidence. The burden of proof, I propose, now rests with those who prefer to stick with dogma instead of data.

In summary, the old consensus is no longer viable, being highly unstable – much like Mount Vesuvius itself proved to be in 79. The only way the old consensus can stand with reference to Pompeii is if every single artifact presented in parts 3 and 4 of this book has been systematically misinterpreted. Even if only one of those artifacts has been correctly interpreted, the consensus view is no longer defensible. Some might find it easy to believe that all of these artifacts have no relation to Jesus-devotion. On this occasion, call me a skeptic, but I cannot conjure up the necessary belief.

---

8. Kuhn 1970: 85 (citing Herbert Butterfield). See also Hanson 1958: 4–32.

15

Here and Beyond

I now rest my case for the existence of Jesus-devotion in Pompeii, as testified to by a gamut of primary and supplementary evidence from that Vesuvian town. If the case has been made, there are, nonetheless, a few supplementary issues that require brief engagement at this point. Five such issues are registered here.

The Apotropaic Attraction of Jesus-Devotion

We have seen that the propensity of crosses in Pompeii gravitate around the use of the cross as an apotropaic symbol. The cross for which this is the least obvious is the cross in the stamp ring of Meges, but even that cross could easily have been devised to bring apotropaic protection to its wearer. In fact, three places where apotropaia were frequently found in the ancient world are precisely the three places that the Pompeii crosses are found: that is, at entryways, on jewelry, and at intersections.

- Whereas entryways were guarded by apotropaic devices of various kinds, Jesus-devotion left its mark in that same location within

Pompeii (the bakery cross together with street crosses 1, 2 3, 12, 13, 16, and 17, together with the late-noticed cross 19).

- Whereas jewelry would include charms and rings of apotropaic protection, Jesus-devotion in Pompeii includes a cross on a personal ring, perhaps for apotropaic defense (the Meges ring).
- Whereas neighborhood intersections were frequently adorned with phallic and snake apotropaia to increase levels of protection and well-being within districts, Jesus-devotion in Pompeii left its mark at these same strategic locations within the town (street crosses 4 through 11, 14, 15, and 18).

Evidently, then, Pompeian Jesus-followers made use of the cross in much the same way that their Greco-Roman contemporaries made use of noncruciform apotropaia.

This gives us unprecedented insight toward answering a question that has continued to perplex the historical mind: What was the attraction of Jesus-devotion for the average person in a Greco-Roman urban environment? Why would a Greco-Roman urbanite find appeal in a message about a Jew who was crucified in Jerusalem but raised to life by the deity of Israel? In view of the crosses of Pompeii, historians now have unique, unparalleled, and exceptional data from the ancient material record with which to address that question. That data suggests that, whatever oddities it might have been perceived to include and however much it might have seemed "foolishness" (1 Corinthians 1:18, 23; 2:14), the message of the early Jesus-movement was indeed seen as "good news" by some in the first century who understood it as a means of defense (both personal and corporate) against the foreboding suprahuman powers that were seen to shape so much of life. The testimony of the Pompeii crosses suggests that this apotropaic axis needs to be placed near the top of any explanation of the allure of the "good news" proclaimed by advocates of Jesus-devotion in the first century (and beyond). That allure lay precisely in the power expected to derive from Jesus-devotion, thereby increasing security in life and, ultimately, in the life beyond.[1]

When Did Jesus-Devotion Arrive in Pompeii?

The arrival of Jesus-devotion in Pompeii precedes the eruption of Vesuvius in the second half of 79. Most of the artifacts we have considered provide no specific clues as to when they appeared on the material realia of Pompeii. At least one street cross, however, offers us some traction in this regard. Incised where Via Consolare meets Vico di Mercurio, street cross 4 is embedded within the rut carved out by ancient cart wheels (as we saw in chapter 12 above). This characteristic enables us to pin down a rough approximation for the incision of that cross.

As we saw in chapter 13, Eric Poehler has demonstrated that Vico di Mercurio was changed from an eastbound to a westbound street at some point after the construction of the Central Baths began.[2] Can we, then, determine whether an eastbound or westbound direction of Vico di Mercurio's traffic best explains the location of cross 4? If so, we can arrive at an approximate date for that cross.

In fact, cross 4 is best explained as having been inscribed while Vico di Mercurio was an eastbound route. As carts entered the town through the Herculaneum Gate and moved south along Via Consolare, some turned east along Vico di Mercurio, where they would pass along the back of the Insula Arriana Polliana (avoiding the bottleneck south of cross 4 and north of cross 6 on Via Consolare). Placing an apotropaic cross in the wheel rut of that southbound-to-eastbound intersection makes perfect sense, as a means of "spiritually disinfecting" the traffic moving along the back of the Insula Arriana Polliana. There would have been far less impetus to inscribe an apotropaic cross in what had become a northbound wheel rut once Vico di Mercurio changed to

---

1. Of course other factors would have been involved too – not least a corporate life in which enriching relationships were initiated and support networks were maintained. What Small says of advocates of the mystery religions (2007: 200) may well apply to advocates of Jesus-devotion as well: "To a large extent they must have found comfort in the closed communities of the mystery cults that offered salvation. . . . [M]any ordinary people, especially slaves and freedmen, . . . must have found comfort and a new sense of identity in their ready-made societies." Note, for instance, the importance of care for the needy among early Jesus-groups; see Longenecker 2010.
2. Poehler 2005; 2006: 69 ("westbound during Pompeii's final phase").

a westbound route, with traffic predominately leaving the town in a westbound-to-northbound direction.

Accordingly, cross 4 makes much better sense when it is seen to predate the change in traffic direction along Vico di Mercurio. Prior to that change, incoming carts that turned along Vico di Mercurio almost inevitably came into direct contact with the apotropaic cross, with their wheels rolling over it as the cart moved along toward the back of the Insula Arriana Polliana. (There was, of course, no need for physical contact in order for the apotropaion to be effective, so cross 4 would have served the same purpose in relation to eastbound pedestrian traffic.) That situation ceased to exist when the construction of the Central Baths caused traffic problems and, as a result, Vico di Mercurio was changed to a westbound route.

We cannot know for sure when that change happened, but the westbound cart-wheel wear on the curbstones along Vico di Mercurio is significant enough to suggest that carts must have been moving westbound along that road for approximately a decade. Probably the traffic flow changed along Vico di Mercurio at some point in the late 60s or early 70s. This would place Jesus-devotion within the town by the late 60s.

Another street cross is also datable, using similar observations about the change of directional flow along streets in region 9. Cross 15 resides in a location that seems to target traffic flowing westbound-to-northbound through the intersection at Vico di Balbo/Via Stabiana (that is, between insulae 9.1 and 9.2). Tucked close to the side of Via Stabiana as if it were referencing Vico di Balbo, cross 15 makes better sense if it were incised after the change in traffic direction along that street. As Poehler has demonstrated, Vico di Balbo changed from an eastbound to a westbound street after the construction of the Central Baths. It is, of course, possible that cross 15 was incised to protect a residence to the east of Via Stabiana along Vico di Balbo, as cart traffic moved east along Vico di Balbo after leaving Via Stabiana (e.g., one of the four entrances from 9.1.30 through 9.1.34). In this scenario, cross 15 would have been incised prior to the change of traffic direction. But in view of the concentration of crosses along Via Stabiana, it is more likely that cross 15 was incised to offer protection to Via Stabiana. This means that cross 15 was probably incised in reference to westbound traffic turning north onto Via Stabiana from Vico do Balbo – a situation that arose only after the construction of the Central Baths. Situated so as to connect with westbound-to-northbound traffic, the purpose of cross 15 was to add protection as westbound traffic along Vico di Balbo spilled out and headed north along Via Stabiana, where Jesus-devotees are now known to have lived. This means that we can date the crosses along Via Stabiana (assuming that they were all incised at roughly the same time) a few years later than cross 4. Between the incision of cross 4 and the incision of cross 15 lay the onset of the construction of the Central Baths.

Dating the Via Stabiana crosses to the time after the construction of the Central Baths concurs with conclusions drawn in chapter 12. There it was noted that the absence of the cross at Vico 9.3/9.4 may well be explainable by the minimization of that route once the Central Baths were constructed. None of the other artifacts of Jesus-devotion are datable, however, except by way of speculative scenarios pertaining to cross 4 (by the late 60s) and cross 15 (sometime within the 70s).

How did Jesus-Devotion Spawn within Pompeii?

Although Jesus-devotion is evident in region 6 by the late 60s, we cannot be sure how it arrived there.[3] Nonetheless, some aspects of

---

3. Earlier I considered options in which Jesus-devotion may have arrived from Puteoli or Rome (Longenecker 2015: 144–47). Another interesting option is that it may have arrived from Jerusalem. One possibility is as follows. Jewish Christians in Jerusalem found themselves unable to participate in the rebellion against Rome (66–70 CE) and, experiencing disdain, relocated elsewhere early in that rebellion (so Luke 21:20–21), some perhaps going to Italy. Connections between Jerusalem-based Christianity and Rome-based Christianity had been notably strong prior to the destruction of Jerusalem (see, for instance, Richard Longenecker 2011: 67–84) but Christians in Rome were being persecuted by Nero at precisely the time when Jerusalem-based Christians were relocating (say, 67–68 CE), so Italian urban centers other than Rome were clearly preferable, and Pompeii might have been one such locale. There they would be known as Christians who did not take arms against Rome, which would not have hurt their reputation among the majority of Pompeii's residents. The attraction of this scenario is that it would link the Pompeii crosses to the "Jewish cross" of Ezekiel 9, evidenced on Jerusalem ossuaries of this time and soon to be referenced in the Christian text of Revelation not much later. It would also correlate with the appearance of the Christian cross in Pompeii by the late 60s. This scenario would require further

the spawning of Jesus-devotion within Pompeii might have looked something like this.

The bakery at the southwest corner of the Insula Arriana Polliana probably served as a base for Jesus-devotion within Pompeii.[4] Either the Ankh-like cross on the wall of the bakery or (some of?) the ten street crosses of region 6 may have been the first material signs of Jesus-devotion within Pompeii. A good number of the street crosses of region 6 appear to have been incised in a pattern encircling the Insula Arriana Polliana by the late 60s. They may have been thought to increase security within the neighborhood as well. Some crosses may have been added later (perhaps cross 3 outside 6.17.22).

We cannot know the date for the construction of the bas-relief cross that appeared on the wall of the bakery. It may have predated or postdated the street crosses of region 6.[5] With the Ankh-like cross on the wall at the time of the eruption, we can assume that this baker had been operating in the same location from at least the late 60s (as testified to by street cross 4) right up to 79 (as testified to by the cross on the wall). That ten-year longevity attests to his success in business – a fact that might have played a role in the spawning of Jesus-devotion with Pompeii. If Jesus-devotion was advertised as a deterrence against malady and a promotion of the good, the baker's own long-term success in business might have been pointed to as evidence of that fact. "It works for me," he might have been heard to say to others, articulating the success of his apotropaic faith.

With a strong foothold in the Pompeii bakery, Jesus-devotion began taking root elsewhere within the town. Someone in insula 1.13 ingeniously embedded a cross of protection into a graffito that declared "he lives" (*vivit*) in relation to the one who had died on a cross. Meanwhile, an artisan in 6.17.22 (a self-contained room presumably

---

demonstration, but I mention it here as a potentially fruitful alternative to the Puteoli and Rome scenarios.
4. It was large enough to serve as a place of gathering, and its space was not complicated by use within a large household, which might have impeded the privacy and/or intimacy of the gathering of Jesus-devotees.
5. Incidentally, stucco decoration "is one of the most significant aspects of the artistic production" during the last quarter-century of Pompeii's existence (i.e., during the "Fourth Style" of artistic decor); so Lessing and Varone 1996: 142.

rented by the householder of the magnificent three-level house at 6.17.23/25) adopted the baker's devotion, as testified to by street cross 3. As street crosses 9 and 10 might testify, a few Jesus-followers may have resided within insula 6.12 – either as residents in one of the shops on the insula's outer ribbon or as slaves within the House of the Faun (with other slaves in that household being devotees of Isis, as noted earlier). Jesus-devotion also spread into other residences along Via Stabiana. Cognizant of the street crosses of region 6, those Jesus-followers incised similar equilateral crosses within the street's paving stones for similar apotropaic protection of their residences and, perhaps, their local district. Their efforts were thought to help fortify a dyer's shop (cross 12 at 9.3.1–2), a nearby residence of notable size (cross 13 outside the House of Lucretius at 9.3.5), a residence just south of that (with the late-acquired cross 19 outside either the shop at 9.3.8 or the bakery at 7.2.3), and another residence further down the street (crosses 16 and 17 at 9.1.12).

Toward the tail end of Pompeii's existence as a viable Greco-Roman town, someone in 7.11.11 wrote a graffito making reference to Christians, who had made their presence known within the neighborhoods of Pompeii. That graffito also advertised a curious double circle (together, perhaps, with the Greek letter chi, for "Christ"). The same double circle also made its way onto the stamp ring of a Jesus-follower by the name Meges. He was probably a slave (his ring shows no sign of his name having been changed upon manumission), but one with enough influence in a Pompeian household to conduct business on behalf of his master. This Jesus-follower linked a cross with the double circle in order to associate Jesus' death with an affirmation of life (much like the linking of death and life motifs within the *vivit* graffito). The double circle was not to have much longevity as a Christian symbol, although it pops up as such within the material record of Ostia about two centuries later. Evidently, one symbol of Jesus-devotion within Pompeii was shared by other Jesus-followers on the Italian peninsula and, for that reason, survived for a time within pre-Constantinian Christianity instead of being eliminated by the eruption of Vesuvius.

A Laboratory for Historical Study

It has been said that historians "have more information about Christianity in Corinth than in any other first-century city."[6] This was true when it was written in 2010. It remains true in relation to the literary evidence testifying to the development of Christianity in that city over the second half of the first century – texts such as 1 Corinthians, 2 Corinthians, and *1 Clement*. But the urban center about which we now have the most material evidence pertaining to Jesus-devotion is not Corinth; instead, it is Pompeii. We do not know where Jesus-followers resided in Corinth; we know where they lived in Pompeii. We have no material data from Jesus-followers in Corinth; we have artifacts left by Jesus-followers in Pompeii. We cannot reconstruct the specific environment in which Jesus-followers lived in Corinth; we can make good headway into the specific environment of Jesus-followers in Pompeii (since in this regard I have only scratched the surface).

In fact, in some ways Pompeii presents itself as a new laboratory in which to undertake experiments regarding early Jesus-followers and the attractions that the good news of the early Jesus-movement might have offered first-century audiences. How Jesus-followers might have found attraction in the "good news" of the early Jesus-movement, how they conducted their meetings, how they might have related to one another and to outsiders, and how they might have read Christian texts circulating among early Jesus-groups – these have all been given close attention in scholarly literature focusing on the first urban Christians. Those interests might now be better served by reframing inquiries of this sort in relation to the hard data of Jesus-devotion that Pompeii provides.

This is, for instance, where we might try getting clarity on the

---

6. Hubbard 2010: 3.

matter of exclusivism and syncretism (to name just one among many potential areas of consideration). What were the chances that Jesus-devotion in Pompeii conformed to apostolic expectations regarding exclusive allegiance to Jesus, especially when Jesus-groups there may not have enjoyed a strong apostolic presence or influence? To what extent would a "cultural drag" have been inevitable among Jesus-followers who lacked a notable apostolic influence?

There must have been a hundred and one permutations to this. Several scenarios help to demonstrate how those permutations might have been in play among Jesus-followers in Pompeii.

We start where we already began considering this issue – that is, in the Insula Arriana Polliana bakery. We have seen that the bakery cross is difficult to pin down on a scale ranging from exclusivism on one hand to syncretism on the other. We can, however, ask further questions regarding the baker (probably a freeman or a freedman). Was the small lararium in the oven room left vacant after the baker devoted himself to the crucified but risen deity? Or did bronze figures of deities still reside there until the eruption of Vesuvius – figures of the baker's own choosing? Did the baker place any trust in "the divine protection of Fascinus," represented by the phallic symbol above his oven? Did he continue to revere the protective spirit (represented by a snake) that overlooked his baking ingredients next to the bakery oven? Moreover, if the bakery provided ample space for a weekly gathering of Jesus-followers, would they all have shared the same perspective regarding the "pagan" features of the bakery?

We might ask similar things about the apostle Paul, who embedded himself in workshops during his stay in urban centers around the Mediterranean basin.[7] Inevitably those workshops would have exhibited artistic or architectural features that ran contrary to Paul's exclusivist Jesus-devotion, but can we really imagine him having those features removed from the workshop to suit his particular brand of Judeo-Christian religiosity? More likely, Paul simply adopted an apathetic attitude toward those features (compare his advice to

---

7. We see this, for instance, in Acts 18 and elsewhere.

Corinthian Jesus-followers in 1 Corinthians 8:4–6) and/or used them as teaching props to bolster the good news that he proclaimed. Might Paul's example provide a parallel to the baker's situation?

What might we say about the slave Meges? With symbols of Jesus-devotion taking a prominent position on his stamp ring, and without any other signs of religious affiliation, we can be fairly sure that this Jesus-follower was content to align himself prominently with the Christian deity. But questions immediately present themselves. Could this enslaved Jesus-follower have forsaken all other forms of religious affiliation, even if he were disposed to do so? If we also assume that his master was not a Jesus-follower, Meges would have found himself in a highly conflicted situation if he tended toward exclusive devotion to Jesus. As a member of a household, Meges would have been expected to participate in the religious observance of his non-Christian householder.[8] Did Meges cross his fingers when the household gathered around the lararium to offer sacrifices to the householder's chosen deities?

Perhaps the "apostolic voice" regarding exclusive devotion mixed in Meges's head with other articulations of the apostolic voice that may have complicated the situation. For instance, Meges may have heard through the grapevine that a prominent Christian apostle had charged his communities *not* to avoid contact with non-Christians, but to be fully engaged with them, even "the immoral of this world, or the greedy and robbers, or idolaters" (1 Corinthians 5:10). Or perhaps he had heard the apostolic instruction that Jesus-followers are to "remain in the condition" that they were in when they became Christians – whether that condition was freedom or slavery (1 Corinthians 7:24). Or maybe he had heard that the apostolic voice charged female Jesus-followers to remain married to their nonbelieving husbands (1 Corinthians 7:13; 1 Peter 3:1–2). No stipulation is attached to that instruction. We might have expected the apostolic directive to include an important antipagan qualification: "If her husband agrees to empty the household lararium of all of its deities, then she may stay with

---

8. On slaves being expected to participate in household worship, see, for instance, Rives 2007: 121.

him, even if he is unbelieving." Instead, female Jesus-followers are simply to remain married to a pagan, idol-worshiping husband. In fact, the husband and the offspring of that marriage are said to be made "holy" as a consequence of the wife remaining with her pagan husband (1 Corinthians 7:14)![9] If that was true for the wife, might a similar sanctifying influence pertain to a slave? That would at least cohere with the apostolic instruction that Christian slaves should obey their "earthly masters in everything, . . . wholeheartedly, fearing the Lord" (Colossians 3:22; cf. Ephesians 6:5–6; 1 Timothy 6:2; Titus 2:9) – a directive reinforced by a second prominent Christian apostle who commanded that slaves should "be subject" to their masters "with all reverence, not only to those who are good and gentle, but also to those who are perverse, for this is what finds God's favor" (1 Peter 2:18–19).[10]

How might Meges have tried to negotiate these confusing relational permutations? Should we expect Meges to have exemplified a clarity of monotheistic resolve that outstripped the lack of conceptual clarity within the growing traditions of the early Jesus-movement? This would probably be too much to expect.

The Jesus-followers residing in 6.17.22 (protected by cross 3) might have enjoyed a less complicated situation if they, like the baker (we assume), were free or freed. If we imagine them within a small household of their own, they could have been unconstrained in their Jesus-worship, with an exclusive commitment to their risen deity emerging relatively freely, if they were so inclined. Perhaps their petite residence would have served as a base for a small group of Jesus-followers devoted to their crucified deity of life. (The same might also

---

9. On this fascinating passage, see especially Hodge 2013. On page 244, she concludes noting that in the second and third centuries many "unpublished" Christians "recognized in 1 Corinthians 7:12–16 a scriptural warrant for their mixed marriages, and attempted to integrate their faith and practices into their polytheistic households." She continues: "the ancient household . . . may have lent itself to the sort of mixing of religious traditions that would have been involved in such marriages, . . . [because] . . . boundaries were not always clear between Christians and non-believers."
10. I am, of course, conscious that these stipulations derive from texts whose dating is disputed. I imagine that Colossians dates to the time between the mid-60 and the mid-70s, while Ephesians dates to the time between the mid-60s and the mid-80s. First Peter may be from a slightly later period, but even so, it records a view whose origins precede the composition of the text. These articulations of "the apostolic voice" may already have been circulating in the 70s, in either written or oral form.

have been true of those of 1.13 who were protected by the *vivit* cross, although their residential situation remains unclear.)

The likelihood is that some Christians were exclusive in their devotion to their crucified deity. This is probably reflected in the adjective "cruel" that was likely used against them in CIL 4.679. That adjective seems less suited as a chide of polytheistic Jesus-followers and more suited as a chide of Jesus-followers whose devotion was exclusivist in character. Unlike a syncretistic Jesus-devotion, an exclusivist Jesus-devotion would have run against the grain of polytheistic culture, being seen as holding back civic progress by compromising the worship of the civic deities. If Christians were later deemed "atheists" because of their failure to participate in standard forms of worship, perhaps some Christians in Pompeii were deemed "cruel" for similar reasons. In plotting estimates of Jesus-devotion on a scale of syncretistic to exclusivism, at least some Jesus-followers in Pompeii seem to have positioned themselves somewhere toward the exclusive end of that continuum.

A different scenario might have pertained to the Jesus-devotee(s) who resided in 9.3.5, the House of Lucretius (where cross 13 was placed). Within that grand house, archaeologists recovered small figures of Jupiter, Hercules, Isis, another deity (either Asclepius or Neptune), and a household *genius* in a small peristyle lararium.[11] Was the Jesus-follower in 9.3.5 the householder himself? If so, he seems only to have added Jesus-devotion to the mix of his otherwise typical worship practices within his household. However, the Jesus-devotee in 9.3.5 was more likely to have been a lesser member of the household, probably not a member of the householder's family but, instead, a slave (or slaves, but I will retain a singular referent for convenience). There is no way a slave could have maintained exclusive devotion to Jesus while continuing the practices required of him/her within the household. The same would have applied to the enslaved Jesus-devotee(s) who, if our suspicions are correct, may have resided in 6.12.2

---

11. Boyce 1937: 82, no. 406.

(the House of the Faun), and perhaps to someone similarly entrenched within the house at 9.1.12 (where crosses 16 and 17 are embedded).

Could such slaves have enjoyed corporate fellowship with other Jesus-followers beyond their households? Could they have extracted themselves from their households in order to attend a celebration of Jesus-worship beyond the households to which they belonged?

Answering this fully would require a good degree of nuancing that would take us too far afield at this point. It is fair to say, however, that such a scenario would have been possible in many cases. There were, of course, different kinds of slaves embedded within different kinds of situations. Some held positions of some prominence and authority within households, while others simply carried out menial tasks. If we imagine the slaves in insula 6.12 and 9.3.5, for instance, to have been menial slaves, their contact with Jesus-followers beyond the household might only have been sporadic at best.

Other situations are just as viable, however, especially for supramenial slaves within a household. Contrary to our stark impressions of ancient slavery, many supramenial slaves seem to have been allowed certain levels of autonomy, enabling them to pursue involvements beyond the household. At a most basic level, for instance, this is testified to by Pompeii graffiti proclaiming love or sexual relations between slaves embedded within different households.[12] But it is also evident in other ways as well. The business tablets of Pompeii's prosperous auctioneer-banker Caecilius Jucundus include five financial arrangements undertaken by a slave, Hesychus. Of those five transactions, two were undertaken on behalf of Hesychus's master and three were undertaken on behalf of Hesychus himself, including the lending of sizable amounts of his own money (no doubt, officially part of his *peculium*) to a free(d)man.[13] Clearly Hesychus the slave had time for his own pursuits beyond his obligations to his master's household.[14]

---

12. This seems to be the scenario behind *CIL* 4.8171: "Nicopolis, you've been fucked by me and Proculus and Fructus from the household of Holconius." Perhaps also *CIL* 4.2457: "Methe of Atella, slave of Cominia, loves Chrestus. May Venus of Pompeii smile favorably on their hearts and let them always live in harmony."
13. See Martin 1990: 18–19.
14. See also *CIL* 4.3340.6, which reads as if Salvius (identified as a slave of the heirs of Numerius

This is precisely the scenario represented in Jesus' parable of the unmerciful slave (Matthew 18:23–35).[15] In that narrative, a slave is required to repay the great sum of money that he owed to his own master – the money evidently having been given as a business loan (a situation that rarely appears in our conceptualization of ancient slavery). Having received mercy from the master, the slave goes and requires a fellow slave to pay back a smaller sum of money that the fellow slave owed him. While the parable displays signs of hyperbole, the situation must have been realistic enough in its basic contours to have been recognizable to a first-century audience. The situation of the slave described by Jesus would not have come close to the experiences of many menial slaves, but some slaves nonetheless enjoyed clearance to undertake initiatives of their own. As Dale Martin notes, many slaves at the upper end of the household structure "lived very much like most of the free population surrounding and mingling with them," even being "fairly independent of their owners' day-to-day control."[16] Some slaves even lived apart from their master in order to conduct business on the master's behalf – no doubt conducting some business for themselves at the same time.[17]

Managerial slaves, then, would have had enough freedoms to permit some movement beyond the master's household. And perhaps lesser freedoms were extended to other enslaved members of households. But one way or another, it is not a stretch to imagine that certain slaves within non-Christian households had the occasion to embed themselves within Jesus-groups beyond their master's household (a scenario that seems to be assumed in 1 Peter 2:18–21, for instance).

The same was all the more true for ex-slaves, of course. Perhaps this is how we are to imagine those Jesus-followers who understood

---

Nassenius Nigidius Vaccula) were performing a business transaction of his own rather than for his master's household. The pertinent part of the transaction record reads "I have received from Lucius Caecilius Iucundus on account of my auction the sum" (translated by Cooley and Cooley 2004: 184). Along other lines, it is interesting to note that one slave (Nymphius) conducted business on behalf of his master (Junius Aquila) in the very act of auctioning himself off to another master; see *CIL* 4.3340.7, as discussed by Keegan 2014:240–42.
15. This was helpfully pointed out to me by Lyn Osiek.
16. Martin 1990: 3.
17. See Martin 1990: 2–3, 189.

themselves as beneficiaries of the apotropaic protection offered by cross 12 outside the dye shop at 9.3.1–2. The residents there might well have been former slaves of the householder in the insula's main residence (9.3.5), remaining clients of their former master, who subsequently acted as their patron.[18] In this scenario, those Jesus-devotees would have been free agents, despite their ongoing responsibilities toward their former master. Moreover, being on the periphery of their former master's household in 9.3.5, they would have enjoyed access both to members within that household (where a slave may have advocated Jesus-devotion) and to other Jesus-followers elsewhere in the town.[19] Perhaps, as an outpost of the household based in 9.3.5, the Jesus-followers in 9.3.1–2 could host a Jesus-group that allowed the slave in 9.3.5 to worship with other Jesus-followers beyond the household of 9.3.5.

These are just a few scenarios that the Pompeii laboratory enables us to ponder. Other scenarios are possible and should be considered, but this is not the place for that.[20] The task of testing scenarios requires a larger cadre of informed discussion partners, if our Pompeii laboratory is to prove beneficial in efforts to refine our understanding the emergence of the early Jesus-movement. The task of testing scenarios

---

18. Sometimes slaves and former slaves resided in business properties owned by their masters or former masters (respectively). That the dyer's shop was in the same insula as the House of Lucretius makes this a viable prospect, since there would seem to be precedent for the same elsewhere in Pompeii. As Oakes notes, for instance, 1.10.6 is an ideal candidate for this, in relation to 1.10.4 (2009: 8). Similarly, 7.4.59–62 looks to have been a bronze worker's complex (see Gralfs 1988: 71–75). It probably began life in a single property (say, 7.4.59) and progressively expanded to the adjoining properties (say, 7.4.62, with a new property being created between them at 7.4.60–61). The purchasing of adjoining properties might explain the relationship of the crosses outside both 9.3.1–2 and 9.3.5. On relationships within 9.3, see Viitanen and Ynnilä 2014. They note (2014: 151) that the shops originally connected to 9.3.5 (and 9.3.15) "were originally connected with the main house and only later on made physically separate entities," and that in this way "the separation of the elite house and the commercial activity was made clearer, although the ownership of the property continued unchanged."
19. This scenario would also apply if, instead of being former slaves of their master in 9.3.5, they remained slaves within his household, but slaves who frequently operated beyond the master's place of residence.
    Scholars have at times linked 9.3.1–2 with the dyer's shop directly across the street, at 7.2.11, imagining that the same person owned both dye complexes (e.g., Fiorelli 1875: 184–85; Maiuri 1957: 126; della Corte 1965: 156). As Moeller points out, that both were dyer's shops is "hardly a sign of common ownership" (1976: 36). Moreover, it was often the case in urban centers that those belonging to the same profession would operate out of properties that were in close proximity to each other; see Kloppenborg 1996: 24.
20. For instance, I have not been able to incorporate the late-acquired cross 19 into this scenario.

also will involve correlating the literary corpus of early Christianity with social realities on the ground. As Peter Oakes articulates the point, "surely the primary task of the commentator is to investigate what the [text] would have meant in practice," which includes relating the text "to a fairly detailed examination of its socio-cultural context" and exploring how it "would be received" by those whom we know to have been among its primary audiences.[21]

Oakes has been at the forefront of this enterprise, asking how particular texts could have been interpreted by Jesus-followers in particular locations.[22] In one of his projects, he deftly builds up character portraits of people from Pompeii and transfers them to Rome in order to read Paul's letter to Christians in Rome through first-century eyes. But that kind of project can now be much more straightforward in its execution. Since Paul's letter to Jesus-followers in Rome no doubt circulated beyond its original recipients, we can simply ask how that letter might have been heard by the various Jesus-followers of Pompeii about whom we now know a little bit. That exercise, in turn, might help us to reflect more practically on how aspects of that letter would have had particular force in a first-century urban context. This, in turn, might enable us to craft a better understanding of the rhetorical context of the text. In particular, we could explore the extent that a text's reception by ordinary people like the Jesus-followers of Pompeii might have played a role in influencing what was written and how it was presented.

Exercises of this sort, which could well represent a growth point in the study of early Christianity, will go beyond Paul's letter to Jesus-followers in Rome, of course, and will include other genres beyond epistolary texts. They will include, for example, narrative Gospels, not least Mark's Gospel, which was composed probably a decade or so before Vesuvius's eruption and may have circulated widely among early Jesus-groups after its composition.[23] About this Gospel we have

---

21. Oakes 2009: 176, 178.
22. Oakes 2001; 2009. See also Jewett 2007.
23. Regarding the widespread circulation of Gospel narratives among Christian communities, see especially Bauckham (ed.) 1997.

been told, "Readers need...to use knowledge of the first century to understand the story in light of its cultural and political context, and to test interpretations."[24] Similarly suggestive is Richard Hays's perceptive comment that "Mark has crafted the story to gain hermeneutical control over the traditions of Jesus as miracle-worker." Traditions of this kind might have been precisely the sort of thing that gained traction in Pompeian Jesus-devotion, where apotropaic benefits of Jesus-devotion are at the forefront. Perhaps urban Jesus-groups like those in Pompeii were what the first evangelist had in mind when he sought to "control...traditions of Jesus as miracle-worker." The Markan evangelist wanted to ensure that traditions about Jesus as "divine protector" (which might be an improvement on the term "miracle-worker") needed to be placed in a larger narrative, and one that included the formation of communities in relation to the full narrative of their protector deity's own sufferings and apocalyptic triumph.[25]

Pauline studies are especially primed and ready to move forward in applying *realia* from Pompeii to the interpretation of early Christian communities. Recently, for instance, it has been said that Pauline scholarship has reached "a very opportune time" in which "new currents of scholarship are reassessing the Roman context of Paul."[26] Another voice has called scholars to ground our interpretations of Paul "more securely in the actual realities, so far as we can assess them, of Roman life and culture."[27] Such voices are hardly novel.[28] Although we may regret the extent of our ignorance about the urban centers where Paul based himself, that deficiency (we have recently been told) "can be made good, to some extent at least and with due caution,

---

24. Rhoades, Dewey, and Mitchie 2012: 153-54.
25. For an early exploration of this issue, see Longenecker 2016b. Hay's quotation is from 1996: 80.
26. Harrison 2014.
27. Wright 2013: 312.
28. Compare Judge's estimate from 1960, now found in 2008: 8-9: "[I]deas are never satisfactorily explained merely by discovering their philosophical connections. They must be pinned down in relation to the particular circumstances in which they were expressed. . . . [Early Christian literature was] collated and formulated in Greek for the information of religious societies in Hellenistic cities. If [this Christian literature] is to be understood properly, it must be understood from their point of view" – that is, the point(s) of view of the urban dwellers who received them.

by exploring the one place which has been remarkably preserved for posterity: Pompeii."[29] And with Jesus-devotion present in that urban center, our new perspective on Pompeii offers fresh avenues of investigation.

Between the Earthquake and the Eruption

Prior to his death in 65, and around the time that Christians in Rome were being slaughtered by Nero for allegedly starting the fire that razed much of the imperial city, the Roman philosopher and statesman Seneca (himself a tutor to Nero) published his extensive book examining the natural world, *Naturales quaestiones*. In that work, Seneca included several paragraphs on the ruinous earthquake of 62 or 63 that "laid low" Pompeii and "all the adjacent districts" in Campania (6.1.1). Outlining the extensive devastation that the earthquake caused, Seneca commented on the emotional state of the people left behind in the area. He painted a picture in which the inhabitants were shaken to their core, suffering from what we might almost label a "stress disorder."

It is important for our purposes to recount his pseudo-psychological description of the inhabitants of the area in some detail (6.1.4–5).

> Some people were so shocked that they wandered about as if deprived of their wits. . . . It is necessary to find solace for distressed people and to remove their great fear. Yet can anything seem adequately safe to anyone if the world itself is shaken, and its most solid parts collapse? Where will our fears finally be at rest if the one thing which is immovable in the universe and fixed, so as to support everything that leans upon it, starts to waver; if the earth loses the characteristic it has: stability? What hiding-place will creatures find, where will they flee in their anxiety, if fear arises from below and is drawn from the depths of the earth? There is panic on the part of all when buildings creak and give signs of falling. Then everybody hurls himself headlong outside, abandons his household possessions, and trusts to his luck in the outdoors. What hiding-place do we look to, what help, if the earth itself is causing the ruin, if what

---

29. Wright 2015: 264. He continues: "in recent years much more has been made of the social significance of 'space' – that is, the urban space occupied by dwellings of different sizes, and the domestic space within the households. We can learn a lot from these, not least in the areas of power and honour."

protects us, upholds us, on which cities are built, which some speak of as a kind of foundation of the universe, separates and reels?[30]

Seneca's reconstruction of the psyche of the area in the immediate aftermath of the earthquake is poignantly evocative. Distressed people without solace. Anxious people deprived of their wits. People immersed in great fear – fear, drawn from the depths of the earth. As Seneca notes, "many people fear this kind of death most of all, in which they go down into a pit with their own houses, and while still alive are carried off from the number of the living" (6.1.8).

No doubt the immediate effects of the disastrous earthquake wore off with time, and things slowly began to return to normal, relatively speaking. But Seneca's portrait suggests that something more fundamental than the fear of the moment was in play among the populace who had lived through the terrifying earthquake. He captures people's sense of deep-seated insecurity, a fearfulness about the very realities that they had taken for granted. The world itself had been shaken. Its most solid parts were shown to be unstable. The very thing that they imagined to uphold them, perhaps even the very foundation of the universe, had shown itself to be untrustworthy and potentially menacing. For this reason, some of Seneca's contemporaries had "renounced Campania and . . . emigrated after this catastrophe," determined that "they will never visit that district again" (6.1.10). Seneca himself saw no sense in that, since every location is subject to disasters of one kind or another. Nonetheless, the people had been exposed to the hazardous realities of existence. Some of them chose to leave the district altogether, removing themselves from the constant reminder of the precarious fragility of their lives in the grip of much larger forces of destruction all around them.

What can we say about the many who stayed behind in Pompeii, with destroyed temples reminding them of their own precarious place in a dangerous world? According to Seneca's own observations, earthquakes such as the one that laid Pompeii low in the early 60s (and those that continued to shake Pompeii's foundations in the remaining

---

30. Seneca, Loeb 457 (Corcoran): 129.

years of Pompeii's life) "inspire religion in men's minds" (6.3.3). Seneca's point is testified to by marble reliefs found within the house of Lucius Caecilius Jucundus (5.1.26, a house protected by a canine spirit, as evidenced in a sleeping dog mosaic at its entryway). Depicting the devastation caused by the earthquake, these marble reliefs were embedded within the household's worship shrine. Evidently, from the mid-60s or so, the religious devotion of that household was fashioned with specific reference to the earthquake and the fragility of life that it impressed on the minds of Pompeii's residents. We cannot know whether these reliefs were meant simply to testify to the power of the deities or whether they prompted residents of the household to request that disasters of that magnitude should not happen again – or both. Nonetheless, if Seneca's claim is taken seriously, it would seem that Jucundus's Pompeian household was not alone in practicing its piety in relation to a heightened consciousness of life's precariousness in the aftermath of the earthquake.[31]

With these points in view, we need to consider whether data from within various strands of the historical record are coalescing, like pieces of a puzzle that slot together to reveal a bigger picture. Do assorted parts of the historical record cohere in a way that allows us to recognize a convergence of factors that more readily facilitated the rise of Jesus-devotion with Pompeii? I close this book outlining the possible shape of the rise of Jesus-devotion in Pompeii, as suggested by an interrelation of the diverse pieces of historical data.[32]

A devastating earthquake wreaked havoc in Pompeii in the early 60s, reinforcing a sense of life's fragility among many of the inhabitants of the region. As a consequence of this nagging sense (and repeated earthquakes prior to the eruption of 79), some residents decided to leave the area. Many who remained, seeking to enhance their sense

---

31. Butterworth and Laurence (2005: 332) suggest that "among the vast majority who stayed on in the city into the late AD 70s, . . . some appear to have been driven to superstition and the more obscure reaches of religion" because of the anxiety of living in the troubled town in the aftermath of the earthquake. Against any tendency to downplay Seneca's claims about the effects of the earthquake, Milnor rightly notes: "One of the events whose impact . . . we still do not completely understand, was the devastating earthquake which rocked Pompeii in 62 CE . . . [when possibly] as much as a third of the city was rendered uninhabitable."
32. For further expansion of these ideas, see Longenecker 2017.

of security in the face of the potential ravages of life, lived with a heightened sense of religious devotion. But for some, that heightened sense of devotion also resulted in a heightened sense of religious exploration. The traditional deities were still recognized as valid recipients of Pompeian devotion, but religious devotion also needed to be refreshed and reenergized within the town.[33]

While temples to the traditional deities were in the process of being refurbished within Pompeii, it was the temple of Isis that captured the early funds for restoration.[34] The last decade of Pompeii's life saw the flourishing of Isis worship.[35] As "the city's semi-official religion," Isis worship went hand in hand with the "veritable craze" of "Egyptomania."[36] The fear that, according to Seneca, had seized residents of Pompeii and led to an increase in religiosity in the town may have contributed to this entrenchment and augmentation of Isis-devotion within Pompeii. Quite simply, her devotees were promised an enhanced life both in the present and beyond death.

Many became enthralled with the Egyptian deity who promised life enhancement to her devotees, including some of the town's influential politicians and elite. By contrast, a few of Pompeii's residents, and relatively inconsequential ones at that, began to devote themselves (in one form or another) to a different deity of life beyond death. While

---

33. Maiuri reconstructs a different but related scenario in the aftermath of the earthquake. Controversially, he believed that the town saw the influx of the *nouveau riche* and artisans in the wake of the departure of the established aristocrats. He postulates a rise in superstition within the town of Pompeii between the earthquake and eruption. So he writes (1957: 117): "The only protection against the evil-eye, the *fascinum*, was the amulet, and phallic charms rattles with balls were hung and multiplied in number wherever money, riches and gain might be in danger, and wherever man might feel the instinctive need to protect the fruits of his toil against the perils of the evil power of chance. In a city so strongly pervaded by material interest and so changed in its population, formal religion, with its official rites and practices, gave way to the more lively and intimate popular superstitions."
34. By contrast, as Small (2007: 200) notes, "the temples of Apollo and Venus and the Capitolium were still not usable in AD 79." They were, however, in the process of refurbishment, and the temple to Venus was being enlarged beyond its previous footprint. Worship of the Capitoline deities (Jupiter, Juno, and Minerva) had been transferred from the forum to the temple of Jupiter Meilichios (i.e., Asklepius) on Via Stabiana. Butterworth and Laurence (2005: 343) suggest that the rebuilding within the forum "testified only to the civic spirit that saw the city through its difficult times, not a feeling that the danger had passed."
35. As noted by Small 2007: 187; see also Liebeschuetz 1996: 180–82.
36. Here I combine the claims of Lessing and Varone (1996: 125), Etienne (1992: 118), and Bragantini (2012).

Nero slaughtered some of that deity's devotees within the imperial city, many within the empire recognized that those Christians were victims of the unjustifiable wrath of an unbalanced emperor. For some of Nero's subjects, a low-grade form of sympathetic compassion toward Christians embedded itself (as Tacitus claims in Annals 15.44.5; see chapters 2 and 5 above). Persecution against Jesus-followers in Rome stopped altogether with Nero's death in 68, whereupon a period of general tolerance toward them seems to have predominated for a decade or so.[37]

It was during this time, between the earthquake of the early 60s and the eruption of 79, that we have traces of Jesus-devotion within the town of Pompeii. In a Pompeii that was hungry for fresh forms of religious security, a few of its residents welcomed the news of a deity that had defeated a fearful form of death. Their "good news" may have seemed odd to many of their peers, and one resident of Pompeii seems to have described them as cruel. Meanwhile, Jesus-devotees met together – probably in small numbers in a few groups dotted throughout the town. From their risen deity, they sought protection for themselves and, evidently, for their districts. Some may have taken the risk of being exclusive in their singular devotion to their crucified but resurrected deity. Others may have been more sympathetic to the common-sense strategy of worshiping all the deities, with Jesus Christ as a powerful new addition to their collection of deities. But however their devotion was configured, these Christians probably celebrated the newness of life that they enjoyed – life that would extend beyond their own deaths, since they may have heard that "the end is eternal life" (Romans 6:22).

When the end came on that fateful day in 79, one thing might have caused some of them to look different from their contemporaries. Many of their peers, desperately fleeing the doomed town, fearfully clutched apotropaic devices and statuettes of their deities, from whom they sought deliverance from death.[38] By contrast, some "cruel" Jesus-

---

37. The data supporting this paragraph is available in brief in chapter 5 above; see further Longenecker 2015: 121–23; see especially Longenecker (forthcoming) 2017.
38. On statuettes in the hands of Pompeii's deceased, see Connor 2006: 94; Small 2007: 207n119. One

followers may have left their hands intentionally empty. And perhaps a few with empty hands died with one word on their scorched lips: *vivit*.

young girl, for instance, who died in the company of fourteen others outside the Nola Gate, carried a statuette of Isis Fortuna, rings with Fortuna and snake heads on them, and a phallus pendant – all of which were intended to enliven her protection.

Appendix: Positioning Pompeii's Street Crosses

The eighteen street crosses are listed here with pictures depicting their placement in the street (highlighted by a circle) and a description of their placement within their specific environments. Pictures have been used that most advantageously illustrate their placement; the descriptions do not necessarily coordinate with the perspective of the pictures. (A picture might be oriented northward, for instance, while the description might be oriented southward – as is the case for cross 2.)

THE CROSSES OF POMPEII

Cross 1

The photo looks south into Pompeii from outside the Herculaneum Gate.

Stand at the outer edge of the Herculaneum Gate. An imaginary line between the west and east bases of the gate's arch will inevitably hit this cross on the second stone from the west curbstone, about 1.2 meters (4 feet) from that curbstone and 2.1 meters (7 feet) from the east curbstone.

Cross 2

The photo looks north toward the west side of the interior of the Herculaneum Gate.

Entering the town from the north and taking the west pedestrian entry on the right of the large cart entrance, look down and to the left as soon as you pass through the full gate complex. The cross is centered on the second curbstone. Alternatively, walking into town through the cart gate, as soon as the gate complex ends, look down and to the right. The second curbstone displays the cross prominently at its center.

Cross 3

The photo looks west into entryway 6.17.22.

Stand facing 6.17.22 from the street (looking west). The cross is in the middle of a small stone in the middle of the street, approximately 2.1 meters (7 feet) from the west curb, and directly to the east of a deep wheel rut. (Cross 3 is closer to 6.17.22 than the property on the other side of the street.)

Cross 4

The photo looks east between insula 6.2 and insula 6.3.

Stand with insula 6.2 on your left and insula 6.3 on your right, looking into the narrow street ahead of you – Vico di Mercurio. The cross is embedded within the cart-wheel rut that moves from Via Consolare into the narrow Vico di Mercurio. Find the wheel rut and you will find the cross, although the wheel wear has diminished its visibility. The cross is on the northern tip of the second stone away from the east side of Via Consolare. It is about 2.6 meters (8.5 feet) from the west curbstone, and a survey marker is nearby.

Cross 5

The photo looks east where the northeast corner of insula 6.6 meets the northwest corner of insula 6.8.

At the northern intersection between insula 6.6 and 6.8 (i.e., where Vico di Mercurio meets Vico dell Fulonica), four street stones form a fairly straight edge along the middle of Vico di Mercurio. The west stone in that series of four has cross 5 embedded close to its northern edge. (This section of the town was closed during my 2015 visit when I recorded the street cross locations, so this description of the location of cross 5 is reliant on pictures from earlier visits in 2013.)

Cross 6

The photo looks north between insula 6.4 and insula 6.6.

Facing north (with the top of Mount Vesuvius in view on a cloudless day) and with insula 6.4 on your left and insula 6.6 on your right, look to your left and notice the middle stepping stone between insula 6.4 and insula 7.6. Extend an imaginary line from the north side of that stepping stone about 2.7 meters (9 feet) in an eastward direction (toward you). The cross is centered on the south side of the street stone that has a survey marker toward its southern tip, and lies about 2.4 meters (8 feet) away from the south curbstone of Via del Terme.

Cross 7

The photo looks north between insula 6.6 and insula 6.8.

Looking north with insula 6.6 on your left and insula 6.8 on your right, this cross sits on the east side of a stone. It is about 2.6 meters (8.5 feet) from the south curb of Via del Terme.

Cross 8

The photo looks north between insula 6.8 and insula 6.10.

Looking at Mount Vesuvius through the arch, the cross is on a small stone that rises above most of its neighbors and shows obvious signs of cart-wheel wear. The cross is on the southern part of the stone, just south of the cart-wheel damage on the same stone.

Cross 9

The photo looks north between insula 6.10 and insula 6.12.

Looking north with insula 6.10 on your left and insula 6.12 on your right, this cross lies about 1.7 meters (5.5 feet) into the street from the region 6 curbstones and about 2 meters (6.5 feet) into the street from the region 7 curbstones. The cross appears on the east side of a high paving stone, directly in front of the west stepping stone allowing pedestrian access between insula 6.10 and insula 6.12. Two survey markers are 0.8 meters (2.5 feet) east of this cross.

Cross 10

The photo looks north between insula 6.12 and insula 6.13.

Where the west sidewalk of the street between insula 6.12 and insula 6.13 runs along the east side of insula 6.12, extend an imaginary line 2.1 meters (7 feet) into the street. The cross is located in the middle of a paving stone smaller than those around it. (Being 2.1 meters [7 feet] from the region 6 curbstones and 1.2 meters [4 feet] from the region 7 curbstones, this cross is closer to region 7, but there is no insula boundary there, so cross 10 seems to be operating in relation to insula 6.12.)

Cross 11

The photo looks west between insula 7.2 and insula 7.3.

A large curbstone points out into Via Stabiana from the northern tip of insula 7.2, and a slightly intrusive curbstone appears about 1 meter (1.1 yards) to the south of that curbstone. Cross 11 lies between those two curbstones, about 2 meters (6.5 feet) into the street, at the north end of a stone. This cross is in the middle of the street, but closer to region 7 than region 9 (perhaps acting in relation to southbound traffic).

Cross 12

The photo looks east into entryway 9.3.1.

Find the entryway to 9.3.1. Near the middle of the entryway into the shop, the cross is prominently displayed on the south side of a stone less than 1.2 meters (4 feet) from the east curb of Via Stabiana.

Cross 13

The photo looks east into entryway 9.3.5.

This cross is toward the north side of the entryway into 9.3.5. If the black lines of the mosaic in the entryway of the house were extended into the street, those imagined lines would make contact with the cross on the large stone in the middle of the street, about 1.4 meters (4.5 feet) away from the east curb of Via Stabiana. (This cross is closer to region 9 than region 7, so it seems unlikely to have worked in relation to the entrance in region 7.)

Cross 14

The photo looks east between insula 9.2 and insula 9.3.

On the largest stone in the middle of the intersection between insula 9.2 and 9.3 on Via Stabiana, this cross is displayed precisely in the middle of its stone, being the highest point in the intersection (excluding the stepping stones).

As noted in footnote 18 of chapter 12, during my visit to Pompeii in December 2015, a survey team was making use of a survey benchmark approximately one foot away from cross 14. The metal benchmark was, I was told, "about sixty years old." Here are two pictures demonstrating the proximity of the benchmark (which the surveyors used) to cross 14 (which the surveyors did not use, unaware of its existence until I pointed it out and was told that is was a "Roman" mark).

The surveyor's tripod, centered on the benchmark, with cross 14 (highlighted by the added square) approximately a foot away and unused for survey purposes.

Cross 15

The photo looks east between insula 9.1 and insula 9.2.

Between insula 9.1 and insula 9.2 along Via Stabiana, the single stepping stone assisting the walkway along the east side of Via Stabiana points out into that street. Extend an imaginary line from the north side of the stepping stone, and that line will come into contact with the cross mark.

Cross 16

The photo looks east into entryway 9.1.12.

Find the entryway to 9.1.12. Cross 16 is framed by that entryway, near the middle of the street (approximately 2.1 meters [7 feet] from the east curbstone of Via Stabiana and 1.8 meters [6 feet] from the west curbstone). This cross is at an angle and does not follow the direction of the street. (There is no entryway to the west of cross 16, so the crosses here seem to pertain to 9.1.12.)

Cross 17

The photo looks east into 9.1.12.

Refer to instructions for finding cross 16. Then look about 0.6 meters (2 feet) southwest of cross 16. Cross 17 is about 1.2 meters (4 feet) from the west curbstone and about 2.6 meters (8.5 feet) from the east curbstone.

Cross 18

The photo, taken at the intersection of Via Stabiana and Via dell'Abbondanza, looks south toward the Nola Gate.

Stand at the intersection of Via Stabiana and Via dell'Abbondanza. Looking north, stand positioned between (1) the middle stepping stone directly ahead (the middle of three stepping stones crossing Via Stabiana on the north side of Via dell'Abbondanza), and (2) the southern stepping stone to the right (the stepping stone being one of three that cross Via dell'Abbondanza on the east side of Via Stabiana). A diamond-shaped stone near your feet contains the cross at its lower end (as you look north).

APPENDIX: POSITIONING POMPEII'S STREET CROSSES

Cross 19

This photo looks east into 9.3.8.

As explained in a note embedded in the main text of chapter 12, the low angle of the sun in December 2015 brought to light a cross that I

305

had previously been unaware of in my earlier research. In fact, once shadows fell across this mark, it was extremely hard to find again, just as it had completely evaded my gaze when the sun was higher in the sky on earlier visits to Pompeii. I was not able to take precise measurements of its size, unlike the other crosses. It is roughly 6.7 cm in height and 6.5 cm in width, making it larger than the other Via Stabiana crosses except cross 18. At the point of discovery I simply assumed that this cross is to be associated with the shop at 9.3.8, although it seems just as likely that it was associated with the residence at 7.2.3, which interestingly housed a bakery, like 6.6.17/20-21.

To find this cross, stand looking at the shop in 9.3.8. Two large paving stones extend from the curbstones on the east side of Via Stabiana. The cross mark was inscribed on the second of these, sitting in the middle of the street. The photos below show the cross (left) and its position on its paving stone (right, with the added square highlighting its position).

Cross 19.

Credits and Abbreviations

I have presented the load-bearing components of this book's argument at various conferences and symposia, to ensure that my ideas were first tested in academic contexts prior to publication. The essential arguments of chapters 5 and 6 were presented at "The Second Century Seminar" at Texas Christian University on September 8, 2014. The bulk of chapters 7 and 8 was presented at the "Greco-Roman Religions" unit of the Society of Biblical Literature Annual Meeting 2013 (Baltimore, November 26, 2013). The main arguments of chapters 7 through 11 were presented at the "Art and Religions of Antiquity" unit of the Society of Biblical Literature Annual Meeting 2014 (San Diego, November 25, 2014). The essential argument of chapters 12 and 13 was presented in the "Social World of the New Testament" Seminar of the British New Testament Conference (Edinburgh, September 4, 2015).

My thanks for assistance in this project go to a number of colleagues. At Baylor University, these include the following colleagues: Michelle Brown, Derek Dodson, Jeff Fish, Beverly Gaventa, Kelly Iverson, David Lyle Jeffrey, Lidija Novakovic, Mike Parsons, Todd Still, and Jason Whitlark. A number of Baylor graduate students have also been involved in one way or another: Jeremiah Bailey, John Duncan, Grant Edwards, John Genter, Jenny Howell, Stephanie Peek, Scott Ryan, Lindsey Trozzo, Natalie Webb, Mike Whitenton, and Nick Zola.

Special thanks go to Philip Esler (University of Gloucestershire), Martin Henig (University of Oxford), Lyn Osiek (Brite Divinity School), Andrew Wallace-Hadrill (University of Cambridge), Greg Woolf

(Institute of Classical Studies, London), and Tom Wright (University of St Andrews). These six scholars acted as sounding boards for certain aspects of my argument at various stages in the development of this project. Thanks also go to Allison Cooley (University of Warwick), Eric Poehler (University of Massachusetts Amherst), and Greta Stefani (Soprintendenza Archeologica di Pompei), who kindly fielded email inquiries from me.

This study was supported in part by funds from the University Research Committee and the Vice Provost for Research at Baylor University, by the Department of Religion at Baylor University, and by the funders of the W. W. Melton Chair of Religion at Baylor University.

The map of Pompeii in figure 2.1 (and reproduced beyond that figure) is from Bradley 2005: 35, courtesy of Cambridge University Press. Figures 6.6 through 6.9 are used by permission from Princeton University Press (scanned from Jack Finegan, *The Archaeology of the New Testament: The Life of Jesus and the Beginning of the Early Church* [Princeton, NJ: Princeton University Press, 1992]). Barbara McManus provided the photo for figure 7.1 (left), on behalf of the VRoma Project (www.vroma.org). The British Museum granted permission to reproduce the image in figure 7.4. Jeffrey Spier kindly granted permission to use the images in figures 7.5 and 7.6, and supplied the original digital photos of those artifacts. Permission to reproduce figure 7.7 was granted by the Victoria & Albert Museum in London.

The Ministry of Cultural Heritage, Activities and Tourism—Special Superintendency for Archaeological Heritage of Pompeii, Herculaneum and Stabiae granted permission to reproduce the images in figures 1.2 through 1.5; 3.3; 4.1 through 4.3; 6.1; 6.3 through 6.5; 7.1 (left) through 7.3; 7.8 through 7.10; 8.4; 8.6 through 8.14; 9.3; 10.6; 10.7; 11.5; 11.6; 11.9; 11.11; 12.1 through 12.3; 12.5; 12.8; 12.14; 12.15; 12.16 (right); 12.17; 12.19; 12.20; 13.3; 13.4; 13.7; 13.8; 13.10 through 13.12; 14.1; and all the images in the appendix. The reproduction or duplication of these images is prohibited by the Superintendency.

Images (except for those listed above and those credited in footnotes) were photographed (if artifacts) or produced (if graphics) as follows. Bruce Longenecker: figures 1.2 through 1.5; 2.2 through 2.5; 3.2 (right); 3.4 (right); 4.1; 5.2; 6.1 through 6.5; 7.2; 7.3; 7.8 through 7.10; 8.2 through 8.13; 9.3; 10.2; 10.6; 10.7; 11.5; 11.6; 11.9; 11.11; 12.1 through 12.10; 12.12 through 12.20 (sometimes building on works cited); 13.1 through 13.15 (excluding 13.4, 13.7, and 13.11); 14.1; and appendix images. Callum Longenecker: figure 3.3; 8.4. Torrin Longenecker: figure 8.7. Fiona Bond: figure 3.4 (left). Stephanie Peek: figure 8.14. Catarina Belova: figure 13.11 (purchased from Shutterstock). Objects reproduced in the following images are from the author's private collection: figures 2.2 through 2.5; 11.4; 11.8; 13.13 through 13.15.

The author and publisher gratefully acknowledge the permissions granted to reproduce the copyrighted material in this book. Every effort has been made to trace copyright holders and to obtain their permission for the use of copyrighted material. The author and publisher would welcome notification of any corrections that should be incorporated in future reprints or editions of this book.

Ancient literary works are referred to by established English titles, except in instances where English titles are not standard – in accord with the practice established by *The SBL Handbook of Style*, ed. Patrick H. Alexander et al. (Peabody, MA: Hendrickson, 1999). In those instances, the Latin titles are used. Abbreviations used in this book are shown below.

CIL	*Corpus Inscriptionum Latinarum: Consilio et Auctoritate Academiae Litterarum Regiae Borussicae Editum*. Berlin: Berlin-Brandenburg Academy of Sciences and Humanities, 1863–1974.
IG	*Inscriptiones graecae*. Berlin-Brandenburgische Akademie der Wissenschaften, 1873–2012.
MANN	Museo Archeologico Nazionale di Napoli (The Naples National Archaeological Museum).
PGM	Hans Dieter Betz. *The Greek Magical Papyri in Translation, Including the Demotic Spells.* 2nd ed. Chicago: University of Chicago Press, 1996.
RICIS	*Recueil des Inscriptions concernant les Cultes isiaques.* Paris: De Boccard, 2005.

Bibliography

Primary Sources Directly Quoted

Marcus Tullius Cicero. *Pro Archia. Post Reditum in Senatu. Post Reditum ad Quirites. De Domo Sua. De Haruspicum Responsis. Pro Plancio.* Translated by Nevile Hunter Watts. Loeb Classical Library 158. Cambridge, MA: Harvard University Press, 1923.

Diogenes Laertius. *Lives of Eminent Philosophers, in Two Volumes.* Translated by R. D. Hicks. Loeb Classical Library 187. London: William Heinemann; New York: G. P. Putnam's Sons, 1925.

Martial. *Epigrams.* Translated by Walter C. A. Ker. Loeb Classical Library 94 and 95. London: William Heinemann; New York: G. P. Putnam's Sons, 1919.

Pliny the Elder. *Natural History, Volume 8, Books 28-32.* Translated by W. H. S Jones. Loeb Classical Library 418. Cambridge, MA: Harvard University Press, 1963.

Pliny the Younger. *Letters, in Two Volumes.* Translated by William Melmoth; revised by W. M. L. Hutchinson. Loeb Classical Library 59. London: William Heinemann; New York: Macmillan, 1915.

Seneca. *Natural Questions, Volume 2: Books 4-7.* Translated by Thomas H. Corcoran. Loeb Classical Library 457. Cambridge, MA: Harvard University Press, 1972.

Suetonius. *Lives of the Caesars, Volume 2: Books 5-8.* Translated by J. C.

Rolfe. Loeb Classical Library 38. Cambridge, MA: Harvard University Press, 1914.

Tacitus. *Annals*. Translated by Alfred John Church and William Jackson Brodribb. London and New York: Macmillan, 1895.

Secondary Sources Explicitly Referenced

Adams, Edward.

2013: *The Earliest Christian Meeting Places: Almost Exclusively Houses?* New York: Bloomsbury T&T Clark.

Atkinson, Donald.

1951: "The Origin and Date of the 'Sator' Word-Square." *Journal of Ecclesiastical History* 2: 1–18.

Aune, David E.

1998: *Revelation 6-16*. Word Biblical Commentary Vol. 52b. Nashville: Thomas Nelson.

Bagnall, Roger.

2011: *Everyday Writing in the Greco-Roman East*. Berkeley: University of California Press.

Bahn, Paul.

2012: *Archaeology: A Very Short Introduction*. Oxford: Oxford University Press.

Bakker, Jan Theo, editor.

1999: *The Mill-Bakeries of Ostia: Description and Interpretation*. Tübingen: Brill.

Balch, David L.

2004: "Rich Pompeian Houses, Shops for Rent, and the Huge Apartment Building as Typical Spaces for Pauline House Churches." *Journal for the Study of the New Testament* 27: 27–46.

Baldi, Agnello.

    1964: *La Pompei: Giudaico-Cristiana.* Cava de Tirreni: Di Mauro Editore.

Barclay, John M.G.

    1992: "Thessalonica and Corinth: Social Contrasts in Pauline Christianity." *Journal for the Study of the New Testament* 47: 48-72.

Barnard, Leslie W.

    1984: "The 'Cross of Herculaneum' Reconsidered." Pages 14–27 in *The New Testament Age: Essays in Honor of Bo Reicke*, edited by William C. Weinrich. Macon, GA: Mercer University Press.

Barton, Carlin.

    1995: *The Sorrows of the Ancient Romans: The Gladiator and the Monster.* Princeton: Princeton University Press.

Bates, William N.

    1909: "Archaeological News: Notes on Recent Excavations and Discoveries; Other News." *Journal of American Archaeology* 13: 345–86.

Bauckham, Richard.

    1993: *The Climax of Prophecy. Studies on the Book of Revelation.* Edinburgh: T&T Clark.

Bauckham, Richard, editor.

    1997: *The Gospels for All Christians: Rethinking the Gospel Audiences.* Grand Rapids: Eerdmans.

Bauer, Walter.

    1934: *Rechtgläubigkeit und Ketzerei im ältesten Christentum.* Tübingen: J. C. B. Mohr.

Beard, Mary.

2008: *Pompeii: The Life of a Roman Town.* London: Profile Books.

2012: "Dirty Little Secrets: Changing Displays of Pompeian 'Erotica.'" Pages 60–69 in *The Last Days of Pompeii: Decadence, Apocalypse, Resurrection,* edited by Victoria C. Gardner Coates, Kenneth Lapatin, and Jon L. Seydl. Los Angeles: J. Paul Getty Museum.

Beard, Mary, John North, and Simon R. F. Price.

1998: *Religions of Rome,* volume 2, *A Sourcebook.* Cambridge: Cambridge University Press.

Beale, G.K.

1999: *The Book of Revelation: A Commentary on the Greek Text.* Grand Rapids: Eerdmans.

Becatti, Giovanni.

1961: *Scavi di Ostia, IV: Mosaici e Pavimenti Marmorei, Vols. I & II.* Rome: Libreria della Stato.

Bergren, Thomas A.

1990: *Fifth Ezra: Text, Origin, and Early History.* Atlanta: Scholars Press.

2013: "Fifth Ezra." Pages 467-82 in *Old Testament Pseudepigrapha: More Noncanonical Scriptures, Volume 1,* edited by Richard Bauckham, James R. Davila, and Alexander Panayotov. Grand Rapids: Eerdmans.

Berry, Joanne.

2007: *The Complete Pompeii.* London: Tames & Hudson.

Berry, Paul.

1995: *The Christian Inscription at Pompeii.* Lewiston, NY: Edwin Mellen.

Bodel, John.

2012: "Cicero's Minerva, *Penates,* and the Mother of the *Lares:* An Outline of Roman Domestic Religion." Pages 248-75 in *Household and Family Religion in Antiquity,* edited by John Bodel and Saul M. Olyan. Malden, MA: Blackwell.

Bonaventura, Maria Anonietta Lozzi.

    2011: *Herculaneum Reconstructed.* Rome: Archeolibri.

Boring, M. Eugene.

    1989: *Revelation.* Louisville: Westminster John Knox Press.

Boyce, George K.

    1937: *Corpus of the Lararia of Pompeii.* Memoirs of the American Academy in Rome 14. Rome: American Academy in Rome.

Bradley, Pamela.

    2005: *Cities of Vesuvius: Pompeii and Herculaneum.* Cambridge: Cambridge University Press.

Bragantini, Irene.

    2012: "The Cult of Isis and Ancient Egyptomania in Campania." Pages 21–34 in *Contested Spaces: Houses and Temples in Roman Antiquity and the New Testament*, edited by David L. Balch and Annette Weissenrieder. Tübingen: Mohr Siebeck.

Bremmer, Jan Nicolaas.

    2014: *Initiation into the Mysteries of the Ancient World.* Berlin and Boston: Walter de Gruyter.

Brent, Fredrick E.

    2007: "'Great Royal Spouse who Protects Her Brother Osiris." Pages 346-70 in *With Unperfumed Voice: Studies in Plutarch, in Greek Literature, Religion and Philosophy, and in the New Testament Background.* Stuttgart: Franz Steiner Verlag.

Brettman, Estelle Shohet.

    1985: *Vaults of Memory: Jewish and Christian Imagery in the Catacombs of Rome.* Boston: International Catacomb Society.

Brilliant, Richard.

1979: *Pompeii: AD 79: The Treasure or Rediscovery*. New York: Clarkson N. Potter.

Briones, David E.

2013: *Paul's Financial Policy: A Socio-Theological Approach*. London and New York: Bloomsbury.

Brown, Raymond E.

1983a: "Preface." Pages vii–x of *Antioch and Rome: New Testament Cradles of Catholic Christianity*, edited by Raymond E. Brown and John P. Meier. New York: Paulist.

1983b: "Rome." Pages 87–216 of *Antioch and Rome: New Testament Cradles of Catholic Christianity*, edited by Raymond E. Brown and John P. Meier. New York: Paulist.

Bulwer-Lytton, Edward.

1834: *The Last Days of Pompeii*. London: Richard Bentley.

Butterworth, Alex, and Ray Laurence.

2005: *Pompeii: The Living City*. London: Phoenix [Reprint: 2006].

Campbell, Virginia L.

2015: *The Tombs of Pompeii: Organization, Space, and Society*. London and New York: Routledge.

Catalano, Virgilio.

2002 [1966]: *Gli Abitanti e Culti di Ercolano, nuova edizione con gli Indices a cura di Laurentino García y García e Giovanni Panzera*. Rome: Bardi.

Chapman, David W.

2008: *Ancient Jewish and Christian Perceptions of Crucifixion*. Grand Rapids: Baker Academic.

Clark, Francis E. D. D., and Harriet E. Clark.

   1895: *Our Journey around the World*. Hartford, CT: A. D. Worthington.

Clarke, John.

   2007: *Looking at Laughter: Humor, Power and Transgression in Roman Visual Culture, 100 B.C.-A.D. 250*. Berkeley: University of California Press.

Clarke, William.

   1847: *Pompeii : its past and present state : its public and private buildings, etc. / compiled in part from the great work of M. Mazois, the Museo Borbonico, the publications of Sir W. Gell, and T.L. Donaldson, esq., but chiefly from the ms. journals and drawings of William Clarke, esq., architect*. London: M. A. Nattali.

Connor, Peter.

   2006: "*Lararium* – Household Religion." Pages 90–94 in *Pompeii Revisited: The Life and Death of a Roman Town*, edited by Derek Harrison. Sydney: Meditarch.

Cooke, William Bernard.

   1827: *Pompeii, Illustrated with Picturesque Views*. 2 volumes. London: William B. Cooke.

Cooley, Allison, and M. G. L. Cooley.

   2004: Pompeii: *A Sourcebook*. London: Routledge.

Cotton, Hannah M., Leah Di Segni, Werner Eck, Benjamin Isaac, Alla Kushnir-Stein, Haggai Misgav, Jonathan Price, and Ada Yardeni, editors.

   2012: *Corpus Inscriptionum Iudaeae/Palaestinae*, volume 1, *Jerusalem, Part 2: 705-1120*. Berlin and Boston: Walter de Gruyter.

Cramer, M.

   1955: *Das altägyptische Lebenszeichen im christlichen (koptischen) Agypten*. Wiesbaden: J. Auflage.

Cumont, Franz.

> 1896: *Textes et Monuments Figurés relatifs aux Mystéres de Mithra.* Volume 2. Brussels: H. Lamertin.

Curtis, Robert I.

> 2012: "The Garum Debate: Was There a Kosher Roman Delicacy at Pompeii?" *Biblical Archaeological Society: Bible History Daily,* January 25, 2012. www.biblicalarchaeology.org/daily/archaeology-today/biblical-archaeology-topics/the-garum-debate/.

Daniel, Robert Walter, and Franco Maltomini, editors.

> 1990: *Supplementum Magicum.* Opladen: Westdeutscher Verlag.

de Bruyne, L.

> 1945: "La 'crux interpretum' di Erolano." *Rivista di Archeologia Christiana* 21: 281–309.

de Franciscis, Alfonso.

> 1985: *Pompeii-Herculaneum and The Villa Jovis, Capri: Past and Present; Guide with Reconstructions.* Rome: Vision S. R. L.

de Rossi, Giovanni Battista.

> 1864: "Una Memoria del Christiani in Pompei." Pages 69–72 in *Bulletino di Archaeologia Cristiana* 2.9. Rome: Coi Tipi del Salviucci.

della Corte, Matteo.

> 1936: "I Cristiani a Pompei." *Rendiconti Accademia di Archaeologia, Lettere e belle arti di Napoli* 19: 5–30.

> 1942: *Civilta.* Anno III, no. 9.

> 1958: "Pompei: Le iscrizioni scopérte nel quinquennio 1951–1956." *Notizio degli scavi di antichità* (series 8) 12: 77–184.

> 1962: *The Best Guide Book to the Ruins of Pompeii.* Pompeii: Ipsi [originally 1958].

1965: *Case ed Abitanti di Pompei*. Naples: Faustino Fiorentino.

Dinkler, Erich.

1965: "Comments on the History of the Symbol of the Cross." *Journal for Theology and the Church* 1: 124–46. Originally published as "Zur Geschichte des Kreuzsymbols," *Zeitschrift für Theologie und Kirche* 48 (1951): 148–72.

1967: *Signum Crucis*. Tübingen: Mohr [Siebeck].

Dumézil, Georges.

1996: *Archaic Roman Religion: With an Appendix on the Religion of the Etruscans*. Baltimore: Johns Hopkins University Press.

Dunn, James D. G.

1990: *Unity and Diversity in the New Testament*. 2nd ed. London: SCM Press.

2015: *Tertium Genus? A Contested Identity*. Grand Rapids: Eerdmans.

Dyer, Thomas H.

1875: *Pompeii: Its History, Buildings and Antiquities*. London: George Bell & Sons.

Ehrman, Bart D.

2003: *Lost Christianities*. Oxford: Oxford University Press.

Elgvin, Torleif.

2007: "Jewish Editing of the Old Testament Pseudepigrapha." Pages 278–304 in *Jewish Believers in Jesus*, edited by Oskar Skarsaune and Reidar Hvalvik. Peabody, MA: Hendrickson.

Erwin, Philip.

2013: "Viewing Epiphany through Ekphrasis in Philostratus' Imagines." Paper presented in the Greco-Roman Religions Unit, Society of Biblical Literature Annual Meeting.

Etienne, Robert.

    1992: *Pompeii: The Day a City Died.* Translated by Caroline Palmer. London: Thames & Hudson.

Farioli, R. Oliveri.

    1970: "La 'Croce' di Ercolano, Rassegna di studi." Pages 57–71 in *Rendiconti della R. Accademia di Archeologia, Lettere e Belle Arti,* volume 45. Naples: Societa Reale di Napoli.

Feder, Theodore H.

    1978: *Great Treasures of Pompeii and Herculaneum.* New York: Abbeville.

Ferguson, Everett.

    1987: *Backgrounds of Early Christianity.* Grand Rapids: Eerdmans. 3rd ed., 2003.

    2009: *Baptism in the Early Church: History, Theology, and Liturgy in the First Five Centuries.* Grand Rapids: Eerdmans.

Finegan, Jack.

    1992: *The Archaeology of the New Testament: The Life of Jesus and the Beginning of the Early Church.* Princeton, NJ: Princeton University Press.

Fiorelli, Giuseppe.

    1873: *Gli scavi di Pompei dal 1861 al 1872.* Naples: Tipografia Italiana nel Liceo V. Emanuele.

    1875: *Descrizione di Pompei.* Naples: Tipografia Italiana.

    1877: *Guida di Pompei.* Rome: Elzeviriana.

    1898: *Guida di Pompei (con Aggiunte di Antonio Sogliano).* Napoli: Regia Universita.

Fishwick, Duncan.

1959: "An Early Christian Cryptogram?" *Canadian Catholic Historical Association Report* 26: 29–41.

Franklin, David, and Timothy Potts.

2012: "Foreword." Pages 6–7 in *The Last Days of Pompeii*, edited by Victoria C. Gardner Coates, Kenneth Lapatin, and Jon L. Seydl. Los Angeles: Paul Getty Museum / Cleveland Museum of Art.

Franklin, James L., Jr.

1997: "Cn. Maius Nigidius Maius and the amphitheatre: munera and a distinguished career at ancient Pompeii." *Historia* 96: 434–47.

2001: *Pompeis Difficile Est: Studies in the Political Life of Imperial Pompeii*. Ann Arbor: University of Michigan Press.

Fredriksen, Paula.

2002: "Dining with the Divine." *Bible Review* 14 (October): 62.

Frier, Bruce W.

1980: *Landlords and Tenants in Imperial Rome*. Princeton, NJ: Princeton University Press.

Gardner Coates, Victoria C.

2012: "Théodore Chassériau." Pages 100–102 in *The Last Days of Pompeii: Decadence, Apocalypse, Resurrection*, edited by Victoria C. Gardner Coates, Kenneth Lapatin, and Jon L. Seydl. Los Angeles: J. Paul Getty Museum.

Gell, W., and J. Gandy.

1852: *Pompeiana*. 3rd ed. London: Bohn.

Gesenius, Wilhelm.

1910: *Gesenius' Hebrew Grammar*. Edited by E. Kautzsch. Translated by A. E. Cowley. Oxford: The Clarendon Press.

Giordano, Carlo, and Isidoro Kahn.

2001: *The Jews in Pompeii, Herculaneum, Stabiae and in the Cities of Campania Felix.* 3rd ed. Translated by Wilhelmina F. Jashemski. Rome: Bardi Editore.

Goedicke, H.

1968: "An Unexpected Allusion to the Vesuvius Eruption in AD 79." *Classical Journal* 25: 340–41.

Goodenough, Erwin R.

1953 (abridged, 1988): *Jewish Symbols in the Greco-Roman Period.* Princeton, NJ: Princeton University Press.

Gralfs, Bettine.

1988: *Metallverarbeitende Produktionsstätten in Pompeji.* Oxford: British Archaeological Reports.

Grant, Michael.

1971: *Cities of Vesuvius: Pompeii and Herculaneum.* London: Phoenix.

Gray, Thomas.

1830: *The Vestal, or A Tale of Pompeii.* Boston: Gray and Bowen.

Grossberg, A.

1996: "Behold, the Temple: Is it Depicted on a Priestly Ossuary?" *Biblical Archaeology Review* 22, no. 3: 46–51, 66.

Guarducci, Margherita.

1962: "La piú antica iscrizione col nome dei Cristiani." *Ramisene Quartalschrift* 57: 116–25.

Hanson, Norwood Russell.

1958: *Patterns of Discovery.* Cambridge: Cambridge University Press.

Harley-McGowan, Felicity.

2011: "The Constanza Carnelian and the Development of Crucifixion Iconography in Late Antiquity." Pages 214–20 in *"Gems of Heaven": Recent Research on Engraved Gemstones in Late Antiquity c. AD 200-600*, edited by Chris Entwistle and Noël Adams. London: British Museum Press.

Harris, Robert.

2003: *Pompeii*. New York: Random House.

Harrison, James.

2014: "Review of J. Albert Harrill, *Paul the Apostle: His Life and Legacy in Their Roman Context*, Cambridge: Cambridge University Press, 2012." *Review of Biblical Literature* (January).

Hays, Richard B.

1996: *The Moral Vision of the New Testament: A Contemporary Introduction to New Testament Ethics*. San Francisco: HarperOne.

Hengel, Martin.

1977: *Crucifixion*. Minneapolis: Fortress.

Hengel, Martin, and Anna Maria Schwemer.

1997: *Paul between Damascus and Antioch*. London: SCM Press.

Hobson, Barry.

2009: *Latrinae et Fornicae: Toilets in the Roman World*. London: Duckworth.

Hodge, Caroline Johnson.

2013: "'Mixed Marriage' in Early Christianity: Trajectories from Corinth." Pages 227–44 in *Corinth in Contrast: Studies in Inequality*, edited by Steven J. Friesen, Sarah A. James, and Daniel N. Schowalter. Leiden: Brill.

Hoffmann, Adolf, and Mariette de Vos.

1994: "Casa del Fauno (VI 12,2)." Pages 80–141 in *Pompei: pitture e mosaic*, volume 5, edited by Ida Baldassarre. Milan: Arti Grafiche Pizzi S. p. A.

Hoffmann, H.

1974: "Tertullians Aussage über die Christen in Pompeji." *Wiener Studien* 87: 160–72.

Hornik, Heidi J., and Mikeal C. Parsons.

2016: *Acts through the Centuries*. Hoboken, NJ: Wiley-Blackwell.

Hubbard, Moyer V.

2010: *Christianity in the Greco-Roman World: A Narrative Introduction*. Peabody, MA: Hendrickson.

Hurtado, Larry W.

2013: "Interactive Diversity: A Proposed Model of Christian Origins." *Journal of Theological Studies* 64: 445–62.

Jansen, Gemma.

2000: "Systems for the Disposal of Waste and Excreta in Roman Cities: The Situation in Pompeii, Herculaneum, and Ostia." Pages 37–49 in *Sordes Urbis. La Eliminación de Residuos en la Cuidad Romana*, edited by X. Dupré Raventos and J.-A. Remola. Rome: L'Erma di Bretschneider.

2007: "The Water System: Supply and Drainage." Pages 257–66 in *The World of Pompeii*, edited by John J. Dobbins and Pedar W. Foss . London and New York: Routledge.

Jashemski, Wilhelmina Feemster.

1979: *The Gardens of Pompeii, Herculaneum, and the Villas Destroyed by Vesuvius*. New Rochelle, NY: Caratzas Brothers.

Jensen, Robin M., Peter Lampe, William Tabbernee, and Daniel H. Williams.

2014: "Italy and Environs." Pages 379–432 in *Early Christianity in Contexts: An Exploration across Cultures and Continents*, edited by William Tabbernee. Grand Rapids: Baker Academic.

Jerphanion, G. de.

    1941: "La Croix d'Herculaneum?" *Orientalia Christiana Periodica* 7: 5–35.

Jewett, Robert.

    2007: *Romans.* Minneapolis: Fortress.

Johnson, William.

    2009: "The Ancient Book." Pages 257–81 in *The Oxford Handbook of Papyrology*, edited by R. S. Bagnall. Oxford: Oxford University Press.

Johnston, S. I.

    1991: "Crossroads." *Zeitschriftft für Papyrologie und Epigraphik* 88: 217–24.

Judge, Edwin A.

    2008: *Social Distinctives of the Christians in the First Century: Pivotal Essays by E. A. Judge.* Edited by David M. Scholer. Peabody, MA: Hendrickson.

Kaiser, Alan.

    2011: *Roman Urban Street Networks: Streets and the Organization of Urban Space in Four Cities.* London and New York: Routledge.

Keegan, Peter.

    2014: *Graffiti in Antiquity.* London and New York: Routledge.

Kiessling, Alfred.

    1862: "Scavi di Pompei." Pages 92–98 in *Bulletino dell Instituto de corrispondenza archaeologica.* Rome: Salviucci.

Kloppenborg, John S.

    1996: "Collegia and Thiasoi: Issues in Function, Taxonomy, and Membership." Pages 16–30 in *Voluntary Associations in the Graeco-Roman World*, edited by John S. Kloppenborg and Stephen G. Wilson. London: Routledge.

Knibb, Michael A.

1979: "Commentary on 2 Esdras." Pages 76-307 in R.J. Coggins and M.A. Knibb, *The First and Second Books of Esdras*. Cambridge: Cambridge University Press.

Koga, M.

1992: "The Surface Drainage System of Pompeii." *Opuscula Pompeianna* 2: 57–72.

Koloski-Ostrow, Ann Olga.

2007: "The City Baths of Pompeii and Herculaneum." Pages 224-57 in *The World of Pompeii*, edited by John J. Dobbins and Pedar W. Foss. London and New York: Routledge.

2015: *The Archaeology of Sanitation in Roman Italy: Toilets, Sewers, and Water Systems*. Chapel Hill: University of North Carolina Press.

Krodel, Gerhard A.

1989: *Revelation*. Minneapolis: Augsburg Fortress.

Kuhn, Thomas.

1970: *The Structure of Scientific Revolutions*. 2nd ed. Chicago: University of Chicago Press.

Laidlaw, Anne.

2007: "Mining the Early Published Sources: Problems and Pitfalls." Pages 620-32 in *The World of Pompeii*, edited by John J. Dobbins and Pedar W. Foss. London and New York: Routledge.

Lampe, Peter.

2003: *From Paul to Valentinius: Christians at Rome in the First Two Centuries*. Minneapolis: Fortress. German original, *Stadtrömischen Christen in den ersten beiden Jahrhunderten*. Tübingen: Mohr Siebeck; original, 1987; revised 1989.

Last, Hugh.

    1954: Review of *Études d'Histoire Chrétienne. Le Christianisme Secret du Carré Magique: Les Fouilles de Saint-Pierre et la Tradition*, by Jérôme Carcopino. *Journal of Roman Studies* 44: 112–16.

Laurence, Ray.

    1994: *Roman Pompeii: Space and Society*. London and New York: Routledge.

    2008: "City Traffic and the Archaeology of Roman Streets from Pompeii to Rome: The Nature of Traffic in the Ancient City." Pages 87–106 in *Stadtverkehr in der antiken Welt*, edited by D. Mertens. Wiesbaden: Dr. Ludwig Reichert Verlag.

Lessing, Erich, and Antonio Varone.

    1995: *Pompeii*. Paris: Éditions Pierre Terrail.

Levine-Richardson, Sarah.

    2011: "Modern Tourists, Ancient Sexualities: Looking at Looking in Pompeii's Brothel and the Secret Cabinet." Pages 316–30 in *Pompeii in the Public Imagination from its Rediscovery to Today*, edited by Shelley Hales and Joanna Paul. Oxford: Oxford University Press.

Liccardo, Giovanni.

    2008: *Redemptor meus vivit. Iscrizioni cristiane antiche dell'area napoletana*. Berlin: Il Pozzo di Giacobbe.

Liebeschuetz, J. H. W. G.

    1996: *Continuity and Change in Roman Religion*. Oxford: Oxford University Press.

Lindsay, Jack.

    1960: *The Writing on the Wall: An Account of Pompeii in Its Last Days*. London: Frederick Muller Limited.

Ling, Roger.

2009: *Pompeii: History, Life, and Afterlife*. Stroud: History Press.

Longenecker, Bruce.

1995: *2 Esdras*. Sheffield: Sheffield Academic.

2010: *Remember the Poor: Paul, Poverty, and the Greco-Roman World*. Grand Rapids: Eerdmans.

2012: *Hearing the Silence: Jesus on the Edge and God in the Gap - Luke 4 in Narrative Perspective*. Eugene, OR: Cascade.

2015: *The Cross before Constantine: The Early Life of a Christian Symbol*. Minneapolis: Fortress.

2016a: "Philemon." In *Philippians and Philemon*, by James W. Thompson and Bruce W. Longenecker. Grand Rapids: Baker Academic.

2016b: "Mark's Gospel for 'the Second Church' of the Late First Century." Forthcoming in *The Fulness of Time: Essays on Christology, Creation and Eschatology*, edited by Daniel M. Gurtner, Grant Macaskill, and Jonathan T. Pennington. Grand Rapids: Eerdmans.

2017: "The Empress, The Goddess, and the Earthquake: Atmospheric Conditions Permitting Public Displays of Jesus-Devotion in Pompeii." In *Pompeii and Early Christianity*, edited by Bruce W. Longenecker. Minneapolis: Fortress.

Longenecker, Bruce, and Todd D. Still.

2014: *Thinking through Paul: A Survey of His Life, Letters, and Theology*. Grand Rapids: Zondervan.

Longenecker, Richard N.

2011: *Introducing Romans: Critical Issues in Paul's Most Famous Letter*. Grand Rapids: Eerdmans.

Magagnini, Antonella.

2010: *The Art of Pompeii*. Vercelli: White Star.

Maiuri, Amadeo.

1939: "La Croce di Ercolano." *Rendiconti della Pontificia Accademia Romana di Archeologia* 15: 193–218.

1956: *Herculaneum.* Rome: Istituto Poligrafico dello Stato.

1957: *Pompeii.* Novara: Instituto Geofrafico de Agostini.

1958: *Ercolano. I nuovi scavi (1927-1958).* 2 volumes. Rome: Istituto Poligrafico dello Stato, Libreria dello Stato.

1973: *Herculaneum and the Villa of the Papyri: An Archeological Guide of the Town.* Novara: Istituto Geografico de Agostini.

Marriott, H. P. Fitzgerald.

1895: *Facts about Pompei: Its Masons' Marks, Town Walls, Houses, and Portraits.* London: Hazell, Watson, & Viney.

Martin, Dale.

1990: *Slavery as Salvation: The Metaphor of Slavery in Pauline Christianity.* New Haven, CT: Yale University Press.

2004: *Inventing Superstition.* Cambridge, MA: Harvard University Press.

Mau, August.

1895: "Review of H. P. Fitzgerald Marriott, *Facts about Pompeii* (London, 1895)." *Mitteilungen über römische Funde in Heddernheim* 10: 222–25.

1902: *Pompeii: Its Life and Art.* Translated by F. W. Kelsey. Revised [original English translation 1899]. New York: Macmillan.

Mau, August, and Karl F. W. Zangemeister.

1898: *Inscriptiones parietariae Pompeianae; Supplementum 1.* Volume IV.1 in *Corpus Inscriptionum Latinarum.* Berolini: G. Reimerum.

1909: *Inscriptiones parietariae Pompeianae; Supplementum 2.* Volume IV.2 in *Corpus Inscriptionum Latinarum.* Berolini: G. Reimerum.

Mazois, François.

1824: *Les Ruines de Pompeii.* Volume 2. Paris: F. Didot.

McCane, Byron R.

2003: *Roll Back the Stone: Death and Burial in the World of Jesus.* Harrisburg: Trinity Press International.

Meeks, Wayne A.

1983: *The First Urban Christians.* New Haven, CT: Yale University Press.

Meijer, Wim G.

2013: "If It Walks Like a Duck: Ossuary 6 of the Talpiot 'Patio' Tomb Depicts Commonly Used Jewish Symbols." Blog post, Mark Goodacre's *NT Blog*, November 19, 2013. http://ntweblog.blogspot.com/2013/11/if-it-walks-like-duck-ossuary-6-of.html

Meyers, Eric M. and Mark A. Chancey.

2012: *Alexander to Constantine: Archaeology of the Land of the Bible, Volume 3.* New Haven: Yale University Press.

Milnor, Kristina.

2014: *Graffiti and the Literary Landscape in Roman Pompeii.* Oxford: Oxford University Press.

Mitchell, Stephen, and Peter van Neffelen.

2010: "Introduction." Pages 14–15 in *One God: Pagan Monotheism in the Roman Period*, edited by Stephen Mitchell and Peter van Neffelen . Cambridge: Cambridge University Press.

Moeller, Walter O.

1976: *The Wool Trade of Ancient Pompeii.* Leiden: Brill Academic.

Monnier, Marc.

1870: *The Wonders of Pompeii.* Translated. New York: Scribner.

Mounce, Robert H.

1977: *The Book of Revelation*. Grand Rapids: Eerdmans.

Muscettola, Stephania Adamo.

2013: "Religious Life." Pages 84–119 in *Pompeii: The History, Life and Art of the Buried City*, edited by Marisa Ranieri Panetta. Vercelli: White Star.

Myers, Jacob M.

1974: *I and II Esdras*. Garden City: Doubleday & Company.

Newbold, W. Romain.

1926: "Five Aramaic Inscriptions." *American Journal of Archaeology* 30: 288–329.

Niccolini, Fausto, and Felice Niccolini.

1862: *Le Case ed il Monumenti di Pompei; Volume 2, Part 3*. Naples.

1869: *Le Case ed il Monumenti di Pompei; Volume 2, Part 4*. Naples.

1890: *Le Case ed il Monumenti di Pompei; Volume 3, Part 1*. Naples.

Oakes, Peter.

2001: *Philippians: From People to Letter*. Cambridge: Cambridge University Press.

2009: *Reading Romans in Pompeii: Paul's Letter at Ground Level*. Minneapolis: Fortress.

Orr, David G.

1978: "Roman Domestic Religion: The Evidence of the Household Shrines." Pages 1557–91 in *Principat 16.2: Heidentum*. Berlin: Walter de Gruyter.

Osiek, Carolyn, and David L. Balch.

1997: *Families in the New Testament World: Households and House Churches*. Louisville: Westminster John Knox.

Pace, Thomas.

2014: *A Typology of Roman Locks and Keys.* Masters thesis, Charles D. Tandy Institute for Archaeology, Southwestern Seminary, Fort Worth, TX.

Palmer, Robert E. A.

1974: *Roman Religion and Roman Empire: Five Essays.* Philadelphia: University of Pennsylvania Press.

Pillinger, Renate Johanna.

2014: "The So-Called Constantinian Monogram on Late Antique Textiles." Pages 71–76 in *The Days of St. Emperor Constantine and Helena,* edited by Miša Rakocija. Niš. www.ni.rs/byzantium/doc/zbornik12/HTML%20files/Zbornik-XII.htm.

Pirson, Felix.

1997: "Rented Accommodation at Pompeii: The Insula Arriana Polliana." Pages 165–81 in *Domestic Space in the Roman World: Pompeii and Beyond,* edited by R. Lawrence and A. Wallace-Hadrill . Portsmouth, RI: Journal of Roman Archaeology, Supplement Series 22.

Poehler, Eric E.

2003: "Romans on the Right: The Art and Archaeology of Traffic." *Athanor* 21: 7–15.

2005: "A Reexamination of Traffic in Pompeii's Regio VI – The Casa del Fauno, the Central Baths, and the Reversal of Vico di Mercurio." www.pompeiana.org/research/Streets_Research/AIA_2005/EEP_AIA2005_Text.htm.

2006: "The Circulation of Traffic in Pompeii's Regio VI." *Journal of Roman Archaeology* 19: 53–74.

Presuhn, Emil.

1877: *Die pompejanischen Wanddecorationen: Für schulen, sowie Freunde des Alterthums.* Leipzig: T. O. Weigel.

Price, Jonathan J.

2012: "Ossuary of Iesous Aloth with Greek Inscription, 1 c. CE." Pages

501–2 in *Corpus Inscriptionum Iudaeae/Palaestinae*, Volume 1.2, *Jerusalem, Part 2: 705-1120*, edited by Hannah M. Cotton, Leah di Segni, Werner Eck, Benjamin Isaac, Alla Kushnir-Stein, Haggai Misgav, Jonathan J. Price, and Ada Yardeni. Berlin: de Gruyter.

Price, Jonathan J., and Hannah M. Cotton.

"Ossuary of Yehuda with Hebrew/Aramaic Inscription, 1 c. CE." Pages 274–75 in *Corpus Inscriptionum Iudaeae/Palaestinae*, Volume 1.2: *Jerusalem, Part 2: 705-1120*, edited by Hannah M. Cotton, Leah di Segni, Werner Eck, Benjamin Isaac, Alla Kushnir-Stein, Haggai Misgav, Jonathan J. Price, and Ada Yardeni. Berlin: de Gruyter.

Price, Simon.

2006: "Religious Mobility in the Roman Empire." *Journal of Roman Studies* 96: 1–19.

Ramsay, William M.

1895: *St Paul the Traveler and the Roman Citizen*. London: Hodder & Stoughton.

Rhoades, David, Joanna Dewey, and Donald Mitchie.

2012: *Mark as Story: An Introduction to the Narrative of a Gospel*. 3rd ed. Minneapolis: Augsburg Fortress.

Rives, James B.

2007: *Religion in the Roman Empire*. Oxford: Blackwell.

Roberts, Alexander, and James Donaldson, editors.

1885: *The Ante-Nicene Fathers*, vol. 2, *The Fathers of the Second Century*. Christian Literature Publishing Society. Reprinted, New York: Charles Scribner's Sons, 1905; Grand Rapids: Eerdmans, 1983.

Roberts, Paul.

2013: *Life and Death in Pompeii and Herculaneum*. London: British Museum Press.

Rollston, Christopher.

2012: "Review of *The Jesus Discovery: The New Archaeological Find that Reveals the Birth of Christianity*, by James D. Tabor and Simcha Jacobovici (New York: Simon and Schuster, 2012)." *Rollston Epigraphy: Ancient Inscriptions from the Levantine World*, April 12, 2012. www.rollstonepigraphy.com/?p=497.

Romizzi, Lucia.

2006a: *Programmi decorativi di II e IV stile a Pompei. Un'analisi sociologica ed iconologica.* Naples: Loffredo.

2006b: "La Casa dei Dioscuri di Pompei. Una nuova lettura." *Contributi di archeologia vesuviana* 2: 77–160.

Saliou, Catherine.

1999: "Les Trottoirs de Pompeí: Une Première Approche." *Bulletin Antieke Beschaving* 74: 161–206.

Sanders, Ed Parish.

1983: *Paul, the Law, and the Jewish People.* Minneapolis: Fortress Press.

Sanders, Jack T.

1993: *Schismatics, Sectarians, Dissidents, Deviants: The First One Hundred Years of Jewish-Christian Relations.* London: SCM Press.

Schöne, Richard, and Karl F. W. Zangemeister.

1871: *Inscriptiones parietariae Pompeianae, Herculanenses, Stabianae.* Corpus Inscriptionum Latinarum volume IV. Berolini.

Severy-Hoven, Beth.

2013: "Master Narratives and the Wall Painting of the House of the Vettii, Pompeii." Pages 20–60 in *Gender History Across Epistemologies*, edited by Donna R. Gabaccia and Mary Jo Maynes . Oxford: Wiley-Blackwell.

Seydl, Jon L.

2012: "Decadence, Apocalypse, Resurrection." Pages 15–31 in *The Last Days of Pompeii: Decadence, Apocalypse, Resurrection*, edited by Victoria C. Gardner Coates, Kenneth Lapatin, and Jon L. Seydl. Los Angeles: J. Paul Getty Museum.

Shanks, Hershel, and Ben Witherington.

2003: *The Brother of Jesus: The Dramatic Story & Meaning of the First Archaeological Link to Jesus & His Family*. San Francisco: HarperOne.

Shaw, David M.

2014: "Called to Bless: Considering an Under-appreciated Aspect of 'Doing Good' in 1 Peter." Paper presented to the Social World of the New Testament Seminar of the British New Testament Conference.

Small, Alastair M.

2007: "Urban, Suburban and Rural Religion in the Roman Period." Pages 184–211 in *The World of Pompeii*, edited by John J. Dobbins and Pedar W. Foss. London and New York: Routledge.

Snyder, Graydon F.

2003: *Ante pacem: Archaeological Evidence of Church Life before Constantine*. Macon, GA: Mercer University Press.

Spier, Jeffrey.

2007: *Late Antique and Early Christian Gems*. Wiesenbaden: Reichert.

2014: "An Antique Magical Book Used for Making Sixth-Century Byzantine Amulets?" Pages 43–66 in *Les saviors magiques et leur transmission de l'Antiquité à la Renaissance*, edited by Véronique Dasen and Jean-Michel Spieser. Florence: Sismel.

Stähli, Adrian.

2012: "Screening Pompeii: The Last Days of Pompeii in Cinema." Pages 78–87 in *The Last Days of Pompeii: Decadence, Apocalypse, Resurrection*, edited by Victoria C. Gardner Coates, Kenneth Lapatin, and Jon L. Seydl. Los Angeles: J. Paul Getty Museum.

St Clair, William, and Annika Bautz.

    2012: "The Making of the Myths: Edward Bulwer-Lytton's *The Last Days of Pompeii* (1834)." Pages 52–59 in *The Last Days of Pompeii: Decadence, Apocalypse, Resurrection*, edited by Victoria C. Gardner Coates, Kenneth Lapatin, and Jon L. Seydl. Los Angeles: J. Paul Getty Museum.

Stanton, Graham N.

    1993: *Gospel for a New People: Studies in Matthew*. Louisville: Westminster John Knox.

Stefani, Grete.

    2005: "Pompei: Un Panificio." Pages 139–40 in *Cibi e sapori a Pompei e dintorni; Antiquarium di Boscoreale, 3 febbraio-26 giugno 2005*. Pompei (Napoli): Flavius.

Stefani, Grete, editor.

    2010: *Man and the Environment in the Territory of Vesuvius: The Antiquarium of Boscoreale*. Pompeii: Flavius Edizioni.

Stegemann, Ekkehard, and Wolfgang Stegemann.

    1999: *The Jesus Movement: A Social History of Its First Century*. Minneapolis: Fortress.

Sukenik, Eleazar Lipa.

    1947: "The Earliest Records of Christianity." *American Journal of Archaeology* 51: 351–65.

Sulzberger, Max.

    1925: "Le symbole de la croix et les monograms de Jésus chez les premiers chrétiens." *Byzantion* 2: 337–448.

Sweet, John P. M.

    1979: *Revelation*. Philadelphia: Westminster.

Tabbernee, William.

    1997: *Montanist Inscriptions and Testimonia: Epigraphic Sources Illustrating the History of Montanism.* Macon, GA: Mercer University Press.

Tabor, James D., and Simcha Jacobovici.

    2012: *The Jesus Discovery: The Resurrection Tomb That Reveals the Birth of Christianity.* New York: Simon and Schuster.

Thédenat, Henry.

    1906: *Pompéi: histoire—vie privée.* Paris: H. Laurens.

Tuschling, R. M. M.

    2007: *Angels and Orthodoxy: A Study in Their Development in Syria and Palestine from the Qumran Texts to Ephrem the Syrian.* Tübingen: Mohr Siebeck.

Unlisted author.

    1886: "Monumental Evidences of Christianity." *The Church Quarterly Review* 22: 381–409.

van Buren, A. W.

    1947: "Gnaeus Maius Nigidius Maius of Pompeii." *American Journal of Philology* 68: 382–93.

van den Hoek, Annewies, and John J. Herrmann Jr.

    2013: *Pottery, Pavements, and Paradise: Iconographic and Textual Studies on Late Antiquity.* Leiden: Brill.

Varone, Antonio.

    1979: *Presenze guidaiche e cristiane a Pompei.* Naples: M. D'Auria Editore.

    1980: "La Campania e il cristianesimo delle primissime origini: Contributi valutativisulla questione dei cristiani nell'antica Pompei." *Campania Sacra* 11–12: 3–44.

2002: *Erotica Pompeiana: Love Inscriptions on the Walls of Pompeii.* Rome: L'erma di Bretschneider.

Varone, Antonio, and Grete Stefani.

2009: *Titulorum pictorum Pompeianorum qui in CIL vol. IV collecti sunt.* Rome: L'Erma di Bretschneider.

Viitanen, Eeva-Maria, and Heini Ynnilä.

2014: "Patrons and Clients in Roman Pompeii – Social Control in the Cityscape and City Blocks?" Pages 141–55 in *Sounds Like Theory, XII: Nordic Theoretical Archaeology Group Meeting in Oulu 25.-28.4.2012*, edited by Janne Ikäheimo, Anna-Kaisa Salmi, and Tiina Äikäs. Helsinki: Archaeological Society of Finland.

Wallace, Daniel B.

1996: *Greek Grammar Beyond the Basics: An Exegetical Syntax of the New Testament.* Grand Rapids: Zondervan.

Wallace-Hadrill, Andrew.

1994: *Houses and Society in Pompeii and Herculaneum.* Princeton, NJ: Princeton University Press.

2008: *Rome's Cultural Revolution.* Cambridge: Cambridge University Press.

2011: *Herculaneum Past and Present.* London: Francis Lincoln.

Ward-Perkins, John, and Amanda Claridge.

1976: *Pompeii AD 79.* Bristol: Imperial Tobacco.

1978: *Pompeii AD 79: Treasures from the National Archaeological Museum, Naples, & the Pompeii Antiquarium.* Volume 1. Boston: Museum of Fine Arts.

Wayment, Thomas A., and Matthew J. Grey.

2015: "Jesus Followers in Pompeii: The Christianos Graffito and 'Hotel of the Christians' Reconsidered." *Journal of the Jesus Movement in Its Jewish Setting* 2: 102–46.

Weber, Volker, et al., editors.

    2011: *Corpus Inscriptionum Latinarum, Supplementum 4.1: Inscriptiones Parietariae Pompeianae.* Berlin: de Gruyter.

Welch, Katherine E.

    2007: "Pompeian Men and Women in Portrait Sculpture." Pages 550–84 in *The World of Pompeii*, edited by John J. Dobbins and Pedar W. Foss. London: Routledge.

Westerholm, Stephen.

    2013: *Justification Reconsidered: Rethinking a Pauline Theme.* Grand Rapids: Eerdmans.

Wood, Alice.

    2008: *Of Wings and Wheels: A Synthetic Study of the Biblical Cherubim.* Berlin and New York: Walter de Gruyter.

Woolf, Greg.

    2012: *Rome: An Empire's Story.* Oxford: Oxford University Press.

Wordsworth, Christopher.

    1837: *Inscriptiones Pompeianae; or Specimens and Facsimiles of Ancient Inscriptions Discovered on the Walls of Buildings at Pompeii.* London: John Murray.

Wright, N. T.

    2013: *Paul and the Faithfulness of God: Christian Origins and the Question of God.* London: SPCK; Minneapolis: Fortress.

    2015: *Paul and His Recent Interpreters: Some Contemporary Debates.* London: SPCK; Minneapolis: Fortress.

Yarbro Collins, Adela.

    1983: *The Apocalypse.* Wilmington: Michael Glazier.

Zahn, Wilhelm.

1852: *Die schönsten Ornamente und merkwürdigsten Gemälde aus Pompeji, Herculaneum und Stabile.* Berlin: Georg & Dietrich Reimer (1828–1829, 1842–1844, 1849–1852).

Zingales, Luigi.

2012: *A Capitalism for the People: Recapturing the Lost Genius of American Prosperity.* New York: Basic Books.

Index of Ancient Sources

Hebrew Bible
Genesis
6–9......185
18–19......24
22......110

Deuteronomy
28:22......222n9
28:28......222n9
32:35......14

1 Kings
3......257

2 Chronicles
28:24......233

Job
9:7......93

Psalms
91:9–11......99

Ezekiel
4:3......90
9......89–92, 92n18, 94–96, 95n25, 149, 150, 186n21, 239, 265n3
9:4......89, 90, 92, 95
9:6......90
9:4–6......88, 90, 91, 93, 93n20, 94–96, 105, 150, 222, 238, 239
20:12......90
20:20......90
39:15......90

Zechariah
11:7......89

Old Testament Apocrypha and Pseudepigrapha
Apocalypse of Adam......21n3

Apocalypse of Moses
42:1......93

Jubilees
22:16–17......225n14

Odes of Solomon
27......73

Prayer of Manasseh
3......93

Psalms of Solomon
15:6......89

Sirach
17:22......93

Sibylline Oracles
4.102–29......21
4.130–36......21

Testament of Moses
12:9......93

Testament of Solomon
1:6–7......93n19
10:6......93n19
15:7......93n19
17:1–3......226

Dead Sea Scrolls
Damascus Document
19:9–13......89

Isaiah Scroll......91n15

Josephus
Jewish Antiquities
20.141–44......257n2

New Testament
Matthew
6:13......15
6:31–34......15
15:17......241
18:23–35......274
28:19–20......28n20

Mark......276–77
1:27......16
5......227
5:2–3......227
7:19......241

Luke
21:20–21......265n3

Acts
2:10......26n13
8:9–24......138
16:11–15......142n44
16:25–34......142n44
18......269n7
18:2......26n15, 27n18
18:5–8......142n44
19:9–10......157
19:11–20......138
19:26......14n10
23:12–24:27......257n2
24:26......257n2
28:13–14......20, 40n5, 76

Romans
1:23–25......14n10

6:22......282
8:31......15
12:19......14
16......26
16:3–4......26

1 Corinthians......268
1:18......16, 262
1:23......262
2:14......262
5:1......137n35
5:1–13......137n35
5:10......270
6:12–20......137n35
7:12–16......271n9
7:13......270
7:14......271
7:24......270
8:4–6......270
8:6......136
10:14......14n10
10:14–22......132n25
15:26......17
15:54......15
16:19......26n15

2 Corinthians......268
6:16–18......14n10
9:10......16n13

Galatians
6:2......16n13

Ephesians
1:19–21......16
6:5–6......271

Philippians
1:14......26

Colossians
3:22......271

1 Thessalonians
1:9–10......14
5:15......235

2 Thessalonians
2:4–9......14

1 Timothy
4:4–5......136
6:2......271

2 Timothy
2:19......94n23
4:16......27

Titus
2:9......271

Philemon......142n44

Hebrews......28n20

1 Peter
2:12......235

2:18–19......271
2:18–21......275
2:20......235
3:1–2......270
3:9......235
3:11......235
3:16–17......235
4:19......235

Revelation (Johannine
  Apocalypse)......238, 265n3
1:3......95
2–3......138
3:12......94n25
7:2–3......92, 93, 93n20, 94–96,
  239n38
7:2–8......96
7:9–17......96n29
9:4......92, 93, 93n20, 94, 96, 239n38
13:16–17......92
14:1......94
14:9–11......92
16:2......92
19:20......92
20:4......92
22:4......94

Early Christian Literary Sources
1 Clement......27, 268

5 Ezra......91, 238
2:23......72, 96, 239n38
2:38......96
2:42......96n29

6 Ezra......75

Arnobius of Sicca
Against the Pagans
3.41–42......138n36

Cyprian
Testimonies
2.21–22......91

Epistle of Barnabas 238
9......75, 96, 106
12......75, 96

Eusebius
Ecclesiastical History
3.17......28
4.26......28

Ignatius
To the Romans
3:1......26

Lactantius
Epitome of the Divine Institutes
28......138n36

The Divine Institutes
2.15......138n36

Melito of Sardis......28

Selecta in Ezechielem 9 (MPG XIII
  800–801)......92n17

INDEX OF ANCIENT SOURCES

Tertullian
Adversus Marcionem
3.22......91

Apologies
5......28
13......138n36
16.6–8......79n1
40......39
40.8......20

To the Heathen
1.9.7......20
1.10......138n36

Greco-Roman Literary Sources
Cicero
De Divinatione
1.13......56n17
2.21......56n17
2.59......56n17

Diogenes Laertius
Diogenes Laertius
6.50......125

Homer
Iliad......169n3

Marcus Minucius Felix
Octavius
29.8......79n1

Martial (or Marcus Valerius Martialis)
Epigrams
4.44......4

Ovid
Fasti
1.141–43......234n29

Pliny the Elder
Natural History
28.7.39......127
28.19......13

Pliny the Younger
Epistulae 9.5......11

Letters to Tacitus
VI.16......24n11
VI.20......24n11

Plutarch
Apotheg. Reg.
193–94......234n29

Quaest. Conv.
708–9......234n30

Quaest. Rom.
290d......234n30

Seneca
Naturales quaestiones
6.1.1......278

345

6.1.4–5......278
6.1.8......279
6.1.10......279
6.3.3......280

Suetonius
Claudius
25......27n18

Vespasianus
5.3......242

Tacitus
Annals
15.44......26, 27
15.44.5......28, 76

Histories
4.42......28n19

Virgil
Aeneid
4.609–10......234n29
5.90–96......120n5
9.404......151

Greek Papyri
P46......71
P66......71
P75......71

Greek Magical Papyri
PGM 1.306......93
PGM 3.226......93
PGM 3.266–67......93
PGM 4.1485–86......93
PGM 4.1534–35......93
PGM 4.1561......93
PGM 4.1621......93
PGM 4.2315......93
PGM 4.2326......93
PGM 4.3053......93
PGM 7.220......93
PGM 7.311......93
PGM 7.583......93
PGM 7.595–96......93

SuppMag
1.19......227n16
2.35–36......227n16

Inscriptions
CA-64098......170n4

CIL 1.593.20–55......242
CIL 1.7866......257n2
CIL 1.8224......257n2
CIL 4.60......231
CIL 4.138......43, 44, 46n17, 141
CIL 4.2......241n39
CIL 4.222......242
CIL 4.250......46n19
CIL 4.251......45n15
CIL 4.346......161
CIL 4.679 (*Christianos* graffito) 38, 39, 39n2, 40, 40n6, 59, 76, 153, 155, 155nn4–5, 156–66, 179, 181, 182, 183, 183n17, 184–86,

186n22, 187, 191, 235, 236,
236n34, 237, 237n37, 238, 239,
253–55, 256, 272
CIL 4.787......112
CIL 4.1011......112
CIL 4.1177......46n17
CIL 4.1180......46n17
CIL 4.1222......3n1
CIL 4.1454......123
CIL 4.1507......257n2
CIL 4.1839......161
CIL 4.1840......257n2
CIL 4.1893......162n23
CIL 4.1894......162n23
CIL 4.1939......157n11
CIL 4.2016......157
CIL 4.2310k......151
CIL 4.2457......273n12
CIL 4.2569......257n2
CIL 4.2611......257n2
CIL 4.3149......3n1
CIL 4.3200......39n2
CIL 4.3340.6......274n14
CIL 4.3340.7......274n14
CIL 4.4287......39, 257n2
CIL 4.4976 ("Sodom and Gomorrah" graffito) 39n2, 256
CIL 4.5112......11n7, 29
CIL 4.5244 ("Martha" graffito)......256
CIL 4.5358......213n25
CIL 4.5660–62......257n2
CIL 4.6175......39n2
CIL 4.6641......240

CIL 4.6779......97n31
CIL 4.6990 ("*Iudaicus*") 257
CIL 4.7716......241
CIL 4.7715......241n39
CIL 4.7990......46n17
CIL 4.7991......46n17
CIL 4.8010......257n2
CIL 4.8123......39n2
CIL 4.8171......273n12
CIL 4.8258–59......161
CIL 4.8408......161
CIL 4.8623......39
CIL 4.9757......257
CIL 4.10000......39n2
CIL 4.10062 (*vivit* graffito) 39,
    148–50, 166, 184, 185, 187, 191,
    224, 235, 238, 239, 247, 249,
    253–56, 266, 267, 272, 283
CIL 4.10193......39n2
CIL 4.10477......39n2
CIL 4.10606......243n50
CIL 4.10619......5n3
CIL Supp 8.855......46n17,
CIL 10.846......113
CIL 10.885......242
CIL 10.886......242
CIL 10.890......242
CIL 10.901......242

IG 12.9......222n9
IG 12.955......222n9
IG 12.1179......222n9

Jewish Ossuary
  Inscriptions......85–91, 94–95,
  150, 238, 265n3

Oscan Inscription from Pompeii,
  British Museum,
  1867.0508.76......177

Ostian "*Iesus*" Inscription (Baths of
  Neptune [2.4], Room 6)
  ......68–70, 181, 182, 184, 239, 254

Pompeii paving stone inscriptions
Crosses on Via Consolare......197,
  199, 201n7, 202 201n7, 206, 207,
  208, 211, 218, 221, 221n8, 222,
  224, 226, 227, 227n17, 228, 229,
  256, 263–67, 271, 285–89, 291
Crosses on Via della Fortuna......197,
  201n8, 202, 230, 256, 267, 294,
  295
Crosses on Via delle Terme......197,
  202, 207–9, 221n8, 222, 227,
  227n17, 228, 230, 230n20, 263,
  291–93
Crosses on Via Stabiana (or Via
  Pompeiana) 201, 201n8, 202,
  206, 207, 208, 209, 210, 212, 213,
  221n7, 221n8, 227, 231–33, 248,
  248n54, 249, 256, 264, 265, 267,
  275, 296–304, 306
Crosses on Vico di Mercurio......197,
  202, 207, 211, 222, 227, 227n17,
  262–66, 289, 290

Phallic symbol on Via
  dell'Abbondanza......193, 245

Pompeii Tomb Inscriptions
Gaius Vestorius Priscus Tomb
  inscription (Pompeii, outside
  Vesuvian Gate)......178, 179
Septumia Tomb inscription
  (Pompeii, outside Vesuvian
  Gate)......178, 179

Vesuvian Frescoes (Naples National
  Archaeology Museum
  Inventory)

MANN 976......107
MANN 8836......106
MANN 9105......172
MANN 9978......10
MANN 27695......158
MANN 27844......129
MANN 109688......13
MANN 109982......12
MANN 113197 ("The wise judgment
  of Solomon")......258

Index of Modern Authors

Adams, Edward, 102, 166
Aune, David E., 93n19

Bagnall, Roger, 186n22
Bahn, Paul, 60, 204n14
Bakker, Jan Theo, 68
Balch, David L., 57, 58n22, 97, 98n32, 141n43, 142nn44–45, 230n18
Baldi, Agnello, 105n6, 134n29, 147n4
Barclay, John M.G., 140n40
Barnard, Leslie W., 35, 56, 65–67, 147n4
Barton, Carlin, 125n14
Bates, William N., 40n4
Bauckham, Richard, 93n20, 95, 95n28, 276n23
Bauer, Walter, 67n8
Bautz, Annika, 24n10
Beard, Mary, 5n3, 57n18, 59, 127, 128n22, 155n5
Beale, G.K., 92n18, 93n20, 94
Becatti, Giovanni, 68, 70

Bergren, Thomas, 72nn16–17, 96n29
Berry, Paul, 6n4, 154n4, 159n15, 180, 181, 187
Berry, Joanne, 5n3, 58, 135n30, 204n12, 225, 234
Bodel, John, 137n36
Bonaventura, Maria Anonietta Lozzi, 50n4
Boring, Eugene M., 93n20
Boyce, George K., 272n11
Bradley, Pamela, 8, 29n21
Bragantini, Irene, 114n25, 281n36
Bremmer, Jan Nicolaas, 108n8, 138n37
Brent, Fredrick E., 108n8
Brettman, Estelle Shohet, 185n19
Brilliant, Richard, 29n21, 45n14, 167, 204n15
Briones, David E, 140n40
Brown, Raymond E., 56, 61n32
Bulwer-Lytton, Edward, 24, 24n10, 139
Butterworth, Alex, 8n6, 58, 76n22,

349

99, 108n10, 114nn23–24, 128n23, 189, 193n2, 218n2, 280n31

Campbell, Virginia L., 225n13
Catalano, Virgilio, 56n12
Chapman, David W., 85n6
Chancey, Mark A., 88n8
Cinquantaquattro, Teresa Elena, 58
Claridge, Amanda, 257n3
Clark, Francis E.D.D., 24n10
Clark, Harriet E., 24n10
Clarke, John, 125nn12–14, 128nn23–24, 155n4, 164n25, 224
Clarke, William, 42n8, 204n10, 229
Cooke, William Bernard, 119n4, 121n9, 204n10
Cooley, Allison, 274n14
Cooley, M.G.L., 274n14
Connor, Peter, 282n38
Cotton, Hannah M., 81n4, 88n9
Cramer, M., 108n11
Cumont, Franz, 95n27, 138n37
Curtis, Robert I., 257n2

Daniel, Robert Walter, 227n16
de Bruyne, L., 56n12
de Franciscis, Alfonso, 50
de Jerphanion, G., 56n12
de Rossi, Giovanni Battista, 154, 154nn3–4, 155nn4–5, 156n8, 157, 158, 162, 163, 179n11, 183n17
de Vos, Mariette, 230n18
della Corte, Matteo, 43n11, 49, 49n2, 50, 55, 55n12, 56n16, 120n6, 145n1, 146n4, 147, 147n4, 149, 155n6, 186n23, 275n19
Dinkler, Erich, 63, 67, 88–90
Donaldson, James, 137n34
Dumézil, Georges, 237
Dunn, James D.G., 67n8, 72n16
Dyer, Thomas H., 134, 138

Eck, Werner, 81n4
Ehrman, Bart D., 67n9
Elgvin, Torleif, 72n16
Erwin, Philip, 132n25
Etienne, Robert, 29n21, 58, 113, 234n31, 281n36

Farioli, R. Oliveri, 57, 138, 139n38
Feder, Theodore H., 108n9, 126n16
Ferguson, Everett, 57, 95
Finegan, Jack, 39n2, 85n7, 86, 87, 88n10, 91n15, 108n12
Fiorelli, Giuseppe, 29, 40n4, 56n16, 154, 155n5, 157, 162, 183, 183n17, 204, 204n13, 205, 212, 231n24, 275n19
Fishwick, Duncan, 56
Franklin, James L. Jr., 46n17, 141n41
Franklin, David, 1
Fredriksen, Paula, 132n25
Frier, Bruce W., 141n41

Gardner Coates, Victoria C., 44n13
Gell, W. And J. Gandy., 123, 204n9
Gesenius, Wilhelm, 88n10

Giordano, Carlo, 151n9, 161n21, 257n2
Goedicke, H., 21n3
Gralfs, Bettine, 275n18
Grant, Michael, 29n21, 251
Gray, Thomas, 22, 23, 24, 76
Grey, Matthew J., 183n17
Guarducci, Margherita, 159, 159n16, 162, 163n24, 183n17

Hanson, Norwood Russell, 260n8
Harley-McGowan, Felicity, 75
Harris, Robert, 21n4
Harrison, James, 277n26
Hays, Richard B., 14n12, 28n20, 277
Hengel, Martin, 138n36, 273n13
Herrmann Jr. John J., 108n11
Hobson, Barry, 242n45
Hodge, Caroline Johnson, 91n15, 271n9
Hoffmann, Adolf, 230n18
Hoffmann, H., 20n1
Hornik, Heidi J., 257n2
Hubbard, Moyer V., 136n32, 234n27, 268n6
Hurtado, Larry, 67n8

Isaac, Benjamin, 81n4

Jansen, Gemma, 242, 243, 243n50
Jashemski, Wilhelmina Feemster, 44, 133n27
Jensen, Robin M., 146n2
Jewett, Robert, 26, 27n17, 276n22

Johnson, William, 91n15
Johnston, S.I., 234nn28–30
Judge, Edwin A., 277n28

Kahn, Isidoro, 151n9, 161n21, 257n2
Kaiser, Alan, 218n4, 243, 243n52
Keegan, Peter, 58, 59n29, 63, 97, 113n20, 162n23, 274n14
Kiessling, Alfred, 153n1, 154, 155nn4–5, 156, 156n8, 157, 158, 161n21, 162, 163n24, 164, 179, 179n11, 180, 183, 183n17, 187, 236
Kloppenborg, John S., 275n19
Knibb, Michael A., 96
Koga, M., 243n50
Koloski-Ostrow, Ann Olga, 241n40, 242, 242n46
Krodel, Gerhard A., 94n21
Kuhn, Thomas, 259, 259n7, 260n8
Kushnir-Stein, Alla, 81n4

Laidlaw, Anne, 145n1
Lampe, Peter, 20n2, 25n12, 39n2, 40n5, 57, 102, 103, 146n2
Last, Hugh, 20n1
Laurence, Ray, 8n6, 58, 76n22, 99, 108n10, 114nn23–24, 125, 128n23, 189, 193n2, 218n2, 226, 231n22, 237n35, 243n51, 280n31
Lessing, Erich, 1, 112, 241n41, 266n5, 281n36
Levine-Richardson, Sarah, 159n16
Liccardo, Giovanni, 143

Liebeschuetz, J.H.W.G., 112n19, 281n35
Lindsay, Jack, 56, 125, 125n15, 162n22
Ling, Roger, 8n6, 46n19, 135n30, 141n41, 241n42, 258n4
Longenecker, Bruce, 7, 16n13, 26nn13–14, 26n16, 27n18, 31n22, 69, 71n15, 72n16, 75nn20–21, 85n7, 91n16, 99n1, 137n34, 142n44, 150n8, 175n6, 181n15, 263n1, 265n3, 277n25, 280n32, 282n37
Longenecker, Richard, 26n13, 265n3

Magagnini, Antonella, 8n6
Maiuri, Amadeo, 8n6, 52–55, 55n12, 57, 64–67, 128, 275n19, 281n33
Maltomini, Franco, 227n16
Marriott, H.P. Fitzgerald, 192n1, 195, 209, 210, 248, 248n54, 249, 250, 254
Martin, Dale, 243n49, 274, 274n17
Mau, August, 8n6, 39, 40, 40nn4–6, 102n3, 166, 178nn9–10, 192n1, 248–50, 257n2
Mazois, François, 41–42, 44, 47, 51–54, 103, 104n5, 118, 119nn3–4, 133, 134nn28–29, 136, 138, 225
McCane, Byron R., 91n14
Meeks, Wayne A., 224n11
Meyers, Eric M., 88n8
Milnor, Kristina, 35, 114n23, 132n25, 157n11, 162n23, 177n8, 186n22, 224, 250, 251, 280n31
Minervini, Giulio, 154, 155nn4–5, 156, 157, 157n10, 158, 162, 163, 163n24, 164, 165, 183n17, 236
Misgav, Haggai, 81n4
Mitchell, Stephen, 135n30
Moeller, Walter O., 275n19
Monnier, Marc, 118, 133, 138
Mounce, Robert H., 94n21
Myers, Jacob, 72, 96n29
Muscettola, Stephania Adamo, 121n8

Newbold, W. Romain, 160, 160n18, 161nn20–21, 162, 164
Niccolini, Fausto, 167, 168, 169n2, 170, 170n4
Niccolini, Felice, 167, 168, 169n2, 170, 170n4

Oakes, Peter, 14n11, 135n31, 275n18, 276
Orr, David G., 120n5
Osiek, Carolyn, 57, 58n22, 97, 98n32, 142nn44–45, 274n15

Pace, Thomas, 170n4
Palmer, Robert E.A., 234n28
Parsons, Mikeal C., 257n2
Pillinger, Renate Johanna, 112n17
Pirson, Felix, 43n10, 46n19
Planck, Max, 259n7
Poehler, Eric E., 213, 214, 218,

218nn2–4, 219n5, 221n6, 230n19, 263, 264
Potts, Timothy, 1
Presuhn, Emil, 248n54
Price, Jonathan J., 88n9
Price, Simon, 135n30

Ramsay, William M., 25
Rhoades, David, Joanna Dewey, and Donald Mitchie, 277n24
Rives, James B., 270n8
Roberts, Alexander, 137n34
Roberts, Paul, 5n3, 8n6, 218, 242, 242n45, 243n49
Romizzi, Lucia, 46n19

Saliou, Catherine, 192n1
Sanders, Ed P., 16n14
Schöne, Richard, 156n7
Schwemer, Anna Maria, 138n36
Severy-Hoven, Beth, 81n3
Seydl, Jon L., 24n10
Shaw, David M., 235n33
Small, Alastair M., 38n1, 56, 97, 112n19, 128n23, 230n21, 234n26, 257n2, 258n5, 263n1, 281nn34–35, 282n38
Snyder, Graydon F., 58, 74, 137n33, 154n3, 185n19
Sogliano, Antonio, 56n16
Spier, Jeffrey, 99, 110nn14–15
Stähli, Adrian, 24n10
Stanton, Graham N., 72n16
St Clair, William, 24n10

Stefani, Grete, 58, 82n5, 108n9, 120n6, 209nn19–20
Stegemann, Ekkehard, 11
Stegemann, Wolfgang, 11
Still, Todd D., 26nn13–14, 26n16, 27n18
Sukenik, Eleazar Lipa, 53n10, 64–66, 85n7, 87
Sulzberger, Max, 138, 139n38
Sweet, John P.M., 94n24

Tabbernee, William, 68, 74n18, 146n2
Thédenat, Henry, 248n54
Tolkien, J.R.R., 19
Tuschling, R.M.M., 125n13

Unlisted Author, 158–59, 159n15, 164

van Buren, A.W., 46n17
van den Hoek, Annewies, 108n11
van Neffelen, Peter, 135n30
Viitanen, Eeva-Maria, and Heini Ynnila, 275n18
Varone, Antonio, 1, 112, 118, 139, 139n39, 145n1, 146, 146n3, 147, 147nn4–5, 148, 149, 162nn22–23, 180, 185n19, 187, 209nn19–20, 213n25, 241n41, 255, 266n5, 281n36

Wallace, Daniel B., 90n13

Wallace-Hadrill, Andrew, 8n6, 58, 101, 132n25, 217, 242n48
Ward-Perkins, John, 257n3
Wayment, Thomas A., 183n17
Weber, Volker et al., eds., 153n1
Welch, Katherine E., 231n22
Westerholm, Stephen, 16
Williams, Daniel H., 146n2
Wood, Alice, 125n13
Woolf, Greg, 4n2
Wordsworth, Christopher, 24n9

Wright, N.T., 277n27, 278n29

Yarbro Collins, Adela, 93n20
Yardeni, Ada, 81n4

Zahn, Wilhelm, 204n11
Zangemeister, Karl Friedrich Wilhelm, 40, 40n6, 156n7, 166, 178nn9–10
Zingales, Luigi, 259n6

Index of Vesuvian Locations

Herculaneum
4.15......121n10
House of Galba (7.1–2)......80, 81
House of the Beautiful Courtyard
    (5.8)......82, 83
House of the Bicentenary
    (5.15–16)......38, 41, 50, 52–54,
    55n12, 59, 60, 64–66, 97, 102, 103
House of the Inn (3.1–2,
    18–19)......82
House of the Skeleton (3.3)......84
House of Wattlework
    (3.13–15)......132n25
Palaestra Pool......80
Samnite House (5.1–2)......83
Shop (4.17)......128
Temple Area (seafront suburban
    district)......172

Pompeii
1.8.8......173
1.10.4......275n18
1.10.6......24, 275n18
1.13......145, 145n1, 235, 253, 255,
    266, 272
1.13.7......146n1
1.13.8......146n1
1.13.9......146n1
1.13.11......146n1
5.1.20......121n10
6.2......289
6.3......289
6.4......291
6.6......254, 290, 291, 292
6.6.19......242
6.6.21......242
6.6.22......242
6.6.23......242
6.7.17......121n10
6.8......230, 230n20, 290, 292, 293
6.10......230, 293, 294
6.12......205n17, 230, 267, 273, 294,
    295
6.13......295
6.14.28......129
6.15.5......81n4
6.15.10......121

6.16.30......257
6.17.22......221n7, 227, 256, 266, 271, 288
6.17.23–25......267
7.1.36......129
7.2......296
7.2.3......221n7, 231, 256, 267, 306
7.2.11......275n19
7.2.26......126
7.3......296
7.3.13......121n10
7.4.48......173
7.4.59......275n18
7.4.59–62......275n18
7.4.60–61......275n18
7.4.62......275n18
7.6......291
7.13.3......245
8.5.24......258
9.1......209, 219n5, 264, 301
9.1.8......248, 248n54, 249
9.1.12......200, 204, 210, 221, 221n7, 231, 248, 248n54, 249, 267, 273, 302, 303
9.1.13......129, 232
9.1.14......129
9.1.26......256
9.1.30......264
9.1.34......264
9.2......219n5, 231, 232, 233, 264, 299, 301
9.2.6......232
9.2.7......232
9.3......275n18, 299
9.3.8......221n7, 231, 256, 267, 305, 306
9.3.1......297
9.3.1–2......199, 221n7, 231, 256, 267, 275, 275nn18–19
9.3.12......256
9.3.15......275n18
9.3.23......213n25
9.3.24......213n25
9.3.25......213n25
9.5.19......213n25
9.5.20......213n25
9.8.7......256

Alleyway between Insulae 3.4 and 3.5......241n39
Amphitheater (2.6)......23, 46n17

Brothel (7.12.18–20)......159n16

Caligula Arch (between 6.8 and 6.10)......293
Capitolium (7.8.1)......281n34
Caupona of Euxinus and gardens (1.11.10–11)......132n25
Central Baths (9.4)......212, 213, 214, 218, 218n4, 219, 219n5, 220, 221, 242, 263, 264, 265

District of the Campanienses......231n23
District of the Forenses......231n23
District of the Salinsienses......231n23

INDEX OF VESUVIAN LOCATIONS

District of the Urbulanenses......231n23

Dyer's Workshop and Residence (9.3.1-2)......199, 256, 267, 275nn18-19

Forum (7.8)......205, 242

Forum Baths (7.5.2, 7, 8, 10, 12, 24)......242

Herculaneum Gate (or Porta Saliniensis)......43, 120, 197, 200, 204n12, 218, 221n7, 224, 225, 225n13, 226, 228, 229, 231n23, 286, 287

House of the Bear (7.2.45)......127n19

House of the Chaste Lovers (9.12.6)......132n26

House/Inn of the Christian Inscription (7.11.11-14)......38, 76, 153, 235, 236, 253, 267

House of the Dioscuri (6.9.6)......46n19

House of the Faun (6.12.2)......29, 205n17, 230, 230nn18-19, 256, 267, 272, 273

House of the Gilded Cupids (6.16.7, 6.16.38)......83, 84, 112, 113, 135

House of the Hebrews (1.11.14)......121n10, 151n9

House of Julia Felix (2.4.3)......112; Praedia of Julia......242

House of C. Julius Polybius (9.13.1)......210

House of Lucius Caecilius Jucundus (5.1.26)......126n17, 280

House of Lucretius (9.3.5)......199, 200, 213n25, 221n7, 231, 256, 267, 272, 273, 275, 275nn18-19, 298

House of the Tragic Poet (6.8.5)......230n20

House of the Vettii (6.15.1)......128, 130

Insula Arriana Polliana (6.6)......41, 43, 44, 45, 46n19, 47, 49, 50, 51, 56, 102-5, 109, 118, 133, 134, 140, 142n44, 143, 184n18, 205n17, 222-24, 226, 227, 263 227n17, 228-30, 230n20, 238, 242-44, 253, 255, 264, 266; Bakery (6.6.17, 6.6.20-21), 38, 41, 43, 43n9, 47, 50, 51, 52, 53, 55, 56, 103, 106, 114, 117-20, 120n6, 121, 122, 128, 131-36, 140, 142n44, 143, 222-24, 226, 254, 255, 266, 269, 306; Back entryway of Insula (6.6.12), 133; Premises around outer ribbon of Insula (6.6.2-10a; 6.6.14-16), 43n9; Small Bakery (6.6.4-5), 43; Separate Residences over Bakery Complex (6.6.18-19), 43, 44, 44n12; Shop (6.6.13), 43n9; Shop (6.6.22), 43n9

Marine Gate......194

Nola Gate......231, 283, 304
Nuceria Gate......225

Republican Baths (8.5.36)......242

Sarno Gate......231n23
Stabian Baths (7.1.8)......242
Stabian Gate......219n5
Suburban Baths (7.16.a)......242

"The Street of Tombs"......120
Temple of Apollo (7.7.32)......114, 194, 243, 281n34
Temple of Isis (8.7.28)......114, 114n24, 115
Temple of Jupiter Meilichios/ Asklepius (8.7.25)......114, 281n34
Temple of Venus (8.1.3)......114, 194, 243, 281n34
Temple of Vespasian (7.9.2)......46n17
Tomb of Eumachia......225n13
Tomb of Gaius Vestorius Priscus......178, 179
Tomb of Gnaeus Vibrius Saturninus......225n14
Tomb of Septumia......178, 179

Vesuviuan Gate......178, 240
Via Consolare......43, 45, 197, 221n8, 227n17, 228, 229, 263, 289

Via dell'Abbondanza......131, 193, 199, 219, 219n5, 220, 221, 221n8, 304
Via Stabiana (or Via Pompeiana)......192, 195, 196, 197, 199, 201, 204, 204n12, 209, 213, 214, 214n26, 215, 219, 219n5, 220, 221n8, 222, 231, 232, 235, 236, 248n54, 264, 265, 297, 298, 299, 301, 302, 304, 306
Via del Vesuvio......192
Via delle Terme......43, 197, 219, 220, 221n8, 228, 291, 292
Via della Fortuna......192, 197, 199, 219, 230
Via di Mercurio......221n8
Via Marina......194
Vico 9.3–9.4......192, 199, 212, 213, 214, 214n26, 215, 265
Vico del Fauno......197
Vico del Labirinto......197
Vico di Balbo......199, 219, 219n5, 222, 264, 265
Vico di Mercurio......197, 199, 211, 219, 220, 221n8, 263, 264, 289, 290
Vico di Modesto......197, 229
Vico Storto......192n1
Via di Nola......192, 199, 213, 219, 283n38
Vico di Tesmo......199, 213, 213n25, 214, 219n5, 221, 232

www.ingramcontent.com/pod-product-compliance
Lightning Source LLC
Chambersburg PA
CBHW052010070526
44584CB00016B/1690